My Journey to the Ocean

Lena Mikado

Brave New Worlds
St. Simons Island, Georgia

Elena Markina-Harrison
207 Marina Drive
St. Simons Island, Georgia 31522
www.bravenewworldsls.com

Publisher's Note: This is a work of fiction. Names, characters, places, and incidents are a product of the author's imagination. Locales and public names are sometimes used for atmospheric purposes. Any resemblance to actual people, living or dead, or to businesses, companies, events, institutions, or locales is completely coincidental.

Book Layout ©2013 BookDesignTemplates.com

Ordering Information:
Quantity sales. Special discounts are available on quantity purchases by corporations, associations, and others. For details, contact the "Special Sales Department" at the address above.

My Journey to the Ocean/ Lena Mikado. -- 1st ed
ISBN 978-1508455493

I dedicate this book to all daring travelers and globe-trotters, who strive to see every corner of our beautiful planet. I dedicate it to my mom, dad and Nan. I dedicate it to my family – my crazy husband and my lovely boys Liam and Max. I dedicate it to my Dalmatian Tex – I miss you very much. And, finally, I dedicate it to my friend, who inspired me to go ahead and finish this novel – to Sylvia Tourkey. I wouldn't have done it without any of you.

Thank you!

One's destination is never a place, rather a new way of looking at things.

– HENRY MILLER

Prologue

What else can be said about love? The poems have been written, the songs have been composed. It seems that anything we might want to express has already been done for us. But I think I'll give it another go.

All of us start this life as tiny, helpless babies, who explore the world around them, make their own mistakes, and come to their own conclusions. And isn't it fun? If we simply followed what has already been learned by the previous generations, with no attempts to contribute little bits of our own experience, life would be so dull and so unavoidably status quo.

I've recently become a mother. Don't get me wrong. I'm not saying this to get the usual "Oh, how sweet! What a cute pumpkin! Sweetie pie!" I honestly do believe that majority of people couldn't care less about somebody else's children unless they have their own offspring of approximately the same age. I sure didn't care. But once you emerge on the other side and become a parent, you can then relate to a lot of notions you previously considered alien. You can even relate to your own parents!

These thoughts are crossing my mind as I follow my 15-month-old son up and down the steps of our friends' house. It's his ninth trip back and forth, and, honestly, never in my life have I imagined that I would be ready to exhaust myself to such an extent for a male human being. And here I am, readily performing Kung Fu jumps over the sofa to prevent him from a bad fall. Why do kids take such big risks? Why are they so reckless? Doesn't he realize what consequences his actions will have? The questions are rhetorical. No, he doesn't realize it. Just as I didn't realize that a person can't be smoking two packs of cigarettes a day without drastically shortening their expected lifespan. How can I communicate to him that he can't be doing this? You can't, Elena. He'll just have to learn on his own mistakes. Now I can clearly see the picture. If you managed to happily survive your adolescent years without causing much harm to your health or criminal record, you might as well get ready to spend the rest of your life wondering how in the world you can protect your children from making the same mistakes you've made. Nobody tells you this when you're getting ready to become a parent. Nobody warns you: "Beware, you'll be tortured by the dilemma forever!" I suspect it's a global conspiracy invented to persuade inhabitants of planet Earth to procreate.

Young people consider themselves immortal and invincible. They are always right and there is nothing you can do to prove them otherwise. It's horribly dangerous, but for some reason, when I look back at my very young self, I only want to smile. My reader, let's imagine that we do have access to the greatest invention ever – a time machine. Let's hop on board and head over ten years back. I want to see myself again – young, naïve, full of life, when the world was definitely my oyster and nothing could take it from me.

June 10, 2004

"Three packs of Marlboro, please!"

I squinted at a plump and grumpy big-haired sales lady as dazzling Moscow sunshine bounced off my eyes. I had to stock up – I heard that cigarettes are extremely expensive in New York City. I was not really dependent on nicotine, but smoking out in the open with no risk of being seen by my parents, relatives, parents' friends, or distant relatives of my parents' friends made my head spin with happiness and freedom. No, it was not the first time I was going abroad alone. I already visited Germany two years ago, just for three weeks. But this time, we were heading over to the United States for four months! I took a deep drag of my cigarette – the second one in the last ten minutes – and closed my eyes in utter enjoyment. As it happens, my fiancé did not know that I smoked either. Oh, didn't I tell you? I was engaged to get married next August! Finally! We had been together for three and a half years and soon we would be tying the knot. I was going to miss him terribly. This was the longest we had ever been apart, and to be honest with you, I was having second thoughts about this trip. But this summer was my last chance to visit the U.S. on the Work & Travel Program for college students. I had only one year left before I graduated, and then, adulthood, here I come! I glanced at the girls standing in line for an airport shuttle right next to me – my travel companions – Diana, Vera and Sonia. I had never even seen them before we were informed by our agency that we would be working for the same company and share an apartment in the U.S. The girls seemed nice, but they were just eighteen years old and all single. Or something along those lines.

I frowned. "Hey, by the way. When we are in the States, puhlease... no making out in the living room."

Every time I traveled somewhere with my single friends, they would bring over their new boyfriends or whatever they were, and make me feel lonely and stupid. I didn't really understand why people couldn't find just one person to dedicate their lives to. They wasted their young years on multiple partners and meaningless affairs. Not me - I definitely knew what I wanted.

"Whatever," said Diana, tossing her bright blond hair. "I'm going to party all summer long till I drop."

When we went to Moscow two months ago for the Work & Travel orientation program, Vera and Sonia were late for their train back to Voronezh, a large but provincial city all four of us called home. As Diana and I were comfortably seated in the train compartment, we stared at each other in disbelief: did the train just move, and the girls were not back yet? Diana mumbled: "If they're that irresponsible, I think I'll be mainly hanging out with you this summer." That was the moment I decided that Diana was definitely funny, in her own wacko way.

My main goal of this trip was to see as much as possible of America – I absolutely loved traveling. I would never forget the moment when I received the visa in the United States Embassy in Moscow. It was a sunny April day. I'd been strolling along Novinsky Boulevard and admiring impressive Moscow high-rises. Early-spring fresh air was gently caressing my hair and filling my mind and body up with the invigorating energy of the large city reawakening after the long winter sleep. I couldn't believe that soon I would see New York, I'd walk Carrie Bradshaw Streets, and I'd take a ferry to the Statue of Liberty. And then... then I would go to Georgia. Georgia and I had a very long history together. I was twelve when I first read Gone with the Wind, and I fell in love. With everything. I was so obsessed, they actually mocked me at high school and called me Scarlett O'Hara. I didn't mind it a bit. I only wished I would be that pretty. I'd never considered myself beautiful: nobody ever told me so, and I'd always seen a very ordinary girl staring at me from the mirror. Alex, my fiancé, liked me, and that was all I cared about. I lit the third cigarette.

"Oh my God!" yelled Diana. If you are going to smoke like a chimney, you'd better do it outside of our apartment.

"All right." I shrugged. "I don't care."

"You look silly," giggled Vera. "With this cigarette stuck between your teeth."

"Oh!" It'd just dawned on me that while I was looking for my cell phone to text Alex, I let the cigarette just hang out of my mouth. Not too lady-like. But then again, Scarlett wasn't a lady either. I couldn't help but smile. Soon I'd see Margaret Mitchell's land! I'd see it with my own two eyes. Believe me, for a middle-class girl from Russia, it was equivalent to a flight into outer space. I was so happy, I felt like my head was going to explode into kaleidoscope of multicolored expectations.

"Ouch!" Somebody elbowed me so hard I nearly flew out of the line. In reality, a notion of a "line" doesn't exist in Russia. It's typically a crowd of very aggressive people who are always looking for some space to squeeze any part of their body into in order to get closer to their destination. I guess I happened to be in somebody's way, as my foot got also suddenly attacked for no reason.

"Easy!! Watch where you're going!"

I turned to look at the evil hooligan and saw a tiny wrinkled old lady – babushka – who was maliciously eyeing me up and down.

"Sorry," I muttered. I was brought up to respect older generations under any circumstances, even though my foot was about to fall off.

"Young people these days!" screamed the babushka. "So rude and promiscuous!! Look at what this brat is wearing!" I caught a few accusing glances from around the line and already got prepared to defend myself (all of us were wearing yellow Star Travel T-shirts with the blue Work &Travel USA 2004 logo – what was wrong with that?), as I saw the shuttle pull up. "Hurry!" screamed Sonia and started elbowing her way to the shuttle through the "line" of people. "The shuttle is here. We've got to catch it! We can't be late for the plane!"

Diana and I exchanged the understanding glances. I really started liking this crowd.

CHAPTER ONE

On Top of the World

I had always been afraid of being eaten by sharks. Or, to be more precise, of my plane crashing on the way from Europe, me falling into the abyss of the Atlantic and then being consumed by sharks. No, no, darling reader. I am not going to get into the intricacies of airplane crashes with you. I know that I probably would not be alive by the time my wretched body hit the non-forgiving waters, but... it is my number one primordial fear, and I have all the rights to drown in the self-pitying waves of my own misery.

I shuddered and grasped at the chair armrest as the plane took yet another tummy-turning cloud dive. My knuckles turned white. I glanced sideways without daring to turn my head and saw that the girls were carelessly snoozing away. Lucky heifers! How can some people sleep during turbulence?

I already thought I was going to die on that plane without involvement of any sharks, when I heard the flight attendant announce that we were beginning to land in the JFK airport. I felt my heart flutter in anticipation. It always does that at landing, my heart. It's a combination of fear and elation, the fizzy sweet taste of future adventures on my lips. I finally got some courage up and peeked out into the window.

Right there, floating under the bubble bath of fluffy clouds, was New York. The new land, an entirely new continent, was right there, sparkling and glittering in the pink evening sunshine.

"Girls! Bitchezzz!" I whispered. "We've arrived! We are here!"

"What? How much is that in rubles?" mumbled sleepy Vera as she yawned and slowly opened one eye.

"Forget about rubles! At least for the summer." I beamed. "We are in America, baby!"

***

"Okay, let's just try to focus and relax. Find your inner Zen and exhale. It didn't go exactly as planned, but I'll be just fine! The only thing I have to do is to calm down..."

We had three extra days in New York City before our employment contract in Georgia started. The girls decided to save some money and take a Greyhound bus down south. Not me! Leaving New York City thirty minutes after arriving didn't fit my idyllic picture of the date with the glamorous metropolis. I figured I could borrow extra $400 from my Dad for a plane ticket and crash at my high school buddy's place in Brooklyn. I'd have to work a bit harder to pay my parents back, but so be it. After all, it was the trip of a lifetime. The high-school "buddy" had called two days before my departure date and casually informed me that she'd be out of town. Now... I stopped for a moment and let it sink in. I had all the tickets booked, I was stuck in New York City for three days, and I didn't have a place to stay. It proved impossible to book a decent hotel room without a U.S. billing address. I already started to believe that I'd have to either sleep on a bench in the Central Park or forget about my mini adventure in New York and join the girls on the bus, when I finally found a pleasant hostel in the middle of Manhattan, whose owner kindly agreed to reserve a room for me without the credit card info. Voilà! Whatever happens, happens for a reason, and in my case, the reason always works in my favor. Ha! I'd be staying in Manhattan! It was a "Sex and the City" dream come true.

Except... here I was. On the floor. Of the hostel living room. With a big cockroach casually strolling by my side. And the worst thing was that I was so tired, upset, and lonely, that I didn't even care about the roach. The "Sex and the City" theme interrupted my thoughts, as if in mockery. I stared at the TV screen without blinking. How many times had I watched the show in Russia, trying to close my eyes and imagine myself thousands of miles away from home? Well, I was here now, and it was nothing I'd imagined it to be.

To start with, the cab from the JFK was the most expensive ride I'd ever had in my life, and the driver wasn't the most polite person in the world. Mind you, I am from Russia, and I deal with militant babushkas on the daily basis. I'm not that easily intimidated by rude people, but once you're in a foreign country, you feel just a touch less secure and more sensitive. When I saw the glittering lights of the Manhattan skyline, my heart jumped once again. I was here, after all; I had made it! I tried to chase the loneliness away as I remembered the quick good-bye with the girls at the airport. I didn't even know them, and it was just for three days. What was wrong with me? Enjoy the glam, Elena!

"We're here!" barked the driver. "50 bucks."

I handed him a new, crispy note in disbelief and quickly calculated how many drinks I could get for it at one of the best Voronezh night clubs. "Don't compare the prices! You're in America now," beeped a tiny, greedy voice inside of my confused head. I walked out of the cab and found myself in the dark street of what seemed to be... Gotham City. The street was pitch-black except for a few streetlamps that were casting ominous shadows on the building walls, and a group of not-particularly-friendly-looking guys were slowly cruising the alley and pounding a basketball on the ground. One of them turned around and looked me up and down. Terrified, I quickly picked my luggage up (it didn't even have the rolling wheels!) and scuttled into the hostel entrance. "Elena Markina checking in!"

The person behind the counter gave me a blank stare.

"We're overbooked. But you can sleep in the living room on the floor, if you like. We might have a room for you tomorrow."

On the TV, Carrie and Miranda were having their usual light and witty conversation and enjoying a stroll. As was my roach. I sighed, turned the TV off, and rolled over on my mattress. Loneliness morphed into a crystallized rock in my throat, but I was too tired to cry. This was the first time I wished I'd never left Voronezh.

***

As the famous proverb states, morning brings wisdom. I couldn't agree more. I woke up, had some breakfast (even though the bread was strangely soft and gooey – what do they make it from here in America?), and climbed out of my batman cave to explore the big shiny city.

After going up the Empire State Building and buying souvenirs for my parents and Alex, visiting the amazing Metropolitan and checking out designer shoes in shop windows, I started to feel better. I was just overwhelmed by the weirdness of the situation. Now everything was back to normal.

Gotham mood started coming back to me when I realized that I was too late for the Statue of Liberty ferry. I took the ferry to Staten Island instead and managed to sneak a closer peak at the famous monument. After the ferry got back to Manhattan, I was definitely back to the dark side of the moon. Where did the pleasant hustle of the Wall Street go? In fact, where were the people? Oh, yes, they were probably with their families... or friends. I wiggled my nose, desperately trying not to cry. I had never got that emotional and home-sick before, and I had to learn to tackle this challenge somehow. I ran towards the flashing yellow lights of the bus and jumped on. The glittering reflections of skyscrapers were racing each other in the window. I had just one day left. One day. And then I would be heading to Georgia. Was it also going to be disappointing?

What I didn't know was that the main surprise was waiting for me back at the hostel.

"We have the room for you!" exclaimed the owner.

"Fantastic!" *I guess my roach will have to enjoy the loneliness of the night without me.*

"The only thing is – it's a men's bedroom. We didn't have any room in the girls' section, but we figured it's better than the living room floor."

"Mhm..." That was the sound I managed to utter as I was contemplating on which of the evils was the worst: sleeping with the harmless roach or a bunch of dudes I'd never met before.

I should have stayed with the roach.

I woke up in the middle of the night from a funny noise coming from the bunk bed above me. I wasn't sleeping well, since I'd been under a very powerful impression of illegal human trafficking stories told me by my grandma. I think she must have watched at least a few hundred of crime shows prior to my trip to the U.S. Even before I left Voronezh, I'd already imagined myself in some dump in Brazil or Asia, miserable, helpless and doomed for the most horrible fate. This could happen to girls simply because they didn't keep an eye on their passports. I'm telling you all this, so that you could clearly see the picture: I was completely dressed (in case I had to quickly run out of the room and scream for help), clutching my precious Russian passport in my hand under the pillow and alert to the point of ridiculousness. And then I heard the sound. It was quiet, repetitive, and remotely familiar. It sounded like... I covered my face with the pillow, refusing to believe the cruel reality. The guy above me was jacking off!!! I opened my eyes, and I swear to you, my friends – I did not close them until dawn.

It could only happen to me! Under any other circumstances, I would have died laughing, but I was too busy being petrified. Exhale, find your inner Zen... It's one thing to try to survive a minute of being scared. Spending all night without moving a muscle is a totally different cup of tea.

With the first rays of sunshine I was out of the hell bedroom, still holding the passport in my hand and sprinting towards the restroom. I typically wake up to pee three or four times a night – yes, it's weird, and the girls had already commented on that one on the plane. They said they'd save up some extra money this summer and would donate the money to buy me a new kidney. Whatever.

My third day in New York City went by as if in the haze. I remember chatting with a very talkative Russian guy I met in the hostel kitchen over breakfast. I told him about my adventure, and we laughed and agreed that the bread was indeed made of a very strange substance. Then he invited me to go to the JFK with him to pick up his friend, who was flying from Ukraine. I joined him, since I was already feeling strangely lost and could not think of anything better to do, and we saw a rat the size of a fat cat strolling on the rails of the New York City subway. (Do all creepy crawlers in NYC take it easy?) In the evening, we had dinner at a sidewalk pizzeria, and it was, actually, quite nice. And that's all I remember. I've heard that people tend to clear their memory of all unpleasant stuff. Perhaps this is why I can't really recall the last part of my "glam city date." Please, don't get me wrong – I'm not trying to offend NYC fans. I honestly think that if one already feels lonely, any big city will only intensify the feeling of being a lonesome green monster in the hubbub of nonstop life and entertainment.

As I was quickly getting on the airport shuttle to La Guardia, Sting kept singing in my head: "I'm an alien, I'm a legal alien..." I was happy to be leaving New York. Maybe one day, I'd be coming back here with a bunch of friends and we'd rock the city like there's no tomorrow. But for now...

As the plane soared over the silky beige clouds, I left Carrie and New York behind me. The first coolest part of my trip was over, and it didn't turn out to be cool at all.

CHAPTER TWO

We Are Not in Voronezh Anymore, Toto

In Voronezh, only in a sauna can one experience the heat that intense. I just walked out of the main arrivals' building of Jacksonville International Airport in Florida, inhaled, and didn't quite believe that human beings could live, eat and breathe in such a hot and humid climate. But then with the corner of my eye I caught a glimpse of bright-green palm trees beside the road, and a big silly smile came over my face. I was in the south, the sun was rampaging like a crazy lunatic, and I was about twenty minutes away from the beach. What could be better? The beach is a very exciting idea for anybody born and raised in central Russia: you don't visit it often, and if you do, the trip doesn't typically last long enough to fully enjoy it.

Our employer was responsible for picking me up from the airport. And let me tell you – we'd been much luckier than your average Work & Travel students. We were hired by an exclusive and super-chic resort – Ocean Isle Company – to be working as servers at one of its restaurants. My Dad was a touch skeptical about my summer work. I believe his exact words were: "You're not even capable of bringing a cup of tea from the counter to the kitchen table without spilling it. What makes you think you'd manage to wait tables?" What could be more reassuring?

Naturally, I'd done a bit of research about the resort, and I was quite impressed. Just three days before, Ocean Isle Company was hosting a G8 Summit – the annual meeting of the world leaders. Imagine that! Celebrity visits were not an unusual occurrence, and judging from the website pictures, the place looked like a Mediterranean palazzo. Compared to the majority of students who were going to work for fast-food companies and share apartments with fifteen of their buddies, we seemed to have drawn our lucky ticket.

I'd been corresponding back and forth with the Human Resources coordinator, Sandra. Sandra hired the four of us after an uncomplicated phone interview at the Voronezh Star Travel office. She was extremely nice, but quite possibly thought I was not all there, since I'd been e-mailing her non-stop with all kinds of different questions. Like, where exactly were we going to work? What would the pay be? Where would we live? And would somebody meet me at the airport? Come to think of it, I didn't get the proper answer to most of my questions, but they were probably very busy with the G-8 and all. The only thing I knew for sure was that there would be somebody picking me up in Jacksonville. I'd even printed Sandra's e-mail confirming the arrangements.

"Excuse me!" I smiled sheepishly and tried to articulate my words better, as I noticed the first signs of "What the hell kind of an accent is that?" on the information booth clerk's face. "Somebody's supposed to be meeting me here. Where would they be?"

"Right there." The girl nodded and studied me suspiciously. "They should be holding a 'meet and greet' sign with your name."

"Oh, okay." I frowned. I'd already looked at the signs, and there was definitely nobody waiting for me. "Thanks!"

That's ok! I'll resort to plan B – I'm going to call Sandra. Brighten up, Elena.

"Good afternoon. Ocean Isle Company. Sharon speaking. How can I assist you?"

"Oh hi! My name is Elena Markina. I'm a J-1 student and I was hired to work as a server for the summer. I'm in Jacksonville Airport, and I was supposed to be picked up, but there's nobody here. Could you help me please?"

"Absolutely! May I place you on a brief hold while I'm checking on your transportation arrangements?"

"Sure!" My spirits were suddenly up. The lady was so polite and eager to help. The background classical music had already started putting me to sleep – I was still suffering from the jet lag

– when the operator's voice pierced through the monotonous melody: "Unfortunately, we do not have your name on our transportation records. May we ask you who took care of it for you?"

"Yes, sure. It's... it's Sandra Hendricks from Human Resources. Can I speak to her?"

"Ma'am, Human Resources is closed on weekends. We suggest that you stay at one of the hotels in Jacksonville and call us back on Monday morning."

"But..." there was so much I wanted to say at once, that the words just congregated into one big confused question mark in my head. And what could I say? "I don't know where the hotels are"? "I'm afraid I don't have money for a hotel"? "I'm freaking thousands of miles away from my home and I'm absolutely, utterly, and totally terrified?!"

"Is there anything else we can help you with, Ms. Martina?"

"Markina. No, thank you."

I hung up, briskly walked outside, sat down on the curve, lit a cigarette, and burst into tears. I'd heard stories of Work & Travel students that were ditched by their employers. I just didn't expect it to happen to me. And I didn't expect to be sitting alone outside of the airport an ocean away from my home. I was half the world away from my parents, my fiancé, and my friends - with only 300 bucks in my pocket. *What should I do?* Through the slumber of my despair I heard an airport announcement, and it seemed as if they called... my name. It couldn't have been right. I must have been hallucinating as a result of three extremely stressful days. Hostel, masturbating roommates, rats and cucarachas of cosmic proportions would do it to you. I turned to my left and realized that there was a guy sitting right next to me. He was staring at me as if I was a run-away nut job on the loose. No wonder. I bet he'd been there all along witnessing me running out of the airport and having a hysterical heavy-smoking fit.

"Did they just say 'Markina'?"

"Yes. Is that you?"

"Yes," I managed to mumble through my clenched teeth. "Would you mind telling me what the announcement was about? I didn't pay attention and I really need to know what they said."

"They said you need to come to the information booth." The guy shrugged. He seemed to have lost all the interest.

"Thanks!"

This time, the girl at the counter was definitely unsure of what to think of me, but she did tell me that there was a vehicle waiting for me in the parking lot. I followed her directions and almost ran to the location.

Has it ever happened to you that all of a sudden you feel like you've walked out of a movie theater room that was showing a horror movie and walked into the room with the romantic comedy on the silver screen? If you have, you'll know exactly what I'm going to tell you about. In the parking lot, I saw a dark green Lincoln sedan with the words "Ocean Isle" engraved in perfect golden italic. Your quintessential driver with graying hair, spectacles and matching dark green uniform was holding the door open for me. He looked at me and gave me a warm Santa Claus smile.

"Are you Elena? I'm sorry, I was assigned to take some of our guests here to catch a flight to DC, and they were late."

"That's okay." *Of course that was bloody okay. A minute ago I was imagining myself sleeping in the airport for a day or two, and now I was about to take a luxury ride in this car with leather seats and mahogany ashtrays.*

I climbed in my glamorous "carriage" and started chatting away. That's what I do when I get overwhelmed. My mom told me that once when I was five and she took me to the dentist's office, the dentist couldn't stop me from talking for good thirty minutes. He finally had to ask my Mom to hold my mouth wide open.

The driver's name was Emmett. After Emmett heard all he could possibly hear about my family, my fiancé, and my brilliant plans for the future, he started telling me about the area and Ocean Isle. I was honestly listening to the first part, but then I started dozing off a little. The stress of the past days had finally let go of me, and I felt secure and happy.

***

"I'm not quite sure where I should be taking you, so I guess I'm going to drop you off at the Beach Club."

Emmett might as well have given me a short presentation on subquantum physics and aether theories – I had no idea what he was talking about.

"Okay. Are my friends going to be there? Do you know?"

"No. I thought it was just you. But I'm sure the folks at the Beach Club will take good care of you!"

"All right!" I beamed. "If you say so."

We pulled up in front of a very pretty and cozy building in the Spanish colonial style. The sign "Private Beach Club. For

Members Only" in the same perfect golden italic adorned the entrance. I stepped inside dragging my big old bag with no wheels and stopped in admiration. I wouldn't have called the place luxurious or opulent, but it was definitely the most charming and upscale location I'd ever been to.

Elegant people dressed in Ralph Lauren and Gucci were rushing through the hallway and stopping to take a look at the wall with photographs that had been taken the night before. To the right there was a large pool, and you could see the orange sunset flickering on the surface of the turquoise water. Pool servers were skillfully maneuvering between the lounge chairs and delivering amazing-looking tropical drinks to the guests, relaxing in lounge chairs. You could hear kids giggle with happiness and you could see dressed-up people heading towards the dining room. And right in front of me, through the Mediterranean arch, I saw the Atlantic Ocean – calm and immense. I could feel the hot and humid breeze on my face and I could taste the saltiness of the ocean on my lips. I love water. Ocean fills me up with the great energy and gives me inspiration to live my life to the fullest and enjoy the ride. I even like the whispering sound of the word – "OCEAN."

"Oh wow! You're from Russia! You're the first Russian I'd ever met." The exclamation came from an enthusiastic looking African-American lady. She had a very attractive smile – one of those that make you like the person at the get-go. "My name is Roxanna. I work here, at the Beach Club Reception Desk."

"It's the first time I've seen the ocean," I said quietly and smiled. "There's always first time for everything."

"And isn't it the truth, honey! Come on, let me get you something to eat. You must be starving! Just look at you – skin and bones! Are you all skinny in Russia?"

I've never thought of myself as skinny. I was quite a plump child, and I believe I still suffer from the fat-kid complex. I started liking Roxanna even more.

"Okay, darling, have a seat right here and choose whatever you like from this menu. Kelly, would you please take care of Elena? She's going to work with us this summer!"

Kelly gave me a polite, but empty smile and nodded. In any other circumstances, I would have been upset that my future coworker didn't seem to be particularly friendly. But at that very moment, I was too busy trying to figure out how much I'd have to pay for this unexpected dinner. I mean, in the place like this it might have cost me all 300 bucks I had. I sighed and ordered buffalo chicken wings (whatever that was) and a Coke.

"Elena? Hi! My name is Rob Dwight. I've been working with Tatyana Bomaricheva on arranging your employment for this summer."

"Oh, hello! Very nice to meet you." I was extremely happy that finally there was somebody who actually knew who I was and what I was doing there. I tried to ignore the fact that my throat was on fire. At least now I knew that "buffalo" stood for "very fucking spicy" – for future reference. I choked and took a huge gulp of Coke.

"So how was your trip?"

Mr. Dwight was a very polite gentleman in his mid-fifties with an easy-going demeanor. I figured he was probably Sandra's assistant or something like that. In just a few minutes, Rob and I were chatting away like two old BFFs. Apparently, we would be working right here, at the Beach Club Dining Room, all the way through September. We were not the only foreign students working at Ocean Isle that summer. There were also a few guys and a girl from Slovakia. Sounded like fun! The more the merrier.

"Well, it looks like you're done? Kelly, I'll take care of the check. Would you like me to take you to your friends?"

"Yes, please!" I wasn't sure what I was mostly relieved about: the news that the girls had made it there safely and I'd see them in a mere moment, or the fact that Rob would pay for the horrible dinner.

***

The monsoon came out of nowhere. One minute it was bright and sunny, and the next – the skies opened up, and down came gallons of water.

Rob and I had been driving around for what seemed to be an eternity. He first took me to our apartment complex (which was gorgeous, by the way), but the girls didn't seem to be in. Rob thought that they might have gone out to grab a bite to eat and kindly took me to approximately ten restaurants to look for them.

"Okay, Elena. I'll just have to take you to the apartment for the last time. If they're still not there, I could drop you off at Monika's. The J-1 student from Slovakia I told you about. She's very nice! Maybe you could share an apartment with her?"

I nodded out of politeness. I wasn't in the mood to make any new acquaintances, and I definitely wasn't inclined to have new roommates.

We ran out of the car and knocked hard on the door. All of a sudden, the high-energy beat of a popular Russian song deafened both of us, and we saw Vera standing in front of us. She was wearing dark-blue boy shorts PJs and was holding a hairdryer.

"Elena! You're finally here! Where have you been? We were worried for you!" Vera nearly knocked me over in her attempt to give me a hug.

"Where have three of YOU been? We've been looking for you all over!" I tried to sound angry, but I was so happy to see her, I couldn't help beaming like an idiot.

I know what you're going to ask me. Why would you be missing somebody who you didn't even know before the trip? And that's a very good question. I only remember that I'd never been happier than on that particular day in June, in Southeast Georgia, in the midst of the tropical rain, when I got reunited with the only three people that connected me to my home, my life, to my own self.

"I was drying my hair," laughed Vera, "and we've been dancing. Oh come on, Elena! Relax, have another cigarette."

"Okay, girls! Now when Elena is here safely, let me get back to my duties." *Oh, gosh! We were so excited we even forgot Rob was still there.* "If you ever need anything, please don't hesitate to give me a call."

Rob handed me his business card, smiled and quickly ran to his car. Vera and I glanced at the card and froze for a second.

The card read: "Rob Dwight. Ocean Isle Company. Vice President."

***

Later that evening, all four of us laughed and talked and told each other the stories of our adventures. We couldn't believe how lucky we were to work at such a high-end place. We danced to the crazy Russian music, sang folk songs, and roared with laughter because we sounded like our grandparents. I guess that was the beginning of a serious friendship, but as it goes in life, we didn't know it back then. As Chris would say, we just rode the wave. But hold on... I'm getting a bit ahead of my own story line.

I found a pay phone at the MacDonald's parking lot about two minutes away from our apartment and called Alex. His voice was so comforting, and I felt a familiar gnawing sense of guilt at the thought that I'd left him all alone. If only he could be here with me, if only we could share the excitement of discovering the new world together, everything would be different. I had to chase these thoughts away. They were not helping me in any way... I slowly walked back to our apartment through the warm darkness of the cricket-filled night. I looked up at the stars and tried to imagine what Alex was doing at the moment. He just woke up, was probably making him and his Dad a cup of tea.

"Elena!" Diana's blond head showed up from behind the door. "Are you smoking again? Keep it up, you might get lung cancer before we go back home!"

She was annoying, but my spirits were well up, so I laughed.

"We're going to bed. Are you coming?"

I inhaled the sweet aroma of magnolia trees for the last time and nodded.

"Sure, Diana-Banana. I'm on my way!"

One of the girls who had been renting the apartment before us wasn't moving out till the next day, and all four of us decided to sleep in one room. We were lying in our beds in complete darkness, listening to the heavy drops of rain hitting the windows, and sharing our dreams and expectations. There was a whole new world ahead of us, and – oh, my! – wouldn't it change our   lives   forever.

CHAPTER THREE

"I Want to Ride My Bicycle, I Want to Ride My Bike"

I think Freddie Mercury wrote this song for me. I would have loved to be able to ride my bike. In fact, it looked like I didn't have much of a choice but to ride my bike, but unfortunately, I couldn't. Yes, my friends, I'm one of those rare Homo sapiens species that cannot ride a bike. My Dad is a very impatient teacher. I fell off my bike a few times at the age of five or six, he announced that I was useless, I burst into tears and ran to seek protection under my mom's skirt. Naturally, my mom demanded that my dad left me alone, and here I was: almost twenty-one, on the student program in the United States, not capable of getting to work. Who would think that they didn't have any sort of public transportation in the US! Not even taxis!

I sighed with frustration as I watched the girls having a time of their life at the idea that I'd have to perform 45-minute walking tours every day on my way to work.

"Okay, Elena, it's all good – I'll teach you!" Exclaimed Diana. "Come on, get dressed! We'll go outside and I'll teach you in no time."

I gave Diana a suspicious look.

"We start working in two days. Are you sure you'll teach me to ride a bike in two days?"

"Of course she will!" Sonia couldn't stop laughing. "I really can't believe you can't ride a bike. Who can't ride a bike? Okay, okay, enough of those Ice Queen stares – you'll learn in no time, you'll see!"

Still having the legendary Queen's hit stuck in my head, I reluctantly dragged my feet outside, into what seemed to have been a 150-degree heat. I looked around and felt a bit relieved: there was nobody around to witness my shame. As I attentively started to listen to Diana's instructions, we heard a car pull up.

"Who the hell can that be?"

That was more of an exclamation than a question, but Diana didn't waste her time to fill me up with the information.

"Milo and Chris. Milo is this gorgeous dude from Slovakia, but he's very standoffish. He thinks he's a Greek god or something. And Chris is one of the servers at the Beach Club.

He was born in London, but he's been living here since he was seven. So, in fact, he's an American –"

"Diana!" I hissed. "Too much information for my poor brain. I don't need to know his full bio. I'd prefer for them not be here at all, because I –"

I got interrupted by a very cheerful voice.

"Hello, girls! Hi, Diana! Is that your fourth friend that was left behind?"

"Yes, guys! This is Elena. She just arrived last night."

I tried to squeeze out the most polite smile I could. I don't like being rude to people even if I'm annoyed with them for this or that reason. After all, it was not their fault that I couldn't ride a bike.

"So what are you girls up to?" I'd already forgotten the name of the guy who was talking, but he had a troublemaker-like white smile, red hair, and A LOT of freckles.

"I'm teaching Elena to ride a bike," giggled Diana.

I pictured slowly killing Diana – perhaps suffocating her with a pillow for a more prolonged and excruciating death.

"You can't ride a bike, really?" The red-haired guy was laughing now.

At that point, I decided to take my words about being polite back. I wanted to murder him as well.

"He he, that's funny! She can't ride a bike!" Snorted the guy from Slovakia.

I was officially in hell.

"Really," I said. "In fact, we've got to get down to business. We don't have much time left. If you excuse us, please," I snarled and tried to get on the bike.

"Sure! Nice to meet you, Elena. We'll see you around."

I briefly caught the glimpse of his smile. Definitely the freckliest person I'd ever met in my life.

***

I should have been more patient and given my dad another chance. In that case, I wouldn't have been dragging my sweaty old self down this beautiful but endless road on St. Simons Island, Georgia, in scorching heat. I felt like I was stuck in the desert and my face had just turned into a plump ripe tomato. And my knees looked like I'd been run over by a trash truck. I'd been trying to conquer this horrid contraption the majority of people refer to as "bike" for the last two days. I ended up falling over like a sack of potatoes right on the cement. It hurt. Oh, crap, it was hot! I tried to distract myself from a very attractive idea of fainting right there and then and looked around. The gorgeous Antebellum building to my left looked exactly like Tara from Gone with the Wind. Or at least like the one in the movie, if not the book. I stared at the grand mansion with magnificent Greek pillars and romantic balconies in utter admiration. I could bet there was a majestic ballroom inside, and the sunlight playfully reflected in the crystal chandeliers. I had already imagined myself gracefully flying down the elaborate curved staircase. The orchestra had just started playing the first notes of my favorite waltz, and this elegant handsome gentleman was offering me his hand to help me down the steps...

"Need a ride?"

I quickly turned into the direction of the voice. I'd heard it somewhere before.

"I'm Chris. We met yesterday. You look like you're very determined to get to work. Do you want a ride to the shuttle stop?"

I desperately tried to put myself together and come back from my ballroom fantasy to the reality of a red-haired guy in his Ford Explorer.

"My mom instructed me to never accept rides from someone I don't know," I giggled, but still kept my distance from the car.

"Your mom is a very intelligent woman. But by the look on your face, it seems like you're about to have a heat stroke. Plus, a serial killer wouldn't be picking you up in broad daylight with so many people as witnesses."

"All serial killers probably say that." I shrugged.

"It's air-conditioned in here."

"Okay!" I jumped in the car and sighed with relief as the cold air brushed all over my body. "Thank you, I really appreciate it."

"It's no problem. You were very funny out there, but it looked like you wouldn't last long. I had to turn around".

His smile was contagious and I had to laugh.

"Yeah, I was probably quite a sight. People don't really walk in America. They're either driving or jogging."

"Ha ha! You nailed that one." Apparently, Chris found my comment hilarious – he couldn't stop laughing.

"I'm sorry. My face probably looks very red and ugly. It always happens to me when I work out."

"I don't know what you're talking about. You look beautiful."

"Yeah right." I rolled my eyes and smiled.

"Quit fishing for compliments. So do you have a boyfriend waiting for you at home?"

"I do, actually." I started nodding proactively. "My fiancé. We're getting married next summer." I was already used to guys asking me questions like that. I just pretended I didn't notice that they were flirting with me, and that way nobody would end up embarrassed.

"How come he's not here?"

I wasn't used to that.

"Well, it's complicated"."

"How complicated?"

I stared at him in the attempt to pass the message along with just my eyes, without saying it out loud: "People don't ask strangers questions like that – it's impolite!" I have a very heavy stare. I inherited it from my dad, and typically it works wonders. Not this time.

"Was too busy to come with you?"

"No. He just... he didn't have money for the program. Plus, he doesn't speak English." Bummer. I sounded defensive. Everything I said was nothing but the truth. What I didn't mention was Alex's... what's the right way to put it? Unwillingness to experience new things in life? No passion about seeing other countries and thinking outside of the box? But I'd never mentioned it to anybody. Not even my parents or my closest friends. I think I had never even admitted it to myself. And I definitely wasn't going to provide an explanation to this guy I'd met the day before.

"I think you're too young to get married. You need to enjoy life first, you know?"

Unbelievable! And now he was giving me The Look.

"Everybody says that! That's just because they've never found their true love."

"Maybe so." Why was he smiling? He must have been enjoying his interrogation. I wanted to have at least a quarter of his confidence. "Looks like your shuttle. Hurry! You don't want to miss it." Chris pulled up in front of the shuttle stop. "I'll see you later!"

"Okay. Thank you, Chris!" I quickly hopped out of the car and tried to avoid meeting his eyes.

***

I showed up at work too early. I took my time changing into the ugliest uniform one could possibly imagine. A striped white and blue shirt that reminded me of the one my dad used to wear in the early nineties, baggy navy-blue pants, and an apron. Plus – picture that! – the *enormous* shirt was supposed to be tucked into the pants. In the end, I looked like a flamboyant bloke with an enormous and strangely uneven ass. Frustrated, I walked away from the mirror and went outside to have a cigarette.

"Elena! It's time to come back in. Let me show you how to fold napkins." It was Laura, one of our supervisors. Laura was a super nice plump African-American lady with a very soft voice and innate inability to withstand any sort of conflict. Or brush it under the carpet.

Fold napkins! I never could fold anything in my life. I'm really awkward and clumsy – always have been. I was only left to hope they wouldn't be staring at me when I was trying to fold those napkins.

"Okay, Elena, have a seat right here. Let me look at the schedule and find out who will be your trainer tonight."

"Her trainer? I could do it, Laura." I couldn't believe my eyes. Standing right in front of me and casually leaning against the hostess stand was... Chris. I didn't even know he worked there! "Would you like to train with me, Elena?"

And then it happened. To explain exactly what happened and how it happened I need to rewind a decade or so back. As a little girl, I used to read a lot of romantic love stories. Starting from Cinderella and Sleeping Beauty in kindergarten, to Danielle Steele in middle school and finally finishing up with Gone with the Wind and Anna Karenina. I'd always been a hopeless romantic. As a teenager, I was not determined to change the planet - however shallow it might sound. I was programmed to find my true love and have this amazing big white wedding with everybody admiring the happy couple. I had everything planned – I chose a store I'd buy my wedding dress at when I was in fifth grade – so when I turned seventeen and still didn't have a steady boyfriend, I started proactively searching for one. I met Alex through my school friends in the movie theater one evening. I remember looking at him and finding him very witty and attractive. I love men who make me laugh. I recall looking at him and thinking, "This is the moment when two of us should be falling in love." And we did! It was just like in the books I read when I was a kid.

But back then, three years ago, in the balmy lilac warmth of the Russian summer evening, I was prepared for that moment. I knew it would happen! Hot and humid Georgia evening with the blood-orange sun reflecting in the Atlantic through the windows of the Beach Club dining room came as a complete surprise. So, my friends, let's go back just a touch.

"Would you like to train with me, Elena?" His eyes met mine, and I saw his white, mischievous smile. In one second, my chest was overwhelmed with so many unexpected emotions that I all of a sudden couldn't breathe. My heart seemed to disappear for a moment, and a weird electrical stream came from my ribcage down my arms and for some reason ended up in the tips of my fingers making them cold and sweaty. And I'm not speaking metaphorically. *What in the world was that?*

"Yes." I heard my voice and didn't recognize it. I was too busy listening to the Gone with the Wind theme that a pretty blonde pianist just started playing. Was this some kind of a set-up? Except... nobody knew about my dreams but me. How could it be happening to me? I had a fiancé and a wedding planned. This was so not like me! I should have learned to ride a bloody bike.

***

I just hadn't had sex for two weeks, and I was feeling horny. That was absolutely normal! And it had nothing to do with falling in love. Remember what Grandma said? Majority of flings happen because of romantic circumstances and don't have anything to do with finding Mr. Right. And she would know! She was cheating on granddad all his life long. And he was cheating on her, too. Maybe I should imagine that Alex and I were having sex. I needed to remember what it felt like. *So, we're coming back home, mom and dad are still at work...*

"Let's ask Elena! Elena, what do you think?"

Crap! I quickly lifted my eyes up just to see Chris and another server, Brendan (very cute, by the way), staring at me and apparently expecting me to give them some sort of answer. Bummer! Why couldn't it be a "yes or no" question? That way, I at least could have taken a 50/50 chance.

"About what?" I pretended to be totally preoccupied by folding a napkin. It wasn't that difficult to pull off, since in the last fifteen minutes Chris and Brendan folded about fifty of them, and I was still on my third. And it looked as if it had been munched on by a tiny Chihuahua.

"About the Iraq War, naturally. We've only been talking about it for half an hour. What have you been up to? Daydreaming about your boyfriend?"

His eyes were laughing at me. *Did he know exactly what I was trying to do? I was going to show him! I was going to prove him wrong.* I put on the most serious facial expression I could muster and said:

"I am a Russian in the U.S. – I can't voice my opinion or they'll think I'm a spy." And then I smiled with my sexy smile.

I had no idea why I did that, and I definitely shouldn't have. Chris gave me this long, heavy, and sensual stare and I felt like a fly stuck in the jam, helpless and desperately trying to get the fuck out.

"Gotta love those Russian girls," he finally said. "Looks like you're not gonna be that popular with the Russkies, Brendan."

"Oh, whatever, Chris. You're just an arrogant asshole."

"All righty then! Enough of BS for tonight. Come on, Elena! I need to show you a few things before the dinner service starts."

And off he went. I waved a quick bye to Brendan and scurried along in an unsuccessful attempt to catch up with Chris's straddle.

"Sorry for leaving in such a hurry. Can't stand spoiled frat boys who think they're king shit of turd mountain. Plus, we've got to keep moving. Remember, if you want to make a lot of money in service industry, you've got to always be on the move. So, how come you happen to be such an intelligent young lady? Are you in college?" Chris started filling up multiple pitchers with ice and water.

"Yes." I was happy he finally quit flirting with me and relaxed a little bit. "I study foreign languages and one day would like to work as an interpreter."

"Wow! That's cool! What languages do you speak?"

"English, German, Spanish, Japanese, and Russian." I'd always liked boasting about my ability to speak multiple languages. I would put a nonchalant face on and simply name all the languages I was fluent in. I'd always tried to keep it humble, as if I was saying, "I can breathe, walk, chew, pee," but in reality, I loved seeing people's astonished reactions. Does that sound very superficial?

"Really? Say something in Japanese!"

"Okay. Hajimemashite! Watashi wa Elena desu. Dozo yoroshiku onegaishimasu." I bowed my head in the traditional Japanese manner of greeting.

"That's impressive. And sexy! I used to have a Japanese girlfriend." Chris was placing coffee powder inside of the enormous industrial coffee makers. It would take me all shift long to figure out how to work those.

"You did? Why did you break up?" I was finally in the safe
waters. Talking about your girlfriends and boyfriends always
makes people seem more friends than possible lovers and takes
that initial flirtatious uneasiness away.

"It appeared she was screwing a bunch of other marines as
well. She was a buy-me-a-drink-girl."

"You were in the military?" It was my turn to be surprised
now.

"That was in my previous life, before I morphed into a peace-
loving musician." Chris smiled and quickly walked away from
the coffee station to the swinging door with the round window.

"Look, we have a table in our section. I'm about to go and fill
up their water glasses. Watch me through this window. Next
table is yours." And off he went again. God, what happened to
him? It was as if somebody turned on an invisible engine in his
butt. Cute butt, by the way. "OUCH!"

"Girl! What're you thinking standing in front of this door!
We're working here!" After I quit seeing little golden stars – the
result of a very painful door attack – I saw Sonia tripping after
Shirley, her trainer. She quickly turned around and whispered
"Fuck!" to me and kept on running. Apparently, Sonia also
didn't find waiting tables easy.

"Your turn!" I was just in time to step away from the evil
door when Chris flew in and handed me the pitcher. "There's a
five-top in the corner. Go over there and fill their glasses with
iced water. Remember, you should be pouring water clockwise,
gentlemen should always come last. Make sure that there's
plenty of ice in the glasses as well, not just water. Come on!"

I stared at him in shock. I might have been able to speak five
languages, but I never ever ever would be able to remember

what he'd just said and coordinate it with gracefully pouring water into the delicate glasses.

"Come on now! I'll be watching you from here. Don't worry, you'll be fine."

Yes, he is right. I shouldn't be freaking out. Just inhale, put the most dazzling smile on and GO!

I walked out of the kitchen and the last rays of the gorgeous Georgia sunset hit my eyes. I slowly approached my table. They looked very nice and extremely well-groomed. There were a mom and dad in their early fifties and three pretty girls of approximately my age.

"Good evening. May I?"

"Yes, please." The mom gave me a very polite smile, and I relaxed.

I managed to successfully accomplish my mission with the ladies. Gentleman last. When I started filling up the dad's glass, only the water came out. I need to shake it just a touch. Shake. Nothing. Shake. Bloody hell! Shake – CRAP! All the ice from the pitcher went all over his pants. His pants... Gucci, D&G, Versace? How long would I have to work to pay for the bloody pants? I didn't know what to say or do. I just stood there like a retarded monkey trying to pretend that it was a very bad dream. Then I looked up and saw red hair and a bright white smile.

"I'm sorry. This is my trainee, Elena, she's from Russia. This is her first day at work. Here are some fresh napkins. May I bring you anything else, sir?"

Oh, how thankful I was to him for being there! Even though now this nice family would think that all Russians were poorly coordinated orangutans.

"Oh, no! I'll be totally fine. It's just water. Russia? Wow! What brought you here all the way from Russia?"

As I started telling them our Work & Travel story, the horror of the last five minutes subsided and I could finally breathe. I couldn't believe I'd managed to get away with murder! Our interesting conversation was rudely interrupted by the loudest sound of breaking glass. In fact, it sounded like a glass factory had just exploded. And then I heard Sonia exclaim "Suka b...!" That's the privilege of working in a foreign country. You can shout taboo words out in public and nobody will ever know.

"Her first day also?" smiled the dad.

I nodded and tried not to burst out with laughter.

**

"Here you go! Have some. You definitely deserved it." Chris was handing me a glass of red wine.

"Are you sure it's fine to drink at work?"

"No, it's not fine. But the dinner's over, all the guests are gone, and you've had a stressful evening. Plus, I do it all the time."

He was partially right. We were polishing silver in the tea station. Tea stations were these three little booths discretely hidden between the grand columns of the Beach Club Dining Room. The guests just naively assumed that it was a mere decoration. In reality, they were servers' stations with everything one might need during breakfast, lunch or dinner. So here we were, polishing silver, drinking wine and chatting away.

"I couldn't believe you actually spilled it all over him," laughed Chris. "Crazy girl!"

"I'm very clumsy. My dad kept telling me I'd never make a good waitress."

"Nobody knows you better than you know yourself. Not even your parents."

Again, that stare. The heart-jumpy finger-tip-sweaty kind. I'd already grown used to it. At least used to pretending it didn't have any effect on me.

"What do you think about going to the beach? We can grab some wine and stargaze?"

That sounded so cool! I loved going to the beach at night. I'd only done it twice in my life. Once when I was twelve with my parents and their friends, when parents got drunk and went skinny dipping and we kids were stuck on the beach, sleepy and wondering how long it might take. And the second time during our college trip to Crimea with my best friend Kate and the guys we met at a night club. The guys played guitar, and we sang and drank wine.

"Sounds like fun! But I've got to come back home and let the girls know. They need to change and get ready."

"Oh. I was actually talking about just me and you."

"Chris." I paused and looked right in his eyes. "I'm engaged. I can't be doing this. Remember?"

There! I said it. It was out there in the open. Now he wouldn't be able to pretend it was fine to flirt with me.

"I know I know." He stood there, leaning against the counter, with the glass of wine in his hand. "But a little bit of fun before the wedding never hurt anyone."

Oh, God! His eyes. How can I explain this? He didn't even have to talk dirty to me. Everything he wanted to say or do was right there, in his eyes. My knees just went weak and soft. Traitors.

"You're horrible." I shook my head and picked up a tray with clean coffee cups and saucers. "Where should I put those?"

"Come on, Mother Superior, I'll show you."

I rolled my eyes and followed him to the dining room.

"They go inside of that cabinet, on the back shelf."

I bent over and tried to put the tray inside.

"Over here?" I yelled from inside of the cabinet.

"A bit farther"

"Here?"

"Just a touch farther"

"Bloody hell! Here?"

"Pretty much. Now arch your back a little bit."

I wanted to kill the crazy mofo! I jumped out, nearly hitting my head on the cabinet, my face all pink from embarrassment, stray hair awkwardly in my eyes.

"You think that's funny?"

But looking at him tilting his head backwards a little and laughing his ass off made me giggle as well. I forgot to tell you – I love men who are not afraid to joke dirty around girls. Call it perversion, but I believe it deserves respect.

"Okay, I'll give you that. It was funny!" I turned around and started walking away. "I've got to go. Shirley's agreed to give us a ride back home."

"Elena!"

"Yes?" I turned on my heel.

"Do you want to come back to my place?"

"Why?"

"We could have really mind-blowing sex."

"You're unbelievable!"

"Does it mean yes?"

"No." I smiled and shook my head. "See you later, Chris. Thanks for everything."

"See   ya!   Elena   the   Paina."

CHAPTER FOUR

1 Dalmatian and
Cruella de Copville

It turned out that getting to work wasn't as hard as it first appeared to be. After the girls told the entire Beach Club that I had to get up at 4:50 in the morning and walk 40 minutes to the shuttle stop, our coworkers started feeling sorry for me and offered to pick all four of us up. They even had this schedule worked out where different people would pick us up on different days. Worked great for the girls, too – no wearing themselves out on a bike, just a comfy car ride. Smartass bitches.

I was slowly getting used to waiting tables. I was actually even getting really good at it. The only problem was – sometimes I just couldn't understand the Southern drawl to save my life! And I hated waking up that early. But I absolutely loved the little break when the breakfast rush was over, and the lunch craziness didn't start yet. I just stood there by the tea station and stared at the immense ocean in front of me. Blue, and calm, and captivating. I couldn't believe we got to work at a place like this. The opulent interior and the spectacular landscape outside made me remember a TV commercial for a soap opera they used to show in Russia in the early nineties. The commercial would start off with amazing video clips of turquoise ocean waters, white sandy beaches, palm trees and dazzling orange sunsets accompanied by some cheesy music. Then the camera would change the focus and zoom in on a magazine-perfect, stunning couple strolling on the beach, jumping towards each other to embrace and lose themselves in a long kiss that would make everybody sitting in front of the boob tube, munching on fried potatoes, green with envy. And then, the deep voice behind the screen would say, "Do you want to see the world's most beautiful places? Do you want to experience whirlwind romance? Do you want to forget about the drudgery of your daily existence? If the answer to all of these questions is 'yes', then switch to Channel 1 every weekday at 7:00 pm and watch the amazing Santa Barbara. Live the life you will never experience in reality."

Talk of inspiring young minds to believe in the great future ahead of them.

I smiled as I thought that I had actually already managed to see quite a few places for my age. I had nobody to thank for that but my parents: they'd done their best to make sure my life wouldn't end on Santa Barbara.

We'd also made friends with the J-1 students from Slovakia. Monika – a very pretty and lively brunette - was working with us at the Beach Club, and Milo – the gorgeous dude – was in Room Service. We already got into the habit of having drinks at their place, which was across the street from our apartment. Pretty much nightly. The day before, for example, everybody was there. As I thought about last night, my treacherous heart that apparently had the mind of its own once again gave an unexpected jump. I'd already named this phenomenon "Chrisoparanoia." Because every time I thought of Chris, all these strange things started happening to me. I still honestly believed that was because I'd been sex-deprived for a while, and I just missed Alex. And Chris had the same sense of humor as Alex did, and I guess I happened to like him. Why not? We were allowed to like other people. Right? And it didn't mean that I was cheating on my fiancé or anything of the kind. Not even close.

I couldn't help but travel back to our chit-chat with Chris as all of us were chilling out at Milo's place and sharing our work stories.

"What time are you working tomorrow, Elena? "At 7 a.m. again! That's horrible! I'm not sure I can survive waking up THAT early every morning." My eyes got wide and sparkly as I looked at Chris. It always happens to me when I get tipsy and carried away.

"Well, you know you don't have to do that. You can just move in with me and I'll take care of you. You will never have to work again." Chris was definitely enjoying messing with me.

"Yeah, right. That sounds like a good plan. I might take you up on that one."

"I'm 100% serious. You want to start moving in right now?"

"Ha ha ha! I don't think so. I live in Russia, remember? All my family is still there and all that fun stuff."

"All right then. Don't move in if you don't want to. You're still welcome to come back to my place tonight."

"Why would I do that?"

"I have orange ice cream."

I stared at him incredulously. I was feeling light and dizzy with wine. There was no tension left, we were just playing around and enjoying each other's company. But... I lost the thread of our game. Ice cream? At that very moment, Chris leaned forward really fast so that his eyes were right in front of mine and our lips nearly touched.

"Deliciously refreshing after hard-core sex." He smiled and got back to his place as fast as he'd come close to me.

Bloody hell. I could only hope I didn't look as horny as I felt.

"Guys! What are you up to?" Drunkenly happy Vera jumped on the couch right between us and handed me a full glass of wine. Thank fuck. I was drowning there. "Chris, are you hitting on our engaged girl?"

Vera giggled and patted Chris on the shoulder. Then she turned to face me and quietly said in Russian, "What the fuck do you think you're doing?" And then again in English: "Okay, I just thought I'd bring Elena more booze. Have fun, kids!" And off she went.

Okay, Elena. Relax. Find your inner Zen. Inhale.

"Are you all right? You look like you've seen a ghost." Chris was surveying me with those intense eyes. Oh mine. I still had to somehow survive three and a half months and stay faithful.

"Yes, I'm fine. I think I have to go to bed. You know, waking up at 5 a.m. and all that." I waved my hand in a not very

successful attempt to seem nonchalant and started to shift off the couch.

"Elena, wait. I thought you might want to have my phone number – just in case." Out of the blue, I felt Chris's fingers on my lower back. Oh no, please don't touch me. I was so full of sexual tension at that moment, Electric Barbarella had nothing on me. Why was he touching me there anyways? I caught his hand and found a post-it with his phone number in my jeans.

"I figured I'd put it somewhere where you can always find it. Nighty night!"

"Guys! Let's take a group picture! Elena, Chris, come here!" This time Diana came to my rescue. "Milo, Monika, Tyler, come on! Group picture of our first party in America!"

Only after the flash blinded me did I notice that Chris's hand was casually rested on my hip. As if it'd always been there. What was wrong with me? Does the flight over the Atlantic chemically change your brain? Or affects one's personality? Note to self – hide that picture from Alex when back at home.

"Elena! This couple's been sitting in your section forever! What do you think you're doing?" The high-pitched voice penetrated the pink bubble of my memories and I felt as if I'd fallen from the sky and painfully hit the ground. The voice belonged to Carla, one of the Beach Club dining room captains, who was eyeing me up and down with reproach. "Come on, go take their drink order. Girl, no daydreaming at work!"

I guess I'd gotten a bit distracted by thinking about last night. To my utter distress, I could already see that these people didn't really like me. Why would they? I had no idea how long they'd been waiting.

"Good afternoon! I apologize for making you wait. I'm new, and I'm not quite used to the way things are here." I gave them the most polite "I'm a new, cute, not-that-bright Russian girl" smile I could possibly muster. "What can I get you to drink?"

"That's okay, honey! I'll take an Awna Pawma, please," the posh-looking woman with big blond hair smiled and swiftly got back to studying the menu.

"Sweet tea for me, please," announced her partner.

Fuck me. What in the world is Awna... What?

"Absolutely!"

I somehow managed to fake a confident smile and walked off straight into the kitchen. Diana was standing in front of the Micros computer, humming a Russian pop song, jiggling her hips left and right in the typical disco fashion, and placing the lunch order in the system.

"Do you know what kind of drink is Awna something?" I grabbed her hand in despair.

"Elena. Are you still hung-over?" She stared at me, calm and casual – the total contrast to my disturbed self. "Are we going to Chris's party tonight, by the way? Everybody at the Beach Club seems to be going."

What? What was she talking about? Why would I care about some stupid party? Realizing she couldn't help me, I rushed towards Carla.

"Carla, what is Awna Pawma?" I've tried to articulate as much I could recall the pronunciation.

Carla just glared back at me as if I was a crazy person talking gibberish. Come to think of it, I guess I was.

"Girl, I ain't gotta a clue what you're talking 'bout!"

"Oh, Diana." I turned back to her, nearly crying. "I can't go back to those people and tell them I didn't know what they ordered. They already hate me, and now they'll just think I don't understand English on top of that!"

"Elena, relax! Just calm down and repeat what she said one more time," said Chris, who stuck his head out from behind the towel room door.

"Awna Pawma," I sounded like a retarded cow.

"Arnold Palmer. The southern accent must have confused you. Half iced tea, half lemonade. Named after a famous golfer." Chris flashed me a smile. "I told you I'll always take care of you. And chill out. You can't be waiting tables and freak out like that with no reason."

How did he manage to always show up at the least expected moment? And act like he was in total control of the situation?

"Here. Take it to the table." Chris handed me the glass and walked off.

"Did you know he's almost thirty-eight? He looks so young!"

Still dumbfounded, I looked at Diana and shrugged.

"I couldn't care less about his age. And no, I'm not going to the party. And you shouldn't be going either – we were not invited."

"Oh, now you're acting bitchy," laughed Diana. "If you don't want any attention from him, quit egging him on."

"What? I'm not egging him on! And I'm not acting bitchy!"

"You are and you are!" Diana was all Mrs. Serious all of a sudden. "I saw you yesterday night at Milo's place. This thing you were doing with your eyes."

"What thing?"

"You know? The thing!" Diana rolled her eyes in an exaggerated flirtatious manner. I knew exactly what she was talking about. Alex had always been making fun of this habit of mine. "You like him!"

"No I don't!" I retorted.

"You do! You like him! You want him! You dirty slut." – Diana was apparently having a time of her life at my expense.

"Whatever. Oh, shit! People with their drink order!"

I quickly ran out of the kitchen with the tray of drinks and thanked goodness. They were at the buffet filling up their plates. I didn't even have to talk to them at that point. Just drop the drinks off and go...

"Easy, mama!" As I turned around in a rush to get away from the table I walked straight into Chris.

I told you. He was everywhere. I lifted my eyes to look at him.

"Thank you for helping me out earlier."

"You're welcome. You were in the weeds. Try to avoid that at all costs."

"What are 'the weeds'?"

"Having too much on your plate when you're waiting tables. It's called being in the weeds. Always stay cool. People can sense when you panic."

That was it. That was what I found so sexy. He looked very young, but his eyes were the eyes of a guy who had lived a little. Everything that he said made so much sense, as if I just started formulating the thought, and he already had the correct solution. It was annoying and attractive at the same time.

"So are you coming to the party then? I didn't quite hear what you told Diana."

Oh, no. He'd been there all the time, listening to me mooing "Awna Pawma" eight hundred times.

"It was the first time I heard about the party. I don't think we're coming, we weren't invited."

"Everybody's invited."

"I don't know about that. In Russia, you can't come to people's parties unless you were personally invited. It's impolite."

"Well, you're in the U.S. of A now, honey bunny! I'm expecting all four of you to be there."

"Well, we'll see."

"No "we'll see" and no excuses. Excuses are like assholes – everybody has one."

"Okay," I snorted with laughter. "We'll be there."

Had I just rolled my eyes again?

***

And there we were. Standing in front of this amazing illuminated swimming pool with approximately fifty already intoxicated people partying away. Three coolers full of beer, a vodka watermelon (a vodka watermelon?!), and extremely loud music. I was pretty sure all four of us felt as if we had suddenly stepped into a scene from American Pie. That's what all Russians of our generation base their beliefs on what American party looks like –American Pie. I couldn't help the silly giggle as I remembered our conversation with the girls when we were beautifying ourselves for the party.

"We've got to watch out," said Sonia. "Everybody screws everybody in America. One minute you have one drink too many, and next thing you know – you've just had sex with somebody you can't remember the name of!"

"You sound like a real expert," I laughed as I was trying to apply the thick eyeliner on my eyes. "Have you done it a lot?"

"No!" yelled Sonia, "But I've watched all three American Pies. Out of the blue, she jumped at me and started tickling me hard on the sides. "Why are you putting so much make-up on, Elena? Oh, let me guess! Chris the Trainer?"

"Aaghhh!!" I was laughing and crying at the same time. "Look at what you've done! I look like bloody Frankenstein! Get off me, you crazy woman!"

"Bitchesssssssssssss!" That was Vera, standing in the doorway and looking all fresh and glamorous. "Should I put these pink stilettos on or these purple ones? What do you think?"

"Hmmm... I don't like either of them. Hold on – try these!" I dove into the dark and scary Loch Ness mess of my closet and managed to dig out my most perfect and favorite wedges with the golden rim. They cost me three times my monthly salary as a part-time foreign language teacher. Needless to say, I loved them to bits.

"Oh, Elena, are you sure?"

"No, but you should grab them and leave this room before I change my mind. Quickly! One, two, three – go!"

"I'm outta here!"

And off she went, just to be replaced by Diana holding my leopard-patterned top.

"Elena." Diana started the sentence really slowly and seriously, like a UN proposal speech. "Do you mind if I wear this tonight." She said it just like that, without the question mark.

"Yes, I do! I'm wearing this tonight! Where did you even get this?"

"I put it in the wash," Diana shrugged and started slowly backing up. "You never wash anything, so I thought I'd help you out."

"Diana." I narrowed my eyes. "Don't mess with me! We're leaving in five minutes and I look like I'm going to the Halloween party thanks to Sonia! Next time, it's yours. I promise."

Apparently, we all ended up looking pretty damn good. We were surrounded by guys of all ages, body types and skin colors. Goodness, American girls have it going on! Russian men never pay enough attention to women. They follow one of the most famous poems of the most prominent Russian poet, Alexander Pushkin, who unfortunately for us, Russian girls, once wrote:

The less we love her when we woo her,
The more we draw a woman in.

As you can probably imagine, the psychology of dating in Russia is quite different from the States. I can definitely understand why so many Russian girls end up getting together with guys from the USA or Europe. Who wouldn't like to be adored like that? All the time!

"So you came here all the way from Russia?" A longish-haired boy named Scott was staring at Vera, googly-eyed. You could actually see strawberry ice cream cones reflected in his eyes instead of Vera's face. "Your accent is so sexy. Say something else!"

Oh, for fuck's sake.

"Elena, quickly! Come here, let's have some vodka watermelon! It's so funny, but it'll make you drunk in no time!" Monika, who was already wearing a bikini, grabbed me by the arm and pretty much dragged me to the edge of the pool.

"Monika! How many slices have you already had?" I rubbed my wrist. "I'll have a bruise here tomorrow, I swear."

"Just five." Monika surely didn't hear the irony in that. "Here, have some! You'll love it!"

"Wowy-zowy! Look at who's here! Mrs. I haven't been invited, I'm too cool for school!"

I looked down in the direction of the voice and saw... a very happily drunk host. How many watermelons had he consumed? Fifteen?

"Elena the Paina!" Chris's voice was at least ten octaves too high, but it worked out all right since the music was so loud, you couldn't hear yourself think. "Why don't you jump in?"

"I'm not wearing a swimsuit," I managed to utter as I was chewing on the juicy watermelon. "Wow! That IS good."

"Well, you should go change, then." Chris pulled himself up and sat on the edge of the pool.

The air was so warm and humid, and the watermelon was so effective, I thought it was actually a brilliant idea.

"My apartment is right there! 2B." Chris waved in the direction of the apartment complex. "The door is open. Help yourself to whatever you can find."

Oh, God. I didn't even want to think what he meant by "whatever you can find."

"Maybe some orange ice cream?" I grinned and tried not to look at him too much. In his swimming shorts on the edge of the pool. Red hair all disheveled. That smile again. Stop!

"Silly Russian! He he!" This time it was Milo. "What orange ice cream are you talking about?"

"The sexy one." Chris winked at me and took a large gulp of Heineken.

"Watch out, Christopher! Elena's fiancé the soccer referee will kick your ass!" Milo apparently found this conversation extremely entertaining.

"He sure will! All right then, I'll go change!"

"Don't change too much. I like you the way you are."

Was everything he said a pick-up line? I had to remember to write them down for my English class back at home. I approached the girls that were still surrounded by what seemed like an even larger group of male Homo sapiens species and asked Sonia if she wanted to come with me.

"Sure! Let's go. I'm dying to jump in this pool. Isn't it cool – a pool party! Nobody will believe us back at home."

"We've got to take more pictures. It's so pretty here – everywhere!" I said as I pushed the apartment door open.

"Dalmatian!" exclaimed Sonia. "Look at this pretty, pretty doggie!

The Dalmatian was indeed very good-looking. And friendly. In fact, when I tried to pet his head, he got on his back legs and gave me a hug. Sweet! I looked around, half-way expecting to see a dirty barren bachelor's dive. Not at all! Chris's apartment had light-orange walls, a yellow microwave and it smelled of those nice multicolored candles that might be confused with food in the state of extreme intoxication. The fridge was completely covered with pictures of Chris's trips around the world and his girlfriends. A lot of them. I had to stand and count them for quite a while when I was waiting for Sonia to change.

"Come on, Elena! Hurry up!"

"That's fine. Just go! I'll see you outside."

"Okay then!"

I quickly changed into my bikini and walked outside. The party was still going on, but something had changed... Who was that guy screaming at Tyler? I came closer to the pool and stopped next to Monika and Milo.

"I'm telling you right now! My grandson was asleep. You woke him up – turn the music off right now! It's 1 o'clock in the morning for God's sake!"

"But sir! We'll turn it down. I promise. We won't bother you anymore."

"Turn the god damn music off, or I'm calling the cops!" Barked the furious neighbor and stormed off.

As soon as these magic words were heard by the people at the party, everybody started slowly jumping the ship. They're so disciplined in America! In Russia, nobody would even notice that the neighbor was there.

"Should we leave?" I asked Monika.

Before I could get the proper answer, I heard a loud splash and then the sound of my own body hitting the pool surface. I got up from underneath the water, my thick eyeliner dripping down my cheeks.

"Ooops, sorry! I didn't hurt you, did I?" Chris actually looked worried. "I thought I grabbed your leg a bit too hard. Are you okay?"

"I'm fine," I said, laughing and trying to get the make-up off my face. "The question is – are you okay looking at the smudged-eyeliner face? Just be honest with me – do I look like the Joker from Batman?"

"No." Chris smiled with this content expression of a very drunk person. "You always look beautiful, I told you."

It was very romantic and all, but the lovely scene was rudely interrupted by the police siren piercing the quiet summer night. All of a sudden, a cop car – just like in the movies – pulled up in front of the pool. And out of the car came this creature. Blond, untidy, overweight. She pointed the flashlight right into our faces and screeched:

"You motherfuckers! Get your fucking asses out of the god damn swimming pool right now!"

As a narrator, I'm trying to limit the usage of curse words in my book to the very necessary minimum. This, however, is a word-for-word quotation that all of us will remember forever.

We all swiftly got out of the pool. All of us but Chris. He seemed to be enjoying himself as he was doing his laps across the pool. Slowly and obviously very annoyingly for the weird female police monster.

"Listen, you fucker. Get out of the fucking pool! Do as I say!"

"I thought we were living in a free country," said Chris as he turned around to do the next lap.

I barely managed to suppress a snort of laughter. This is exactly how I would have liked to act in the situation. In fact, one day I got into such a hot argument with Voronezh militia men, Alex had to bribe them to prevent my imminent arrest. Alex, my superhero. I can't help it: I just get a bit carried away in my attempt to save the world from injustice and start saying things that one is not supposed to say to law enforcement officers. But that was at home. Here I was too scared of deportation. My thoughts were interrupted by Cruella screaming into Chris's face. At that point, Chris was already out of the pool and facing her.

"If you continue to resist arrest, I will have to mace you!"

"But I'm not resisting." Chris shrugged and laughed in her face.

"Sir, if you continue to resist arrest, I'll have to mace you."

"Okay, mace me then, mace me mace me mace me!" Chris dropped on his knees and put his face down on the ground. "Mace me mace me mace me!"

He was mocking her ruthlessly, and he did manage to throw her off her game.

She lost control of the situation and shrieked, "Get this idiot in the car right now! We're taking him to Brunswick jail!"

And off they went. Chris's swimming shorts dripping, him still smiling away – you've got to respect that. Then his head was pushed in the car and they started pulling off.

Monika, Milo, Tyler, and the four of us stared at each other in disbelief. What in the world had just happened? Before we could recover from the initial shock, we heard the brakes screech. A pretty little brunette girl in a bikini was standing by the cop car and apparently trying to convince them to let Chris go. Cruella reappeared from behind the wheel of her hell machine, grabbed the girl, and pushed her in the back of the car. And then they disappeared into the night.

"Who was that?" I heard myself ask.

"It's Farrah," said Monika. "Chris's best friend. They do everything together."

"Everything?" Diana arched her brows with her usual irony and gave me a nasty look.

"Looks like it." I felt a green ugly worm crawling through my chest. *Oh great, Elena.*

"Jealous?"

How did Diana always manage to say the last thing I wanted to   hear?

CHAPTER FIVE

PMS or Potential Manslaughter Syndrome

I am convinced that majority of murder cases occur when one of the parties involved suffers from the **PMS**. Premenstrual syndrome, that is. A lot of research is bound to be done in this area, since somebody has to explain to us, women, how on earth our bodies can become temporary headquarters for a horrendous, spiky-haired, evil monster that we all turn into every twenty-eight days or so. I would like to declare that, contrary to what men may think, we are not capable of controlling the creature in any way, shape, or form. She just shows up, all red-haired, snake-tongued and fire-breathing, and possesses our minds entirely. Believe me. It's true.

The condition may intensify if provoked by the events outside of our control zone. That was the only way I could explain why I was standing in the middle of the Beach Club kitchen, spitting the most horrible Russian profanities I could possibly think of, throwing my arms about in the most insane fashion, and stomping my feet. The target of my aggression was Diana, and I've got to come back to the events of the last evening to justify my unruly behavior to you, my darling reader.

The previous day, after work, Monika invited me to join her for dinner and drinks at Locos, a local bar just a short five-minute walk from our apartment complex. It sounded like a great idea. Something to break up our routine of work and parties at Milo's condo. We had a delicious dinner, a cheese quesadilla with jalapenos (ironically, the best food I discovered for myself in America), and even more delicious beer. I had approximately three of them. Or more. It's always difficult to tell when you're ordering pitchers of beer, how much magic liquid you exactly consume. On the other hand, it makes it very easy to blame it on your friends: "Noooo, I didn't drink at all; now, Monika – what a beast!" Anyhow, by the time the waitress showed up with the fourth pitcher, my vision was already just a touch blurry, and everything around me seemed to be pink and glittery. Like the Barbie doll world. At this exact moment, in walked Ken. AKA Chris. I jumped up in my seat as I saw him plunge in the booth next to me. I hear you. You're thinking: are you psychotic or something? Being extremely fond of somebody doesn't necessarily make one act spastic. I would agree. However, after the night before I decided to try my best to avoid Chris at all costs.

That morning before work I walked to the pay phone behind our neighborhood McDonald's and called Alex. Hearing his so familiar voice was soothing and comforting. Okay, I'm lying – it was more like a refreshing slap on the face that screamed, "What are you doing, crazy brat? Everything that has to do with Chris is in your head. You still have your fiancé, who also happens to be your best friend and who loves you to bits. And who doesn't have a slightest idea about what's been going on in your bug-infested brain. And Chris apparently has Farrah." End of story. It made everything so easy. I couldn't even believe I let a tiny little bit of any other alternative at some point in time visit my sick mind.

So here I was. A new me, free of any sort of silly romantic delusions and one hundred percent wasted. As you can probably imagine, I didn't expect to turn my spinning head and see Chris's face peeking at me through the fog of beer-infused reality.

"Aren't you supposed to be in jail?" That was the best greeting I could think of.

"Uhh, nice to see you too, young lady. What's up, uncle Milo?! Monika, what's going on, beautiful?"

"Have some beer with us, Christ-O-pher." That's how Milo pronounced his name – with a very strong emphasis on "O". Christ-O-Pher.

"I guess I don't have much of a choice. I'm afraid our Russian needs to be cut off before she falls under the table."

"Oh, whatever!" I've got to admit, my "whatever" came out just a little unclear. I tried to suppress a stubborn hiccup to no avail. "I'm perfectly fine. I just had one glass of beer."

"You mean one pitcher of beer, Russian princess?"

"Why are we talking about me, anyway? How did it go in Brunswick jail, Mr. Mace Me Mace Me Mace Me?"

"It was amazing. I was surrounded by a gangster-looking guy covered in blood, a disheveled woman who kept on saying that she'd just knifed her husband, and Farrah in her wet bikini. The last part wasn't that bad, considering." Chris gave everybody around the table the most arrogant boyish smile I'd ever seen in my life.

I'm assuming the sour expression on my face was quite obvious, since Chris quickly added, "She's just my friend."

"Yeah right!" Grinned Milo. "A friend with benefits."

"Don't listen to them, Elena. They're just silly boys." Monika jumped to my help. "Hey, listen, have you ever tried a margarita?"

"No, what is it?"

By the time half of the deliciously sour nectar in my tall glass was gone, our table was all of a sudden approached by a pretty brunette girl wearing spectacles.

"Oh, hi, Lori! I've been wondering what took you so long." Chris got up from his seat and gave the girl a peck on the cheek. "Lori, these are my friends from Slovakia – Milo and Monika. I went to visit them in February? And this is our beautiful Russian princess, Elena."

I immediately blushed. I wish he would stop addressing me like royalty. Especially in the presence of the people I didn't know.

"Would you like something to drink, Lori?"

I shot Monika a look. If one could draw a bubble like the ones they do in comic books, mine would contain one giant question mark. Was she Chris's girlfriend? He certainly was acting like she was. To make things even worse, Milo and Monika got up and announced that they were going outside to smoke. Great.

"Yes, please. I'll have a Corona." Lori sat down in the booth opposite me and smiled. The smile was wide and intended to be polite.

"So, Elena, what brought you here all the way from Russia?"

"I'm on the student program called "Work & Travel USA". I came here to work for four months. And practice my English."

"I see!" Her smile got even wider. "So you're in college! How old are you if I may ask?"

Was I suffering from alcohol-induced evil eye, or was this question really a bit out of place?

Chris seemed to be surprised by the direction of the conversation as well.

"Twenty. One," I quickly added. "Twenty one." I had totally forgotten I was lounging in an American bar drunk as a skunk and underage according to American law. In Russia people quit drinking by the time they turn twenty-one. But... I was in the USA, and as they say when in Rome...

"I see!" Lori's smile couldn't possibly get wider. She looked like she'd had a face lift.

"Yes. Elena is this extremely talented and gorgeous Russian porn star who speaks five languages and can drink a bartender under the table." Chris seemed to be having too much fun. I came to the realization that he in general enjoyed being in the center of controversial situations.

"And she is about 20 years younger than you," Lori was still smiling away. My facial muscles started hurting just from looking at her.

"Seventeen – to be more precise," said Chris as he kept his eyes glued to mine. It occurred to me that neither of us even looked at Lori in the last five minutes.

"I think I'll join Milo and Monika outside for a cigarette." I jumped off my seat nearly knocking over the rest of my margarita.

"Actually, I've got to go." Lori quickly grabbed her purse and car keys.

I looked down at her beer. It was untouched. Just a lonely slice of lime sticking out of the bottle and asking, "Aren't you going to eat me?"

"Okay then, Lori. Nice seeing you. We'll catch up, okay?" Chris lazily took his eyes of mine and nodded to Lori. He didn't even try to stop her.

"See you. Was pleasure meeting you, Elena!"

"It was nice to meet you too, Lori."

When she was gone, I stared back at Chris accusingly.

"You were being rude to your girlfriend."

"She's not my girlfriend and it was her that was being rude. She was implying I was Chester the molester. She's just jealous. Do you want me to walk you back home?"

"I wanted to have a cigarette with Monika first, and I'll be fine. I can get home by myself."

"If I know Milo and Monika, they're nowhere to be seen. Those two are supposed to get married and have five kids, but they don't know it yet. That's for one. Secondly, you can't be walking home alone. It's too late."

"Okay then." I shrugged. "Let's go. I have to get up at the ungodly hour of five in the morning."

We walked out into the plush coziness of the Georgia summer night and I inhaled an unusual aroma I was already getting used to.

"What is this smell?" I asked.

"I farted."

"You are horrible!" I snorted. "It might as well be, but I don't think so. I've noticed it a few days in a row. It's a very pungent and overpowering smell. Not that pleasant at first, but then you grow to like it."

"It's the marsh. The famous marshes of Glynn. So how is Alex doing?"

I quickly lifted my eyes. He was mocking me again.

"As a matter of fact, he's great, thank you. I called him this morning. He just finished playing soccer with his dad and they were drinking beer."

"Nice. Well, we're already here, Mrs. Engaged and Proper."

"Thank you, Chris. I'll see you later."

As I turned to walk away, Chris quickly grabbed my wrist, spun me around and pinned me to the wall. Just like that. Let me tell you, every girl dreams of this moment. Every girl wants to be spun around and pinned to the wall by a guy she likes. It probably has something to do with unconscious inferiority to a strong male species or somewhat along those lines, but the feeling can't be compared to anything else. A woman feels turned on and helpless at the same time. A woman loses her breath and her sanity for one brief moment. And Chris knew that perfectly well.

I could smell his scent and I could feel his warm hands on my waist. He tried to kiss me, and I turned away. His lips touched my neck, and I felt like the whole universe around me was about to explode. It actually did explode, and in the center of the chaos I saw Alex's face. Sad and disappointed. I pushed Chris away.

"No! I can't be doing this, Chris. I'm sorry."

I briskly turned around and shut the door. *That's it. Now, let's catch the breath and go to bed. You haven't done anything.*

As I tiptoed through the black hole of our living room, I hit my foot on something really heavy – probably a portable stereo.

"Shit!"

I jumped to the bedroom I shared with Diana on one foot and blindly tried to search for the bathroom light.

"Elena, is that you, dirty slut?"

That was Diana, obviously.

"Yes, that's me!"

"Did you finally have sex with Chris?"

"No!" I whispered. "I'm engaged, remember?"

"Oh yeah, right. Whatever."

"But..."

"What?"

"He is probably a VERY good lover."

"Sweet dreams then. Elena?"

"Hmm?

"Clean up that horrific mess in our closet, will you? Your side looks like Hiroshima after the explosion."

"Okay, okay. Good night."

The night went by annoyingly fast. I just closed my eyes, and the next minute the nasty alarm clock was already beeping. I got up, hung-over and not quite understanding where I was and why, got dressed with the speed that a trained military officer may envy and ran out with the girls to catch our ride. All our work days started as a big blur. I honestly think I was more asleep than awake until approximately noon.

After waiting my morning tables like a drugged-up zombie and miraculously surviving the breakfast shift, I comfortably perched myself on the chair in the towel room and prepared to enjoy my iced coffee. Suddenly, Farrah and Chris walked into the room laughing their asses off.

"What's going on, Elena the Paina?" Chris nodded, picked up a tray full of silver and walked out. Farrah followed. Was it just a game of my imagination or did Chris seem to be just a touch too confident? Why would he? Shutting the door in somebody's face doesn't typically boost their self-esteem.

I shrugged and figured I didn't really care. It was Alex's mom's birthday and I had to find a way to give her a call. I finished the coffee and was about to go outside for a cigarette, when Monika showed up from around the corner and whispered:

"Elena! I've got to tell you something. About Diana."

Apparently, Chris had come by that morning to our apartment thinking that I was off and wanting to probably try another devilish tactic of his that could take me off my marriage path. He didn't know that all of us, except Diana, were at work. Diana invited him in and they had a nice chit-chat on the couch, during which Diana didn't fail to mention that I thought that

Chris was a VERY good lover. To be more exact, I imagine she actually said:

"Chrrrris!" Diana has a very strong Russian accent, and she always rolls her "rrr" in an accentuated James Bond girl manner. "Elena said that you must be a great lover! Is it trrrue?"

"Elena," Monika kept whispering. "Now Chris is even more determined to ... you know. Get in your pants? He told Milo about this, Milo told me... and I figured you needed to know...."

Now you can see, my darling reader, how I came to this insane state of foot stomping and cursing in the Beach Club kitchen. And yes, my period should have been starting soon, which didn't make me particularly pink and fluffy.

"Why the fuck would you even consider saying anything like that?!" That was the last sentence of my hot and spicy monologue. To be honest with you, I don't remember the beginning of it. I just recall that Vera and Sonia had to hold me back as I was trying to scratch Diana's eyes out.

When I regained consciousness and looked around I saw about ten pairs of eyes staring at me with the expression of total shock and — yes, thank goodness — non-comprehension. At least I was screaming in Russian. I still could get my reputation of a sweet Russian girl back. Now if they'd understood what I'd just said... Better not even go there.

"Why would you do that?" All my negative energy seemed to have left me at once and I simply asked Diana the question. "Why?"

"Because it was true." Diana shrugged.

She wasn't even slightly fazed by anything I'd just said. Not a bit. The picture of pure innocence.

"Elena."

"Yes?" I answered without even looking at her. I was tired and in pain. I wanted to take twenty Advils and pass out until next year.

"How did you meet Alex?"

"What? Why?"

"How did you and Alex meet?"

"My high school friend introduced us at a movie theater. Why?"

"Not romantic at all, is it?" Diana rolled her eyes.

I'm going to kill her.

"You're fucking crazy!" I shrieked and went for her hair as she tried to escape through the hell door into the dining room.

"Stop it!" This time it was Sonia yelling. "Both of you! Break it up! Do you want us to lose our jobs and be sent back home? Let's just relax and discuss it back at the condo, okay?"

We did discuss it back at the condo. We had about five vodka shots each, and Diana apologized for not thinking straight – she didn't quite realize how far gone Chris and I were in our flirting game. And I told her I was sorry for calling her the most horrendous names. And then we had four more shots each and Diana even came outside with me and had a cigarette. I remember thinking that she didn't really know how to smoke, because she didn't inhale, but I appreciated the company. I needed it.

It'd been already an hour since Diana went back inside to sleep. It was a beautiful quiet night, and I was still sitting on the steps and staring at an enormous magnolia tree in bloom. The heavy orange crescent of the moon was hanging right above it, and it seemed like it was going to fall and hit the tree any minute. Big white flowers blurred in my eyes and sunk in the saltiness of my tears. I felt stupid and guilty. It wasn't Diana's fault. I was to blame for everything. I got carried away in my game of hide-and-seek with Chris. I was delusional.

I closed my eyes and tried to imagine Alex kissing me in the rain after his soccer match. He'd just finished his referee work, and I was waiting for him at the stadium. As I saw him come close, the warm summer rain started pouring down and we kissed and laughed.

"Elena! My darling Elena! I can't believe you've been waiting for me in this weather. Come on! Let's go home and have some hot tea and a bite to eat. I'm starving."

And we went. And hot tea was followed by even hotter sex and movie watching in bed. And the rain drops were drumming on the window.

I opened my eyes. The crescent was still hanging over the magnolia tree. Strangely enough, it didn't fall.

I was such a bloody idiot. How could I even think about betraying Alex? And Chris. He had something going on with this girl. What was her name? Farrah. They *were* doing everything together. I never knew she worked at the Beach Club until they walked in the towel room together earlier today. He probably was telling her about me and Diana. I was such a sucker. But I deserved it. It was a nice kick in the hiney to snap me back to reality. I wiped my tears with the sleeve of my denim jacket and was already about to get back in the condo, when I heard him.

"Elena!"

Chris was walking from Milo's apartment. He was barefoot and drunk. He was wearing his Beach Club uniform and carrying the work shoes in his hands. As he approached me, he put his shoes down on the ground and took my face in his palms.

"Elena. You're turning me on. I'm thinking about you all the time. About your eyes. I want to kiss these eyes all night long."

Another flashback took me half a year ago into the freezing cold Russian night. Alex was walking me back home through the dark and dangerous courtyards of the Soviet apartment complexes. The snow was a thick layer of glittering white on tall pine trees, and the stars were cold and distant. The air was so crisp we could taste the frost on our lips. And the only sound that we could hear was the crunching snow under our feet. I was looking forward to coming back home and having a cup of tea with mom and dad, maybe watching a late night movie with mom after dad went to bed.

"You never pay me compliments." I was whining and teasing him at the same time. "I think you're taking me for granted."

"But I love you more than anybody ever will. And I know exactly what I love about you. I don't have to talk about this all the time."

"But women love compliments. It keeps us going you know." I laughed.

"Okay! Let's see. Your eyes are such a deep blue color. Like the ocean. When I look into them, I feel like I might drown."

He was messing with me. I gave him a look from under my eyelashes, and noticed that he was dead serious.

Suddenly his face disappeared and I saw Chris still holding his hands on my cheeks. Eyes... Two different nights. One cold, one warm. White snow, white magnolias. A guy that loves me, and a guy that just plays around with me.

"Leave me alone!" I hissed and threw Chris's hands off my face. "Just go away and leave me alone."

"But wait, Elena! I wanted to tell you – "

"Yes, yes, I know. I'm too young to get married, one kiss won't ruin my engagement. Just go AWAY! You don't know anything. You don't know me. You're nobody. Two weeks ago I didn't even know you existed. I don't even know why we're having this discussion."

"Do you really want me to leave?"

"Yes, I do," I whispered.

"Okay. If you want me to quit bugging you, just tell me to fuck off. And I'll never bother you again."

"Okay then. Fuck off." I said it quietly. With no emotion. Looking him straight in the eye.

Chris's shoulders slumped and he looked at me as if I was guilty of mutilating a thousand innocent kittens. Then, without uttering a word, he picked his shoes up and walked off to his car. Barefoot. As I heard the engine start, I lit another cigarette. I'd done the right thing. Back to normal now.

CHAPTER SIX

Alice in

Wonder-Elevator

I'm falling and I'm scared senselessly. I'm trapped in the tiniest elevator ever, I can't breathe, and I'm falling. Except... I'm falling up. If an ordinary elevator malfunctions and drops, you know you're about to hit the ground. In the misbehaving, constantly accelerating Wonder-Elevator, you're afraid of going up. At first, you're not quite sure what's going to happen. You just know that you're horribly frightened and you're not looking forward to it. And then the realization hits you like a bucket of freezing water. But of course! Silly me. I'm about to hit the roof and fly out into the sky. And as you realize this, the Fear grips your insides, penetrates your heart like a sharp spear and then multiplies into the smallest drops of sweat all over your body. And then you –

"Wake up! Elena, wake up!"

"What? Vera, what are you doing here?"

"Uhh, how about — I'm trying to make sure you are not going to die from a heart attack in your sleep?"

"Oh yes, shit." I sat up in my bed, still half asleep and trying to recover from the nightmare. "It's my recurring dream. I've had it for the last couple of years." I frowned and touched my forehead. Ice-cold.

"I don't envy you on that one." Vera looked dubious. "You want to go to the pool for a swim? It's already 4 o'clock."

Both Vera and I were off today. Exhausted after working seven days straight and waking up before dawn, I decided to take an afternoon nap. I regretted it now. I would have been more useful, if I'd cleaned up the closet. Diana would devour me when she got home and saw that it still looks the same. Ruined. I looked at Alex's photo sitting on my bedside table and rubbed my eyes.

"Let's go to the pool. And then I need to call Russia."

"But you just called him yesterday..." sighed Vera. "How much money are you spending on the calls?"

"I have to call him daily. I need to hear his voice. That's what people call commitment, you know." I sounded too aggravated. "I'm sorry, Vera. I'm just... still not feeling it after the nightmare. Let's go to the pool! By the way, I couldn't find my bikini yesterday. Have you seen it?"

"Yeah, sorry... I borrowed it. But it's clean now! I put it in the wash." Noticing my grumpy expression, Vera quickly added, "I'll let you wear my purple mini skirt next time we go out!"

"Now we are talking, sista!"

***

The pool in the Island Retreat condo complex was amazing. It was located in the secluded area in the refreshing shade of magnolias and palm trees. The lounge chairs were surrounded by plush deep-green elephant ears and some plants with enormous tropical red flowers. The turquoise-blue water sparkled in the sun and was beckoning us – come on, jump in and forget about it all! Milo was also quite a nice addition to the pool. In fact, he looked like he was placed there by the owners of the condo complex in their preparation for the promotional photo shoot. He seemed to be fast-asleep on top of the floating mattress. His tanned six-pack exposed in the not-at-all shy fashion and his eyes covered by dark shades. He looked yummy.

"Shh, Elena!" Vera tapped me on the shoulder. "Shh, quiet. Let's..."

Whispering "one, two, three" we performed a double bomb jump into the pool, causing multiple water explosions and turning Milo's mattress upside down.

"What the f –?" Milo's head, still in sunglasses, showed up on the surface of the pool. "He he, crazy bitches!" He started laughing away.

That's what I loved about Milo. He was never getting too sassy about things like that – he always appreciated a good joke.

After an extremely pleasant and tiring session of swimming and splashing in the pool, we dragged our lazy bones to the lounge chairs. Sunbathing time! I'd just put my stylish but cheap sunglasses on and prepared to enjoy a bit of reading, when Milo said:

"What's going on with you and Christopher?"

"Uhh, I don't know. He's your friend, you tell me."

Even through the blurriness of my shades I could tell that Milo was sincerely confused.

"Well, he just totally refuses to talk about you. As if you... don't exist." Milo gave me an apologetic look and shrugged.

"Yeah. I've noticed! In fact, all the Beach Club had a chance to notice it as well!"

Milo's face distorted, and he suddenly turned into a bemused troll. Damn sunglasses! Next time I would save up for some decent shades that wouldn't mess up my eyesight.

"On Monday," I said, "after finishing my breakfast shift I'm walking into the towel room to get some napkins. The room is full of people. Everybody and their brother is there! Your crazy Brit is too, naturally. Since I've already seen everybody but him that day, I, as a normal polite human being, said, "Hello, Chris!" And what do you think he did?" I tore the shades off my eyes with so much force that I nearly slammed peacefully sunbathing Vera across the face.

"What did he do?" Milo asked. He looked like he was cursing the minute he decided to start this conversation.

"He just looked right through me as if I was a bloody Casper the friendly ghost, turned away, and kept on talking to Farrah. Completely ignored me! Do you recall what the towel room looks like, Milo? It's as tiny as a tuna fish can. Everybody in the room stared at me as if I was a leper!"

"Elena," murmured Vera. "Relax, why don't you? He's upset you've turned him down. It's understandable."

"Upset? Upset?!" My voice reached such a high pitch that even Vera opened her eyes and propped herself up on the elbows. "He's thirty-seven years old, and he's acting as if he's in kindergarten and still needs to be potty-trained! He's been ignoring me all week long! It's humiliating! I haven't seen him for five days already — and I hope not to see him, EVER, till we go back home."

"You pissed him off. But I've already told him that he's in the wrong. I mean, he can't be treating you like this." Milo patted me on the shoulder and lit my cigarette that had been hanging out of my mouth during my hot tirade.

"Elena, chill out. Give him some time, and he'll be fine!" Vera sat up and smoothed my hair with her hand. "Today is our only day off. Let's just enjoy it. Look at this pool! Look at these flowers! Look at this weather!! We are having the time of our lives!"

"He he! Like in the Dirty Dancing," giggled Milo.

"You like Dirty Dancing?" Even though I was stressed out about the whole Chris situation, all my emotions were wiped out clean by the notion of a straight guy who liked Dirty Dancing.

"Yes! I even have the soundtrack on my laptop! Want to listen to it tonight?"

"Sure!" Vera and I yelled in unison.

Little did we know that out pool party would be crashed by Sonia, Diana, and... Lorraine? I would have thought that the vision of our friends dressed in the strange à la eighteenth-century-meets-Marlene-Dietrich uniforms and one of the Beach Club captains magically appearing at our pool was a cruel distortion caused by my cheap shades, but I didn't have them on.

There they were... resting casually on the glass table next to my lounge chair. We stared back at the nasty mirage, blinking fast and hoping for them to vanish immediately.

"Elena, Vera! Hurry up! We've got to work a banquet!"

"Work?" The word sounded so horrible, it gave me a murderous headache. "No-no-no! You're mistaken! We're off today."

"Elena," yelled Sonia. "Remember we told HR that we were interested in picking up as many shifts as possible? Well, tonight there's some sort of reception at the Manor, and they need us! Lorraine agreed to give us a ride. We just need you and Vera to quickly change and go!"

Sonia sounded so excited one might think Lorraine had also agreed to give her a Mustang convertible as a present. She was actually right. Back at Moscow we were advised to find an additional job, maybe two, in order to earn more money during our summertime experience. But that's if the first employer was not giving us enough hours or if we could see that the money wasn't good enough, neither of which was the case. In fact, I hadn't made that much money in my entire life. Call me lazy, but I don't like working myself senselessly. I like to enjoy the results of my work, too. For instance, I consider ruining my days off as the worst possible sin, and I like spending the money that I've earned. Well, what else am I going to do with it? Save it? What if I die an accidental death from a brick falling maliciously on my head as I stroll along the streets of my beloved Voronezh? What then? I wouldn't even be able to enjoy my hard-earned, crisp green notes! So I'd gone to CVS earlier that morning and spent $65 on make-up. Monika told me she couldn't possibly imagine what one can buy for $65 at a pharmacy. I showed her my trophies, and she was impressed. Anyway, I got a bit carried away. What I'm trying to say is – I'm not a workaholic. I make the necessary amount of mullah and then I chill out.

"I'm not going anywhere. I'm off!"

"Elena." Diana got closer to me and hissed in my face. "We've already told them you're coming. They're counting on all four of us to be there. Get your ass up and let's go!"

"But – "

My meek protest was interrupted by Vera. "Elena! Work one night, and get yourself another pair of shoes to show off at the college this fall!"

Blimey. That Vera – she knows how to get to me.

"Okay." I climbed off the chair with the speed of a paralyzed snail and wrapped the pool towel around my hips. "Bye, Milo. We'll do the Dirty Dancing next time..."

"Sure! In another life when you finally get a day off." Milo stretched his GQ body on the chair and closed his eyes. "Enjoy. Crazy Russians."

***

Perhaps, Wonder Elevators can also transport you into a different dimension all together. Except, I didn't feel like I fell into a black hole. I felt as if I had emerged on the opposite side of the universe – the intoxicatingly mind-blowing side of it.

After I finally managed to transform my wet and relaxed self into a relatively prim and proper cocktail server dressed as a transsexual Lord Byron (where did they even get these uniforms from? Halloween stores?) with unruly damp hair, Lorraine drove us to the Manor.

Ocean Isle Resorts could boast two amazing hotels on its premises: The Retreat and The Manor. Our early-morning boot camp, AKA the Beach Club Dining Room, was considered a part of The Retreat complex and was located on Ocean Isle. The Manor was a smaller, golf-oriented property and was situated on the adjacent St. Simons Island. The latter also happened to be a residential town for simple mortals like middle-class American families, well-off retirees, and a tiny percentage of beach bums who got lost in time and partied well into their fifties.

I had done pretty good research on the area back in Russia, and I knew that we would be living on St. Simons. Imagine the extent of my surprise when I realized that I didn't have to take a ferry, or a boat, or use a tunnel to get to St. Simons Island or Ocean Isle. Okay, they were connected by roads, but where was the water? Was there another definition of the word "island" in the English language that I was not aware of? I had spent at least three excruciating weeks trying to solve this puzzle. And now Lorraine was explaining to us that the islands were separated by the marsh. The marsh looked like grass, but during high tide – wait and see – the water would be practically touching the sides of the road. I found it fascinating! The marsh would also change colors: at sunrise, you could admire a pinkish-orange sea of warm sunlight, and at sunset, it would all turn bright-yellow, interspersed by the endless streams and lakes of suede dark-blue ocean water.

"No wonder the area is called the Golden Isles," I whispered to Diana, "All this time I've been thinking it's just a field or a pasture, like in Russia."

"Me too," snorted Diana. "Oh, wow, look!"

"Girls, check this out." Vera was tugging away at my puffed white sleeve.

We looked out of the window and let out a collective gasp. Lorraine's car was going down the road that definitely seemed like it belonged in Alice's Wonderland. It didn't feel real. A green canopy of enormously magnificent trees covered the dazzling blue sky. The branches formed an arch high above our heads, and at the end of the magic tunnel, loomed an old English manor with a tiled roof and masterfully framed windows.

"Wow, these trees look like they can talk."

"If they could, they would tell you a lot of interesting stories," smiled Lorraine. "Some of these oaks are a couple hundred years old."

Suddenly, the world around me spun in a crazy carousel of chaotic memories and threw me out into December of last year. My bum was comfortably seated on the computer chair and my eyes were glued to the screen. I was waiting for Alex to come visit me after his day at work. I was alone at home, and my fingers were pleasantly tickled by the hot surface of my tea cup. My feet were snuggled in fluffy warm socks. I was looking for a summer job in America. I spent the last three hours in a useless attempt to find at least anything decent and save some money on the program. It looked like we'd have to pay the agency an extra fee for finding me an employer. I'd been sending emails after emails, and still had no reply. Ideally, I would have loved to spend the summer in Denver. My parents' friends moved there about six years ago, and all of us would have felt safer if I was closer to somebody who really looked out for me in a foreign country. Well, at least my mom would have felt safer for me. I randomly clicked on a website advertising a resort community. A road that reminded me of an enchanted forest jumped out from the computer screen. I stared at it for a second, stunned. How pretty! A description below read: Avenue of the Oaks, Ocean Isle, Georgia, future host of the G8 Summit 2004. Oh, yeah, right. I exhaled in disappointment, exited the website, and came up to the window. A company that hosts the G8 summit – dream on, Elena. I stared into the dark cold evening behind the window glass. Silver stars of snow were slowly falling onto the windowsill. Through the golden shadow of streetlamps, I saw Alex's silhouette briskly moving towards the entrance. I could recognize him even from the height of the eighth floor – we had been together long enough. I smiled and jumped happily into the kitchen to put the kettle on. I met him in the hallway, his cold hands on my back. His fresh icy mouth burned my lips. We forgot about the kettle.

I opened my eyes and watched the oaks go past me through the car window. Serendipity? Fate? I don't believe in fate. But I do get amazed by the surreal experiences life can present us with. Why would we want to know what the future holds? It's akin to knowing the end of a movie while you are still watching it.

"Elena, are you deaf or something?" My existential pondering was disturbed by Sonia grabbing my wrist. "Get out of the car, let's go!"

Even when I found out that our future employer would be the legendary Ocean Isle, I couldn't dream about participating in an event like that. Yes, I saw something similar in the old movies. Yes, I read books that would describe receptions of the kind. I never could imagine I would see anything like that with my own two eyes.

The spacious room paneled with dark glossy wood was filled with the orange rays of the setting sun. The piano player – a formally dressed Latin American gentleman in his sixties – was complementing the atmosphere with the soft-sounding silky sonata that only a true virtuoso can master. There must have been at least a hundred haute couture-clad guests gracefully moving around the room and socializing. They were drinking exquisite cocktails, and they had that self-confident look of people who were at the top of the world and were perfectly aware of that.

"What are we supposed to be doing now?" I asked and received no reply. The girls were also frozen still with their mouths wide-open. "Hey!" I pulled Sonia's sleeve. "You're Mrs. I'll Arrange for the Second Job – what should we be doing?"

"How do I know?" I must admit, she also looked paralyzed with fear. "And I didn't set it up! It was Diana," she snapped.

"Chickens!" giggled Diana. "Lorraine said we just need to be walking around with trays and ask the guests if they would like a drink. And then take their order to the bar. That's it! Let's go!"

I was the first one who Diana lightly pushed in the direction of the crowd. An elderly couple happened to be passing by and I nearly flew straight into them. I decided I was going to kill Diana after all. I'd come back home and make *her* clean our closet.

"Good evening! May I fetch you anything to drink?"

Okay, I had made quite an unexpected appearance, but that still didn't explain why they were gawking at me as if I was an alien creature from the Moon.

"Yes, dear. I would like a Cosmopolitan, please," said the gray-haired lady, almost blinding me with the sparkle of her gigantic diamond necklace.

"And I'd like some whisky on the rocks, please. With a splash of lime."

"Yes, absolutely. I'll be right back!"

A Cosmopolitan was easy – the girls in Sex and the City drink it all the time. But what was "on the rocks" and "splash of lime""? Can lime splash? My Arnold Palmer incident taught me a good lesson. This time I kept repeating the gentleman's order until I finally reached the bar. Never mind that the bartender thought I was a mentally ill girl talking to myself. I at least got the order right. Drinks on the tray and off I went! Hold on... Where had they gotten to? All people here looked so much alike. Oh, there they were! The gentleman had the same weird-looking shoes on – half-white, half-black. No, not them. This lady's neck was adorned with rubies instead of diamonds... How in the world was I going to find them?

"Elena!" Sonia was waving to me. "Come here. It's so fucking funny!"

"What?" I whispered. "I can't leave." I pointed at the drinks.

"Oh, whatever! Come here!"

I put on the most polite and not-at-all confused cocktail server smile I could muster and slowly walked to Sonia.

"What is it?"

"Well, first of all – have you seen the bartender? He is HOT! Maybe I should invite him to my birthday party?"

"Your birthday is in two weeks! And... –" I sighed irritably. "– I need to find the guests who ordered these drinks. Can we talk about your love life after work?"

"No!" said Sonia. "This guy, he works at the Manor. I might not see him anymore. I've got to invite him today. What did those people look like?"

"I don't know. A diamond necklace and two-colored shoes?"

"That helps, thanks. All the guys are wearing golf shoes – it's a reception for golfers. Why don't you just forget about it? Somebody else will get their drinks. Come on! Let me show you something."

As I couldn't find the couple to save my life, I gave up and followed Sonia. She led me into an imposing and very masculine-looking lobby of the hotel. It was extremely dark and smelled of cigars and whiskey. The lobby was empty at that moment, but you could still easily imagine that normally, these leather sofas accommodated extremely powerful men who discussed the future of humanity while drinking whisky and smoking cigars that cost the entire annual budget of a small third-world country. Sonia stopped in front of a side table and pointed at it. "Look! And tell me it's not the most hilarious thing you've ever seen."

"A bust of a dog with shoulder straps? What?" The laughter seized my chest so hard that I thought I'd suffocate. In fact, I thought I was having a hysterical breakdown. Both Sonia and I were practically crawling on the floor.

"Why...?" I paused to battle the tears in my eyes. "Why would somebody make a bust of a dog with epaulettes?"

"I know!" Sonia was laughing and crying as well. "Like, in Russian museums they have busts of poets and writers, and generals! And here – it's a dog!"

"Nothing wrong with that." I gulped for air. "They like dogs at the Manor!"

We promised to each other that we wouldn't leave the USA until we found out the inspirational reason for this creation, and headed back to the reception room. We found everybody, including Vera and Diana, on the terrace. As we walked outside, we were hit by a wave of a magic sound piercing through the hot air.

"What is it?" I stood on my tip-toes and tried to peek over the people's heads. "What's everybody looking at?"

"It's the bagpiper," said Vera. "They have this tradition at the Manor. Every evening at sunset a bagpiper is playing on the golf course."

As we stood there, our faces lit up by the cherry-red Georgia sunset, listening to the ancient notes of the beautiful melody, we knew that this moment would be saved in our minds for the rest of our lives. The years would go by, the times would change, the whole miniature empire that seemed to be so stable and everlasting would be, quite ironically, gone with the wind, but four Russian girls who happened to witness that era at its peak will share this memory forever.

***

"So after it was all over, all the servers got on this strange means of transportation – a jeep train? It looked like a toy train pulled by a jeep!" I was telling Monika about our Manor adventures as we enjoyed our cigarettes on Milo's porch. Christmas lights wrapped around the porch frame were the only source of light, crickets were singing the familiar song, and we were feeling warm and fuzzy.

"And then the guy who was in charge of the banquets, chased us down before the jeep train pulled off, and gave us all free food and a pink long-stemmed rose for each of us," I beamed.

"Looks like you guys had fun!" Monika smiled.

"We did! The only thing is..."

"What?"

"I'm still not sure why that couple was staring at me in a very bizarre way..."

"Well, what did you ask them then? Do you remember?"

"Yes! I said, "May I fetch you anything to drink?""

"Silly girl!" Monika laughed. "Don't say *"fetch"*. *"Fetch"* is like a command for dogs."

"Really?" I blushed. "But in the books in Russia, they teach you that..."

"I know, I know. The same in Slovakia." Monika shrugged. "I guess the authors of those books have never been to the States."

"Well, maybe I deserved the shoulder straps for my prompt fetching service?"

Our wild laughter was broken up by Chris appearing in the doorway.

"Hello girls! Monika." He gave Monika a peck on the cheek and sat in the chair next to me. "Hi, Elena! What's going on?"

"Uhh, I believe it's going to snow in Southeast Georgia."

"What?"

"Your Kindness finally deigned to greet me. What have I done to deserve your gracious forgiveness?"

"You've got to thank Milo for that. He told me I was being unnecessarily rude and rightly so. I apologize for my behavior. Right here and now – with Monika as a witness."

I have to admit, he looked sincerely apologetic.

"Great! I'm glad you got that worked out." Monika rolled her eyes and stubbed her cigarette. "Excuse me for a sec. Milo is calling me."

"He's not calling you!" protested Chris.

"He is! Listen."

We got quiet for a moment, and indeed, Milo was saying something. In another room. In Slovak.

"Those Slovaks!" Chris shook his head as Monika left the porch. "They've always been like that. Sometimes I think they can hear each other from another house through thick brick walls."

"Maybe it's telepathy?" I suggested.

"Maybe. Elena."

Oh no. Not again. I'd already been smashed by a hot wave of Chrisoparanoia at his unannounced appearance. I couldn't withstand another attack.

"I seriously wanted to apologize. I really like you. When I look in your eyes, I just... want to be with you so much. That's why I was being a bit of a pushy bastard. Alex sounds like a very cool and funny guy. I don't want to mess up your relationship. So, let's just be friends."

"Sounds good." I smiled. It didn't sound good at all, but I was engaged and it was the right thing to do.

"So what have you been up to, my Russian friend?"

I told Chris about the Manor reception, and the dog with epaulettes, and my Wonder-Elevator dream. The dream part made Chris arch his eyebrows.

"I'm into the psychology of dreams, you know. You're talking to the right person."

"Really?"

"Yes, I've read a lot of books on the matter, and all my songs are based on my dreams. Sometimes, I even set my alarm clock to wake me up in the middle of the night. I get up and write my dreams down. And later on, I write a song."

"Hold on! You write songs?"

"Uhh, yeah! You didn't know?"

"No! And why in the middle of the night?"

"Your dreams are the strongest at that stage of sleep."

I lit another cigarette and said, "You're a very interesting person, Chris. I'm really happy we patched it up."

"Me too." Chris stretched his long legs and looked at me. "Do you want to go to the park with me tomorrow and walk my dogs?"

"The Dalmatian, too? Sure!"

"I'll pick you up at ten?"

"Sounds good! I actually have to go. I need to call Alex."

"All right. Say hello to him. Chris grinned.

"Naturally!" I leaned forward to kiss him on the cheek. Even the smell of his skin turned my knees into mush. I'd have to remind myself not to do it next time.

Right before leaving the porch, I turned around and said, "Chris. What do you think my dream means?"

"Only you can unravel your own dreams."

"Yes, but... what do you think?"

"Oh, you don't want to know what I think. You'll get mad."

"Okay, then. Don't make me mad!" I laughed. "Good night!"

"Nighty night! Don't let the bed bugs bite."

CHAPTER SEVEN

You Are Fucking Late, Cinderella

I've gotten to thinking – do we learn to appreciate what we have only in comparison to the shitty experiences we had before or does the level of our gratitude depend entirely on our personality traits? If a person is born already into a well-off carefree environment, is he or she guaranteed to be spoiled? Or, if not spoiled, ignorant to the fact that life is totally different outside of what they might be used to. Or ready to pay up $30 for a pair of the ugliest shoes mankind could possibly design?

"What...?" I helplessly glanced up at Chris and Milo. "What IS this?"

"A pair of work shoes that are appropriate for waiting tables." Chris didn't even flinch, although – and I'm quite sure about that – my face implied that I'd rather eat ten frogs alive than even consider buying this atrociousness.

"Oh, no," I started backing up from the aisle in the direction of the exit. "I'm not buying this, AND, more importantly, I'm absolutely not wearing them. Ever," I added in my attempt to sound more convincing.

"Elena, you need them for work. Didn't Lorraine already tell you that you can't wear the shoes you brought with you from Russia?"

"She did." I looked away and mumbled, "I still don't understand what she has against them. I have a pretty pair that I enjoy looking down on while I'm working. And this... do people even buy these? Really?"

"You can't be wearing high-heeled shoes when you're on the floor. You might slip and hurt yourself," said Chris, "even though your Russian shoes do make you look exceptionally sexy and definitely create a more favorable work environment for the rest of us."

"He he! Sexy waitress," giggled Milo somewhere around the corner. "Hey, how do I look?"

He emerged on the opposite side of the aisle wearing the most flamboyant shades and a multicolored gangster hat.

"Gay!" I snapped. "Let's just go back to the island. Put this ugly creation back on the shelf. Or better – in the trash where it belongs. In what universe do people pay thirty bucks for that?"

I started walking to the register without looking back at my shopping buddies. We had spent at least an hour in this very bizarre place called Walmart. It looked like a large warehouse with so much merchandise that I was completely overpowered by a vicious anxiety attack for the first fifteen minutes in the store. I just stared at the aisles and aisles of various stuff. Some of it, I must admit, I wasn't even aware people needed. At first, I couldn't move. Then, still transfixed, I began slowly maneuvering across the rows of China manufactured – read: "affordable" – goods. I lost Chris and Milo in approximately half an hour while I was trying to decide if I should get two or three pairs of new knickers. Oh my gosh – the jewelry was on sale, buy four, get the fifth free. Who knows how long I would have been stuck in the land of happy shoppers – the transcendental state one goes into when attempting to figure out what they want to flush their money down the toilet for – with my eyes hopelessly glued to the jewelry rack, if Chris hadn't found me right in time to save me from the danger of giving my entire paycheck to the Walmart corporation? Good one, Chris! The ugly pair of shoes he had with him put me off shopping for twenty years to come.

Actually, it all started with shoes. That morning, Chris kept his word and came to pick me up at 10 o'clock on the nose. Frankly speaking, I was still asleep when I heard a very persistent knock on the door. Still trying to open my stubbornly shut eyes, I dragged myself to the door and turned the handle. There he was – wide awake, frecklier than ever with the morning sun reflecting on his face, with the Dalmatian by his side.

"You both have spots," I yawned and rubbed my eyes. "Did you mean to choose a pet that looks like you?"

"Yes. And then I got him fixed to make sure he doesn't steal my girlfriends," laughed Chris. "Are you going to change or is it a traditional Russian dog-walking outfit?"

I glanced down at what I was wearing and my face immediately turned crimson. I'd had this white-cotton nighty for as long as I could remember, which is a pretty long time for a piece of clothing. My mom bought it for me at a "tolpa," a phenomenon that could be considered a post-Soviet open-air relative of Walmart. In Russian the word "tolpa" literally stands for "crowd" – the name speaks for itself, doesn't it? But please, my friends, don't forget that most parts of Russia tend to be just a touch chillier than Southeast Georgia. Only imagine shopping in the 20-degree weather, trying on tight jeans in the back of a merchant's booth, hopelessly attempting to zip them up with frost-beaten hands, and praying to all the possible gods you've ever heard of that your ass doesn't get totally numb and fall off. You will ask me – why go there? Well, why do you go to Walmart? So way back then, before our Voronezh transformed into a modern chic city with thousands of fashion stores and five malls, my mom got me this nighty. It had bright-colored oranges (tangerines, grapefruits?) as a pattern, and it made me feel... at home. Which doesn't necessarily mean that I looked particularly hot in it.

"I'm sorry. You boys, come on in, and I'll go and change. Really quick? Okay?" I was doing my best to sound confident and grown-up, but in reality I was burning up with shame.

"Why are you sorry? I like it." Chris beamed. "It looks different."

After I got ready we headed over to a picturesque park perched on the bank of an intracoastal river. As I admired mysterious Spanish moss dangling above our heads and white dots of endless yachts and boats specked across the blue water, Chris told me about himself. How he lived in London until he was seven, and then all his family – his parents and two brothers – moved to the USA. How he grew up on St. Simons Island, and got the part of Michael in the Marry Poppins school play because of his accent. How he had sex for the first time on St. Simons beach, and his girlfriend was wearing nothing but a bandana on her head (I told him I was jealous – my first time was in my parents' bedroom while my grandma was in the living room watching a Discovery channel show on South American monkeys. Talk about housing deficit). How he spent three years in the U.S. marines, realized that he would rather be a peace-loving musician, did his best to get out, had to spend three months in the military jail in Japan – two weeks out of them in the solitary confinement, wrote his first song and learned to play guitar in jail, and then finally was free from the military. How he moved to London to live with his grandmother and made his living by playing music in the London underground and working in a hospital with a bunch of blue-haired old ladies, who would chain-smoke and eat boiled eggs for lunch. How he moved to Montreal for three years, played in a band, and found his true love. How they went backpacking across Europe, and how he got his heart broken. How he lived in Athens, Georgia, for six years, and how much he loved it until one day he realized that he was having a smart philosophical discussion at a coffee shop that reminded him of the same exact existential conversation he'd had many times before on various occasions with different people. How he moved back to St. Simons with the girl he met in Athens. How it was supposed to be for good, but...

"There was no chemistry, you know. I cared for her, but I wasn't in love. So I broke it off. She left the same day and didn't even take a single thing that belonged to her. She asked if she could take Tex –" Chris petted his Dalmatian's head. "– since we got him together. But I couldn't do it. Tex is my dog."

"I see." I nodded. "But you seem to have something going on with Farrah now. Maybe she's the one."

"No," laughed Chris. "Farrah is like my sister."

"Right," I giggled. "I would say a sister with benefits, but it will sound just a bit too kinky."

"No, I'm serious! We've had sex once. With her and another girl," added Chris and couldn't help flashing that arrogant boyish smile again.

"With two girls?" I stared at him incredulously.

"Well, they didn't seem to mind." He shrugged. "If you don't believe me, I can prove it. I got it on the video."

"Stop it, you pervert!" I nudged him and blushed. "I didn't even know people really did that. I mean..." I stumbled while trying to look for words.

"I'm sorry, Elena. I probably shouldn't be telling you all this." For a second, he seemed genuinely confused. He probably didn't know how to take me yet.

"Don't get me wrong, I'm not a conservative girl in any way. I just like to be the only one, you know. Like... Cinderella." I winked at him. "But you shouldn't worry about this – you have two evil stepsisters who seem to be into that. Enjoy!"

"You gotta do what you gotta do." Chris smiled as he opened the door of his car for me. "Do you want to have some lunch and then go to my place to swim in the pool? Milo will meet us there, and we'll drive to Brunswick right away. You do need to buy khaki pants for the Fourth of July, right? I can take you to the store. Plus, didn't you tell me something about new work shoes?"

Since I didn't have a car to drive myself to Brunswick or any other friends to spend my day-off with, I took Chris up on his offer. We first dropped by Del Taco to pick up the heroin of that summer – quesadillas. With crispy fatty wrappers scattered around us and pleasantly numb with bellyful happiness, Chris and I were kicked back in the deck chairs on the edge of his pool.

"Last time I was here, you were face down on the ground trying to find out if Brunswick police officers had any sense of humor." I squinted at him as the setting sun blinded me for a second.

"Nah, I was just showing off. For you." Chris squinted back at me.

As the sun treacherously disappeared behind the purple clouds, I saw that Chris was staring at my face. His eyes were so intense, I thought he might be penetrating my skull and deciphering my thoughts. That would have been helpful – I wished somebody could tell me what was happening in that head of mine. I honestly had no idea.

"What?" I broke the silence.

"Nothing." Chris shook his head and laughed. "I just remembered how funny you were that night when I was trying to kiss you."

"What was so funny?"

"I don't know. You shook your hair and turned your head right and left, and kept saying, "Chris, no, no!" But your eyes stayed closed and you weren't really trying to pull away." Chris's smile was as enthusiastic as if he just hit the jack pot.

"Well, you know. I'm a hopeless romantic. Sometimes too much of one." I shrugged and laughed. "Once, in high school, I was dumped by a boy, because I was too old-fashioned. I believe his exact words were, "You act and sound like your grandmother."

"Why would he say that?"

"Maybe because when he called to break up with me, I told him that I couldn't be bothered, because my prince charming was still awaiting me at the horizon of my future." I snorted with laughter and covered my blushing face with the beach towel.

"You really told him that?"

"Well, my grandma told me it would be a graceful response that would save my face," I mumbled through the towel.

The plush pinkness of the towel brushed on my face and I saw Chris looming above me.

"You don't have to worry about a thing, Elena the Paina. You're different from everybody else and you should be proud of it."

"You think so only because I am different here, in America. In Russia I'm just a very ordinary girl. Gosh, even my name sounds cool here – Elena. Back at home, it's just Lena, and every second girl in Russia is named the same."

"Well, Lena, you're about to burn and become very different from everybody else. At least your bright-red skin color will stand out." Chris was looking down at my legs that were already turning painfully pink.

"Shit, you're right! Do you have any sun block? I think I left mine at home."

"I have the sun block and a Master's Degree in sun block application." Chris smiled and picked up a bright-blue bottle of lotion.

"No, thanks." I snatched the bottle from him and started aggressively rubbing it on my arms. "You're sneaky!"

Suddenly a loud cracking sound interrupted our laughter.

"Ooops. Somebody was killed again in one of the regular shootings on St. Simons Island." Chris stretched his hand in the direction of the fence, his face all comical, TV presenter-like.

"Oh, Chris!" Now I was bending in half, holding on to my belly and trying to stop the crazy laughter from completely invading my insides and causing me to hiccup. "How can you even react to things like that?"

"Like what?"

"That fast! And so funny." I couldn't stop giggling. "Oh!" I gasped for air and propped myself on the elbows. "You're making me laugh like nobody before!"

Having recovered from the laughter attack, I exhaled, pushed the unruly hair off my face and turned to look at Chris. He was also propped on his elbows, his head turned to face me – serious and focused.

Have you ever felt like you wanted to freeze the moment in time? Just take this precious moment, stick it in the time freezer and leave it there forever? I believe that some moments do so automatically, without human interference. I still remember that warm early evening in Georgia as if it was just yesterday. Lounge chairs, turquoise pool, fragrant magnolias, burning sun on my legs. An invisible electric chain that made it impossible for us to take our eyes off each other. Loud silence that made all possible words redundant. The realization hardened at the bottom of my heart. Messy, warm and heavy realization. We both knew.

"What are you guys doing here in total silence?" Farrah was standing behind us, petite and pretty, with the big deck chair that was almost the same size as her.

She put the chair down next to Chris and stretched her arm out.

"I don't think we've actually been properly introduced. I'm Farrah," She smiled and I immediately thought that I would never in my life be able to get my teeth to look like that. I'd have to wear braces till the end of my life, and then maybe, just maybe, my grandchildren and – let's hope – great grandchildren might enjoy my perfect American smile at the viewing of my shriveled-up body.

"Yes, I've heard a lot about you," I smiled back. "I'm Elena."

"Chris, are you coming to the beach party tonight? Elena, you should come. It'll be a lot of fun."

"Bummer, I totally forgot about it!" exclaimed Chris. "Maybe we should all go? Elena, do you think the girls will want to come?"

"Oh, they'll be over the moon. All of us are off tomorrow, and we can sleep in!"

Farrah's appearance made it easier to cover up the uneasiness of the situation. As if nothing happened. Or perhaps it never did?

***

I'd been remembering all this as three of us – Chris, Milo and yours truly – were patiently waiting in the Walmart line. You'd be surprised how much one can think of while waiting for service in Walmart.

"$33.45," squeaked the cashier.

"Chris!" I yelled as I saw what he was about to pay for. "I'm not wearing these! Plus, you don't even know me – why would you be buying me anything? You're not buying them!"

"Watch me," smirked Chris and swiftly ran his card.

"Oh no, Chris! You didn't have to spend your money on me!"

"Well, you wouldn't let me be your boyfriend. Can I at least buy you some shoes?"

"I don't know..." I started to protest.

"Quit that," snapped Chris. "We need to get you home, Cinderella. You and the girls have to get ready for the ball tonight."

"It's a party, it's a party!" Milo was wiggling his hips as the Walmart cashier looked on, dumbfounded.

"Let's go you crazy Slovak. I've got to stop by my mom and dad's house to pick up my mail. We're running out of time..."

***

"What are those? Shrimp or miniature elephants with whiskies?" I winced and took a step back.

"Oh my God!" exclaimed Diana. "I'm not eating them! They're so huge!"

"And they have eyes," added Vera.

"I think I'll just go and drown my confusion in beer." I turned around and headed towards the keg.

The party was taking place at a scenic part of the beach enclosed by hills of big heavy rocks on both sides. The ocean was curiously flat and serene, glistening with dancing reflections of lilac clouds. The temperature was so perfect, one could easily forget about the existence of their body. Everyone at the party was laughing, joking, dancing to the upbeat music coming from the stereo of somebody's car, and enjoying this gorgeous summer evening. I stared at Jekyll Island floating like a giant green whale in the middle of the ocean. It seemed so close I thought I could swim there in a matter of minutes. But I knew it was an illusion, just like this party. I could pretend to be a part of this life, and perhaps just for this evening, or maybe until the end of September, I could fool everybody into thinking that I was really one of them. But then I'd have to jump on the plane and fly back to my real life, and pretend that none of this had happened. No, I'd rather stay who I was. Plus, you couldn't swim to Jekyll Island – sharks would have you for a snack.

"Pumpkin, do you need any help with the beer?"

I turned around and saw Lori grinning happily at me. I wondered if she ever walked out in public without wearing the essential polite smile.

"No, thanks! Already got it!" I pointed at my plastic glass. "I was just... admiring Jekyll Island. I think I'll go for a walk!"

As I strolled down the beach, hard sand wet and cool on my feet, I tried to figure out why I'd been called a pumpkin. I mean,

I'd been trying to convince everybody today, including myself, that I was the main heroine of the story. But life was not a fairy tale, and I was probably more of a pumpkin than Cinderella. Look at Chris, for example – he preferred two evil stepsisters. And they were not even evil – they were just free, liberated, and open-minded. Cinderella had become an old-fashioned and boring prude these days. I only wished somebody would have told us that fairy tales in real life were a bit more confusing.

"Elena! Did you decide to head back home or something?" Chris caught up with me and touched my shoulder. "Are you all right?"

I stood there, hot humid breeze kissing my neck, and looked into his eyes. I wanted to tell him, that more than anything in this world I would love to be the part of this American fairy tale. I would love to call the condo that we stay at "home". I would love to say "yes" to that kiss he was now contemplating. But I was a visitor from a different universe, I was a Russian UFO, and I had an alter ego and an alter life, so instead I said, "I'm dying to pee. All this beer did me in. Is there a bathroom here?"

"Is that really why you just had such a sad look on your face?"

"Yes. Having a full bladder makes me extremely emotional." I took him by the hand and we started walking back to the party.

"I can't believe you refused to kiss me back then. My friends were watching," Chris pouted and gave me a half-smile.

"Well, your friends will survive it. I won't, if I don't find a toilet in the next ten seconds."

"You really want to pee?"

"YES!"

"Okay, I have an idea. See that house on the left? The girl who is hosting the party lives in it – or her grandparents do, to be more exact. Let's walk over there."

After I finally peed and could think about other things apart from my bladder, I walked out of the bathroom and looked around. I was in the dark living room of an older house decorated with heavy wooden furniture. Two elderly people were sitting in the chairs, chatting and laughing, the endless lavender ocean in the window behind them. My gaze traveled to the yellowish photos on the walls. Two of them, young, vibrant, holding hands and drowning in each other's eyes. Here they were again, more grown-up with two little kids, dressed in their best Sunday clothes, smiling shyly into the camera. In a family Christmas picture, they were already mature and serious, surrounded by tall laughing teenagers. Another group picture at the same table – much more content and calm look on their faces, family considerably larger than in the previous photo. Just like that. Their whole life was in front of me. It suddenly dawned on me that I, too, would be old one day. One day, I would look into the mirror, and would see a tiny wrinkled face with the glazed-over look in my eyes. And I would probably think – what had I done in my life that I could look back on and smile, and feel my heart melt and beat as fast as it did when I was young, reckless, full of fire? Would this lady's husband make her heart race, or was there somebody else? Who knew? Remember the Titanic? "A woman's heart is a deep ocean of secrets."

I walked out of the house as the ivory-colored moon was just coming up in the fresh sky. The winds were picking up, and the people started slowly crawling back to their cars. The party was almost over. I rubbed my arms and hurried towards the stairs that would take me back to the beach. As I was awkwardly stepping down, my strappy sandal fell off, hit the sand and landed right into... Was that a pile of doggy doo-doo? Before I could realize what had just happened, Chris walked up to the end of the steps.

"Did everything come out all right? Are you ready?"

"Yes... Can you wait for just a sec? I think I lost my shoe..."

"Elena, didn't I already tell you? I'm ready to wait for you all my life." He winked at me, got on his knee, and picked up the unfortunate shoe. "Would this happen to be yours?" He banged the shoe on the wooden beam of the stairs and announced, "Your shoe is officially shit-free, Cinderella."

As he was sliding the sandal back on my foot, I couldn't help but notice a burning sensation of somebody's eyes on my face. I looked up and saw a tall dark-haired girl hugging a big box of cheap morning-headache-guaranteed wine.

"Chris," I whispered. "Who's that girl? And why is she so determined to drill a hole in my head with her eyes?"

"Oh, that's Emma."

I gave Chris a blank stare.

"The second evil stepsister. She stole my wine because I didn't want to go to the after-party."

"Well, maybe you should go then?"

"No, she'll be fine. She'll have the party on her own. She's got the potion that gets the evil sisters going." He grinned and added, "Come on! The girls are already in the car, we're going home."

***

"Guys, these burgers are so good!" mumbled Vera. "I've never thought I'd say that, but I just couldn't bring myself to eat those gigantic shrimp they had at the party. They looked like there were alive and could start crawling in my stomach any minute."

We were back at the condo, watching Sex and the City, drinking wine, and greedily devouring Burger King Whoppers Chris had bought for us.

"I'm glad you like 'em, but I think I need to go home," yawned Chris. "It's already a few minutes before midnight, and I'm working lunch tomorrow."

Twelve plus eight equals EIGHT! No, my friends, it's not the weird Russian mathematics – that's how one learns to calculate what time it is at home when they're miles away from it.

"Oh, fuck!"

"Well, I'm really happy you don't want to see me go. Or is it an invitation?" Chris looked quite amused.

"Fuck! It's about to be eight in the morning in Russia! Alex's leaving for three weeks to work at a soccer tournament in Moscow. I promised him I'd call him before he leaves."

"What time is he leaving then?" asked Diana.

"Eight!"

I was sure they didn't hear my answer, since I was already halfway to the McDonald's pay phone. Breathless from running and hot with shame, I started punching in the numbers of my pre-call card. Ok, one ring, two, three, pick up, pick up, pick up!!!

"Hello!"

"Oh, Yurij Petrovich! Hi, it's Elena."

"Oh, hi Elena! How are you doing? You wouldn't believe it, but he just left! Literally, the door closed behind him about five seconds ago."

Alex's dad's words resonated in my head and left a nasty gnawing feeling in my chest.

"Okay then!" I tried to sound cheerful, but I was sure I sounded phony. A phony on the phone. "I'll try to talk to him later then! Have a good day, Yurij Petrovich."

I hung up, slowly drooped down the wall, and sat on the ground, my burning face cupped in my hands. You're fucking late,   Cinderella!

CHAPTER EIGHT

Pink Ice Cream

Independence

There is nothing more invigorating and exciting in this world than walking down spring roads of the big city on the way back home from school and drowning in the deliciousness of pink ice cream. Yes, the spring is officially here. We can wave farewell – at least for six months – to snow-covered, slippery roads, unforgiving northern winds, and hats! I snatched off the yucky woolen hat that had been annoyingly making my forehead itch, and was enjoying the fresh breeze with notes of stubborn winter in my hair. My mom would eat me alive if she saw me now, not only hatless, but devouring the forbidden fruit – ice cream. I haven't been allowed ice cream, especially outside, since

I was unluckily prone to pneumonia in my early childhood. But it's late February, I'm already sixteen, the city is alive with the techno-pumping force of spring, youth, and love. I wanted to let my hair down. I've never felt that free, that happy, that independent. I'm happy, happy, happy!

"I'm happy!" I jumped up on my bed in Island Retreat, totally awake and ready for the day ahead of me like never before.

"At least someone is...," grouched Diana and covered herself with the pillow.

"Banana, don't mess up your make-up!" laughed Vera. She was also awake, cup of steaming coffee in her hands. "Elena, did you know that Diana puts her make-up on *before* she goes to bed? So that she could sleep extra ten minutes the next morning?"

"Shut up! Really?" I hopped off my bed and attacked Diana, who was peacefully snoozing under the covers. "Oh my God! She's naked, and made up! The girl is totally LOCA!"

I giggled and happily skipped to the bathroom successfully avoiding the pillow that Diana had sent flying in my direction. As I put my red Fourth of July Beach Club T-shirt on and stared at my reflection in the mirror, I was stunned. I never looked more beautiful. I know it sounds horribly shallow and standoffish, but I honestly never did! Even though the T-Shirt was three times my size, and the pants were saggy, I still liked myself. I let my hair down, and couldn't help but notice that it was oddly curly. My hair had never been curly... I applied bright-red lipstick to match my uniform on my burning lips, and closed my eyes. Last night, before finally falling asleep, I kept pressing the replay button on in my mind. The replay of the last evening...

***

"This movie isn't that funny," I exhaled the minty smoke, stubbed the cigarette, and leaned across the porch doorway.

"Stupid Russian!" moaned Milo. "You've got to quit smoking menthol cigarettes! They'll weaken your heart."

"I thought I was already weakening my heart by smoking, genius!" I lightly popped him on the head and landed on the soft cushions on the couch next to Chris.

"I expected more from a movie with Ben Stiller. Come to think of it, it's the only Ben Stiller movie I don't find funny." Chris shrugged in disappointment.

"Milo, I'm going to the pool. You're coming?" meowed bikini-clad Monika and lazily strolled towards the door.

"I'm on my way!" Milo jumped over the back of the couch faster than the speed of light and gave us a cocky wink.

As the door slammed shut behind them, Chris and I looked at each other and laughed.

"What are they going to the pool for at 2 a.m., I wonder?" I smiled and picked up my wine glass.

"Trainee, I've given you more credit for intelligence." Chris stretched his arm over my shoulders in a mockingly friendly manner. "Milo will perform one of his gay dances for Monika..."

I started feeling ticklish from fuzzy laughter, and Chris went on.

"Then they will have some of that crap beer they're always buying in Winn Dixie, followed by a quickie in the pool – that's going to be fast and embarrassing. Contrary to the common belief, sex in the pool isn't that great."

"Well, I wouldn't know. I'm the Mother Superior, remember?" I turned my head and looked him straight in the eye.

"I know! Cold-blooded Russian virgin."

We both laughed, and I rested my head on his shoulder. As I did it, I realized that I wasn't sure why it had happened. All of a sudden, I could see the picture as an outsider would – if they were present in this dark magnolia-infused room with reflections of Along Came Polly on the walls: a girl happily curled up under a guy's arm, both are laughing and having a hell of a good time. An outsider would see a couple. Before I could conceive the thought that this picture was morally wrong – my fiancé was far, far away, and I shouldn't have got too comfortable around my new "friend" – I lifted my head and looked at him. And then I lost all my thoughts. I only remember that he was getting closer and closer as if in slow motion, and then his lips touched mine, and it felt so painfully right, that I didn't even think about resisting. His hands were cupping my face, my hair was a hot mess, curly for some mysterious reason, my heart was just about to jump out of my chest, hit the floor, and shatter. I thought that I was so happy I could have died right there and I wouldn't have minded. But hold on... was I actually *kissing* somebody else? Not Alex? As the thought cut through my pleasure, my old love started to bleed and I opened my eyes. I was on my back on the couch with Chris on top of me. He must have sensed it too. My guilt was palpable, and he stopped.

***

Why do little kids always leave everything in such a mess? Why? I mean, do they deliberately and maliciously break food in microscopic pieces and spread it around the whole table and the floor under the table? Do they plan to spill apple, orange and grape juices on the white tablecloth and top it off with coffee from their parents' cups? Do they strategically distribute melon chunks on all four corners of the table to defend their fortress from an evil Russian waitress who will definitely spend at least an hour on cleaning up after their royal breakfast? *When I have a kid, I would never allow this to happen. If my child does not have manners to be in public, I will not take him or her out to eat. That's it – end of story!* I sighed with frustration as I was unsuccessfully trying to scrape off a piece of unidentified gooey object off the polished pine-tree wooden surface of the table. I was going to miss my lunch break – by the time I'd finish up cleaning my section after the breakfast shift, the lunch shift would start. I would starve again! I straightened my back out and stared at the violet-blue ocean. There was Africa. Right there, just across the Atlantic. This is where I wanted to be – Africa. Away from Alex, away from Chris, and away from this damn table. No, my darling reader, I wasn't frustrated. My feelings rather bordered a weird combination of extreme elation and the bitter-sweet happiness that made it difficult to breathe. I knew that I was supposed to be burning in the hellish flames of remorse, and never in my entire life had I imagined that I wouldn't, taking into consideration what I'd done yesterday, but I was not! Every time I remembered our kiss, an unstoppable twenty-foot wave of happiness swooped up in my chest, and no matter how hard I tried, I just couldn't even think about Alex. I was longing for guilt, but I couldn't find it. Was I a cold-hearted, ruthless woman? I had certainly never thought of myself as one... And then I heard his voice. I could recognize his voice anywhere and anytime. It sent shivers down my spine and tickled the ends of my fingers with sweaty electric sensations. Oh no. I wasn't ready to face him just yet. I didn't decide how I was going to behave around him. *I want to be in Africa, I want to be in Africa.*

"Elena! Are you going to have lunch?"

I turned around to face him still chanting my African wish in my head and... burst out laughing.

"Chris! You look like a ten-year-old boy! What's the deal with this shirt?"

"Laura told me she only had a small size. It's a touch tight, isn't it?" He beamed. "What's going on with your T-shirt? Or is it a dress?"

"Ms. Laura told me she only had large ones." I rolled my eyes. "What are we going to do?"

"We'll go to the bathroom and get naked."

"Oh, yeah, right, sure."

Even though I could definitely deal with Chris's jokes much better than anybody at the Beach Club, the image flashed so vividly in front of my eyes, that I had to stop and count till twenty in my head. Just to chase off that... whatever that was that I felt.

"Don't get too excited. I'm joking." He laughed. "At least for now."

The last phrase was nonchalantly whispered in my ear. I inhaled and tried to act like I hadn't just mentally screwed his brains out.

"What are you talking about, Chris?"

"Well, we need to go to the bathroom and swap the shirts!"

"Ah! That's a good idea!"

"Duh, genius! Let's go."

"Chris, I can't go. I just finished cleaning the tables, and I'm about... five water glasses short. I need to polish an extra rack. So go on – go have lunch without me. And we'll swap shirts later on. What are those?"

"Those are the glasses for you. I knew you'd be short. You always are. Did I tell you that you are a horrible waitress?"

"Oh, I know!" I nodded. "Where did you get the glasses?"

"I stole them from Diana's section." I tried to give Chris a jokingly reproachful look. "What? She always polishes a few racks too many. I'll tell you, you wouldn't want to get stuck in a lifeboat in the middle of the ocean with Diana as your companion."

"What?"

"I'll tell you about it one day. One of my songs is called Lifeboat. Who eats who if there is nothing else to eat? Are you coming?"

"Hmm, that does make sense, you know..."

***

I was lost somewhere deep in my thoughts while Chris was having a lively conversation with a cute girl with curly, blond hair. We were in the smoking area in front of the Beach Club, and I was fully enjoying my break. I watched Chris laugh, and I realized that his smile was quite possibly the most contagious smile I'd ever seen. Honestly, it would make anybody want to laugh. I couldn't be falling in love. I just couldn't. It didn't fit in my plans for the future, nor did it fit into my overall view of love, relationships, and life. Wasn't I the person who would always preach to my friends about loyalty and uselessness of spontaneous love affairs? Yes, I specifically remember one occasion. My best friend Katya once asked me how I could stay with Alex for three years. Didn't it get boring? What happened after the first, say, six months when you all of a sudden quit seeing the person you were with in blinding iridescent pink light? I had a definite answer to this question. Love was overrated. No, don't get me wrong! I'd always believed in love. It exists, but it's not as complicated as people claim it to be. Friendship, respect and good sex – this is the formula of love. Twenty-year-old Elena had it all figured out, and nobody could convince me otherwise. But now... all my theories were falling apart, crumbling down like a cardboard wall of self-inflicted illusions. I bit my lower lip, and inhaled hot ocean air of Independence Day and Chris's cologne. We had swapped T-shirts from behind the door of the ladies bathroom in the Beach Club. Even though neither of us had seen each other, this T-shirt swapping added a feeling of strange intimacy. Could he also smell me on my shirt?

"So what do you do back at home?"

I pulled myself out of the philosophical la-la land and looked back at the girl who was smiling at me – politely and curiously.

"I'm in college. Studying to be an interpreter."

"Oh wow! Are you going to work for the United Nations?"

"Mmm, no, not sure... I don't think so..."

"Why not?"

"Because she's planning to get married, give birth to ten ruddy-cheeked Russian boys and live happily ever after." Chris crossed his tanned arms and leaned against the palm tree, the brilliant smile deliberately positioned to disarm and defeat.

I shot him a mortified glare that could have stopped a fascist army dead in their tracks and nervously picked another cigarette out of the pack.

"Oh my gosh! You're engaged? Congratulations! When are you getting married?" The blond girl seemed to be more excited about my wedding than I was. It was not right. I was in desperate need of an attitude change.

"Next summer. We're planning on a big wedding with both extended families and friends present. A band and lots of gourmet food." I tried to wind myself up and actually get into the early bridal mood.

"I'll be there too," announced Chris. "Yes, I'll be right there in the room. I'll *watch* you get married."

I stared back at Chris and suddenly there was a complete silence. We just looked at each other, both frustrated with the impossibility. Here we were – blood, flesh and bones – and we couldn't be together, even though it felt like the most natural thing.

"Well, I think I'd better go." The girl gave us an "Okay, now it's really awkward" look and took off.

"Nice talking to you!" I yelled in my attempt to save some dignity and stay polite.

"Come on, Paina! All this love and marriage conversations make me hungry."

"Oh, what do you know about love?" I retorted. "Love is commitment and the only thing you're doing is trying to mess up people's lives!"

"You got it all wrong, trainee. Love is not bloody commitment. Love is letting people be."

I lifted my eyes and was about to reply with something bitter and sarcastic. And then I caught the glimpse of the American flag dancing in the wind. Independence Day. What is independence? What is freedom? What is love? Do I even know? Do the majority of people know or do they just think they do?

Jesus Christ, I was so tired, I couldn't feel my feet, and the only thing I wanted to do was to sit the fuck down.

***

"So, Elena, are you enjoying the Fourth of July?"

Monika and I were invited to Tyler's parents' house for the holiday celebration dinner. Since we were the only two people from our crew that were not scheduled to work the dinner shift, we gladly accepted the offer. Plus, wasn't it wonderful and culturally enriching to spend a traditional American holiday at a typical American household?

"Oh yes! It's very interesting! "

I tried to sound elated – Tyler's mom was so sweet and had cooked all this delicious food and a cake with white, red, and blue frosting – but in reality, my whole body was aching. The lunch shift had simply killed me. I might as well have run a marathon and climbed the Everest on the same day.

Chris had messed with the hostess's charts and I ended up working outside. That was what Chris did. When we didn't work at the same station, he just went to the hostess stand, erased somebody else's name and put mine in. I normally didn't mind (even though I should have), but that day I was outraged. The temperature outside must have reached 110 degrees, plus an impossible humidity index. I couldn't believe that guests actually wanted to sit outside. But they did. Tons and tons of them. They just kept coming in, and asking for stuff, and asking for stuff again and again and again. I was going crazy. I was in a haze of a server's nightmare. At some point, I started running in front of the guests. This was when Ms. Laura stopped me, her face all stern and serious.

"Elena, you can't be running on the floor!"

"Oh, I'm sorry, Ms. Laura. It's just, I mean... I don't have time to do anything. I forgot to get half of the drinks, the kids are screaming. I will NEVER have kids, I swear."

"Trainee, quit your crying and whining and let's go!" Chris swiftly grabbed my wrist and swooshed me away from shocked Ms. Laura.

Before I knew what was going on, I found myself inside the server's station. Chris poured a tall glass of pink lemonade and handed it over to me.

"Drink it. Relax."

"It's pink." I was about to cry. The stupid, stupid tears stubbornly filled my eyes and just wouldn't go away.

"Hmm... What?" Chris looked puzzled.

"Pink. It's pink. I have some weird pink synchronicity today. Never mind."

"What happened to you there?"

"Nothing, I just got busy and I couldn't handle it. And then I realized I was totally useless and lost. And Africa is right there!" I waved my arm in despair.

Okay, now he'll definitely think that I'm crazy. I'm not making any sense.

"Africa, you know? No problems for me if I was in Africa."

"Hunger? Malaria?" Chris arched his eyebrow and gently patted my shoulder. "Take a few minutes to relax. I'll take care of everything. Get back to the floor when you're ready, okay?"

"Ok," I sniveled.

"And Elena?"

"Yes?" *Oh God! If he asks me one more question I won't be able to say a word with all this snot in my nose.*

"I'll miss you, Scarlett."

"What?"

"Every time I leave you to tend to the tables – even if for just a second – I'm going to tell you "I'll miss you, Scarlett". And you should respond, "I'll miss you too, Rhett!""

"You're a nut job!" I laughed.

"Hold on. Is that a booger that I see?"

"Oh, shut up!"

"I'll miss you, Scarlett!" And off he went.

The pink lemonade was absolutely delicious and magically invigorating. I was on the floor in a matter of minutes – energetic and super-fast! Even the little kids didn't pose such a threat to my well-being anymore.

***

"It's been a lot of fun so far!" I smiled at Tyler's mom and stretched my legs. "But the Beach Club was SO busy! I'm in pain from all the running."

"Well, you can relax now, love. Have some food."

"Yes, Elena, it's all behind you now," added Monika who was already sipping on a glass of white wine. "Relax and enjoy the holiday!"

The food was indeed delicious, and we had a good laugh talking about Chris's party and how he'd got arrested. Tyler's dad was a judge, and Tyler told him about everything that had happened that evening. Mr. Smith couldn't get into the details of the case (naturally), but I was sure he'd helped Chris out by not completely believing every word of Cruella de Copville.

"Excuse me, Tyler? Where is the bathroom?"

"Oh, just around the corner to the right. Hurry up, Elena – we're about to leave to watch the fireworks."

"Tyler, don't be ridiculous. Let the girl use the bathroom..."

Mrs. Smith's words faded away as I shut the bathroom door behind me. Okay, where was the switch? Ha! Found it!

I suppressed a yell for help by clamping the hand to my mouth and silently staring at the monster in front of me. There it was, casually crawling in the bathtub – the largest cockroach that ever walked the surface of the Earth. Well, the largest I'd seen, at least. It was of a reddish color and so disgusting, I felt as if millions of them were crawling all over my skin.

"Oh my god, oh my god, oh my god!" I gulped for air. I couldn't move.

If there was a God, I was being punished for cheating. Even though, strictly speaking, we just kissed. Kissing surely doesn't constitute cheating. The roach must have heard my shameful thoughts and started moving towards me. I needed to make a retreat. I needed not to panic. *Think pink. Think pink lemonade. Ok, now – go!*

Out I went from the bathroom and straight into the dining room.

"Oh wow! That was quick," laughed Tyler. "See, mom? It worked. Had I not told her to hurry up, she'd still be there, freshening up, curling her eyelashes..."

"I doubt it," I muttered.

'What?"

"Never mind. Are we going to see the fireworks?"

"No, we're not going, we're running. It should start any minute, and we can't drive, all the roads have been blocked off."

"Thank you for the wonderful dinner, Mr. and Mrs. Smith! It was amazing!" I managed to squeal as I was disappearing through the door.

We ran towards the pier, through the still persisting humidity and starry night. Tyler and Monika were laughing happily (well, they hadn't seen the giant roach, had they?) and talking about the whole night of celebration in front of us. And then we heard the popping sound of the fireworks. The sky exploded in pink bubbles of light as we stood there, heavily panting after the long run. We could hear people around us cheering and laughing. People like freedom. People like independence. That's what makes the world go 'round. I looked up into the sky and thought that the pink globe might hit me on the head and then everything would be over. I looked around and saw that everybody around me – Tyler, Monika, and hundreds of other people I didn't know – had strawberry ice cream glow on their faces. I remembered how Chris had gotten back to the server's station earlier this afternoon. I was pouring iced tea in one of the pitchers and didn't see him. *"I've missed you, Scarlett."* His hot breath brushed on my neck and I spilled half of the pitcher out on the counter. *"I hate being here today. You know where I'd rather be?"*

I stiffened and quit breathing for a while. He couldn't see my face – which was a good thing, considering – and I could close my eyes.

"I'd rather be at my house. In bed. With you. All day long. All night long. I want to kiss you all over. I'll make you c – "

"Okay, stop right there! I think I know what you mean." I turned around and handed him the ice-cold pitcher.

"So did you miss me, Scarlett?"

"Horribly!"

And then the multi-colored constellations covered the whole sky   above   me.

CHAPTER NINE

Dancing with an Alligator

"Okay, so let's see what we got. Ten bottles of wine, four twelve-packs of beer..."

"Crappola beer," I mumbled as I was applying sparkly bright-pink nail polish on my toe nails.

"Elena, just shut up and get busy with the floor cleaning," retorted Vera and continued with the party inventory check. "A box of pink wine and five gigantic bottles of vodka. Should be enough, don't you think?"

"And people accuse Russians of consuming excessive amounts of liquor!" exclaimed Diana. "Most Russian village alcoholics would have a heart attack if they saw a vodka bottle of this size. And what is it called? "Russkova – Vodka Imported from Russia". Have you ever heard of Russkova vodka?"

I awkwardly heel-walked to Diana, trying not to mess up my princess toes, and peeked from behind her shoulder.

"Mmm... No, never heard of it. But we'll definitely give it a try tonight." I smiled and attempted to disappear in the kitchen.

"Elena!" Vera stopped me in my tracks, her accusing eyes staring me up and down. "Everyone here has already done what was assigned. Everyone but you. When are you going to clean the floors?"

"Oh, come on! What is it, a boot camp? I'll get it done, don't worry."

"When?" Vera's arm was still stretched across the kitchen door, blocking the way to the freedom of my bedroom.

"In a second!"

"Elena! The guests will be here in an hour – you haven't cleaned anything, you're not dressed, and you don't have your make-up on. You spent the last hour doing your toenails!"

"Chris is coming. She wants to make sure she looks drop-dead from head to toe," said Diana and gave me a conniving smile.

"What's that have to do with Chris?" I shot Diana a warning look.

"You tell us!"

"Elena." Vera looked like she was about to kill me with the broomstick she was holding. "I couldn't care less even if you were going to do a bikini wax for this party – but for fuck's sake clean the damn floors!"

"Girlzzz, how do I look?"

All three of us turned our heads in unison and momentarily forgot what we'd been arguing about. Sonia looked as if she'd just got back from an expensive spa where she had been pampered like there was no tomorrow. Her short, highlighted hair was stylishly blow-dried and straightened, her lips were full and shiny, and she was wearing a pair of extremely high-heeled stilettos.

"Wow! You did it yourself?" I couldn't hide jealous notes in my voice. "You look amazing!"

"Your bartender will be blown away." Diana came closer to Sonia. "How did you apply this eyeliner? It's awesome!"

"Oh, Sonia! You surely are a birthday girl!" Vera gave Sonia a friendly hug and added dreamily, "Nineteenth birthday in the USA."

Sonia's content face suddenly changed and she glared at me with an expression of utter horror.

"Elena! You haven't cleaned the floors! Daniel will be here any minute, and our place looks like a dumpster."

"It doesn't look like a dumpster!"

"Elena, there are three dried-up dead cockroaches in the living room. It's disgusting!"

"Exactly, why do I have to get the roaches?" I pouted.

"Because you're never doing anything in this apartment," said Vera. "So we had an agreement that when we're getting ready for Sonia's birthday party, you'll be doing the hardest part."

"I don't see how that could possibly be fair." I shrugged. "But I'll clean the floors... right after I take a shower..."

"Elena!" Sonia attacked me, her eyes angrily penetrating my skull. "YOU ARE DOING THE FLOORS NOW!"

"Oh, whatever! You should just calm the fuck down! Daniel is going to be looking at you, not at our carpet. And I am NOT listening to you, eighteen-year-old chicken heads, telling me what I'm going or not going to do. Okay?" I paused for a second, inhaled and went on. "Actually, you know what I'm going to do? I'm going to smoke. Yes! Smoke! And when I'm ready and if – only if – I'm in the mood for this – I will clean your stupid floors! Sonia, quit twitching, you'll get a heart attack. I'm getting enough of "'clean this, clean that"' at home from my parents. Can you just leave me alone for these four months? Jesus Christ!"

I finally stopped and looked at the three astonished faces staring at me with ill-hidden mockery.

"Wow, Elena. You clearly have some sort of cleaning-up issues. Maybe you need to see a therapist," Diana suggested meekly, the corner of her mouth jumping from suppressed laughter.

"You know what? Forget about the party! I'm not going!"

"Oh, yes? And where are you going, may I ask?" giggled Vera. "You still don't know how to ride a bike, and Chris & Co. taxi requires a pretty expensive fare you can't afford."

Fuming, I briskly turned around and rushed towards the door. Vera quickly caught up with me, grabbed my elbow, and whispered, "You know how excited Sonia is about this Daniel guy. And today is her birthday. Why do you have to be such a bitch?"

"This is just stupid, if you ask me. We're on summer vacation – we need to party, instead of spending half of the day on cleaning up. But whatever, I'll do it."

I slammed the door shut behind me and sighed with relief. *When I live by myself, I'll never clean up, I swear. Or maybe I'll become very rich and hire a cleaning lady. Yes, that is exactly what I will do!*

***

"Okay, so I guess he's not coming." Sonia's eyes were watering, and her voice sounded an octave higher than usual.

"It's too early to say," I screamed over my shoulder. I was in the kitchen on all fours, scrubbing the floors. "We told everybody the party will start at eight. It's only half past seven. Don't freak out!"

"But he said he'll be here an hour early to help us set everything up!"

"Well, maybe he got busy," yelled Vera.

"Vera, where are you?" I stopped scrubbing and looked around. "You sound like you're in a cave or something."

"I'm peeing!"

"Oh, well, that explains it." I got up and proudly checked out my work. "Shinier than we ever saw it! Your dance floor is ready, Cinderella!"

I landed on the couch next to Sonia and exhaled heavily. Smoking and floor scrubbing in this exact sequence didn't go particularly well together.

"Cheer up, beautiful! He'll be here in no time."

"Ladies, drinks!" Diana placed four enormous plastic cups filled with an unidentified liquid of dangerously red color on the coffee table in front of us. "Sonia, just gulp yours down. Quit sweating small stuff."

"Bitchesss, can you bring me some toilet paper?"

"No, cave girl, we can't – we're out of it!" I yelled back. "Mmm, Diana, that's yummy. What is it?"

"Vodka mixed with a drink called Fruit Punch – we have them in four strangely bright colors: I can only imagine the chemical reaction they will come with the bacteria in our stomachs."

"Elena! Can you get me some tissue paper from my room? And how are we going to have a party without any toilet paper?"

"I wanted to get some from the Beach Club, but Chris told me it would be looked at as stealing and said he'd bring us some toilet paper," shouted Sonia and indecisively picked up one of the plastic cups. "Maybe vodka will counteract the fruit punch chemicals?" She sighed and drank up half of the glass-full, her eyes still glistening.

"Of course it would be stealing!" I stared at Sonia in disbelief. "Why would you want to take toilet paper from the Beach Club? It's toilet paper, for God's sakes!"

"Exactly," retorted Sonia. "Why on earth would we pay seven dollars thirty cents for a pack of toilet paper?"

"Anyone, please!! Tissue!"

"I'm coming!" I cried back and rushed to Vera's bedroom.

As I was going through Vera's toiletry drawer, I suddenly heard Chris's voice in the living room:

"Toilet paper delivery guy is here! Anybody needs wiping assistance?"

"Oh, Christopher," laughed Diana. "You and your dirty jokes!"

My poor, poor heart missed a few beats. I slowly crept into the hallway.

"Vera." I tiptoed into the bathroom, handed Vera the tissue, and whispered, "Go out there, and tell him I'm in the shower."

"Why can't you say hello first?"

"I look like shit. I need to get dressed first. And do my hair..." I was waving Vera off. "Come on, go!"

Vera kept looking at me quietly, without uttering a single word. She had an amazing ability to look serious and patronizing even sitting on the toilet with her knickers around her ankles.

"What? Who brought you the tissue, chica? If not for me, you'd still be stuck in here, dripping around the floor like a coffee machine."

"Elena." Vera seemed unfazed by my joke. "You're dancing with fire."

"What's that supposed to mean?"

"You know what it's supposed to mean. I warned you. Go get dressed, but give me back this drink!"

"Thanks, Vera! Love you!" I whispered and quietly disappeared in my bedroom.

***

The party would have turned out to be a total success, but Daniel the Hot Bartender never showed up. Sonia was destroyed and decided to take a trip to the Magic Forget-All Land on board of a booze-mobile. Desiring nothing else, but to express our friendly concern and support, Vera, Diana and myself ended up getting equally trashed.

"Oukaaaay, my glam bitchezzz!" I yelled. "Time to take another shot. Let's try this genuine Russian vodka!"

I swiftly poured four shot glasses full and looked around. The place was a mess. Crushed tortilla chips were scattered around the dirty carpet with multicolored splashes of fruit punch, and spinning ceiling fans were adorned with flying strips of toilet paper. I silently stared at Chris, who seemed to be so intoxicated and absorbed in throwing toilet paper up in the air and jumping up and down to the crazy Russian music, he didn't even notice landing on Jennifer's foot. Jennifer, a tall succulent brunette with a Brazilian rear end that made most men salivate like little puppy dogs, scrunched her face in agony and turned around to face her opponent only to suddenly see Sonia running straight into her arms:

"Jennifer! I'm so happy to see you!"

"Thanks, Sonia, but... uhmm, I've been here for like three hours..."

"Whatever! I'm SO happy to see you! Let's have a shot of vodka. Come on!"

"Thank you, but I'm fine. I only drink vodka with cranberry juice." Jennifer smiled.

"Elenaaaaa!" yelled Sonia. "Have you heard of anything more ridiculous? Vodka and cranberry juice? Yuck! Let's make it vodka without the rocks with a splash of vodka!"

"HA!" I yelled in ecstasy. "HA HA HA! This is the most hilarious thing I've ever heard! Vodka without the rocks with a splash of vodka." I staggered and dropped my drink on Diana's foot. All of us shut our eyes closed and when we re-opened them, we were completely covered in cherry-red fruit punch explosion. Including Jennifer's light beige pants.

"Elena! Watch what you're doing, crazy slut!"

Jennifer looked paralyzed. After the first few seconds of pure shock, she attempted a weak smile and started backing off.

"I think I'd better go. I'm working a breakfast shift tomorrow..."

"Verka Serduchkaaaaaaa!" Sonia's voice hurt even my ears. "Let's dance, Jennifer, let's dance!"

Jennifer looked like she'd rather hop on a plane and head over to a third-world country for the next couple of years, but it was too late. Vera and Diana locked their elbows and started spinning in a traditional Russian dance, their arms waving up in the air, screaming and laughing. Sonia swooshed Jennifer, who at that point seemed to have entered a state of a deep coma, and joined the girls. Everybody else was exchanging "check out those crazy Russians" looks and awkwardly stepping from one foot onto another. But when Milo jumped in and began his hip-thrust-belly-dance-shimmy performance, and Monika followed with her sexy groovy moves, the people seemingly relaxed and also joined in the dance. The astoundingly loud music, an upbeat mix of Ukrainian folklore and modern pop, flooded our Island Retreat living room. Verka Serduchka deserves a special attention in my story. It represents a kind of a band that erased the boundaries between the generations; it represents music that made all Russian teenage boys and girls jiggle to their ancestors' tunes. It essentially made all of us not ashamed to come from where we were coming from. And believe me, the

young generation of Russia needed a serious self-esteem boost –
not individually, but as a nation. Funny familiar songs sounded
especially warm and nostalgic when you were so far away from
home, surrounded by so many people that couldn't quite
understand you. I felt goose bumps on the back of my neck and
turned around. And right there, above the waves of popping
heads and wailing arms, I met the eyes of one person that
understood me. Never mind years and miles and cultural
differences that separated us - he knew me better than I knew
myself. Even though he'd just finished throwing a whole pack of
toilet paper rolls on the ceiling fans and was happily beaming at
me with a drunken smile – he was like... family.

I don't remember the last cheerful notes of Verka Serduchka.
I recall slowly moving through the crowd, my eyes fixed on his.
He was walking towards me as well. We started slowly dancing
to the sweet sounds of Let It Be. The vodka without the rocks
with a splash of vodka was definitely coming into effect; we were
both stumbling and Chris stepped on my foot. I laughed and
looked up at him. I thought, "Oh who cares? I am
SOOOOOOOOOOOOOOOOOOOOO happy, how can it be
wrong?" We kissed and the whole world around us came to a
complete stop. We were alone, and John Lennon was
encouraging us to keep on going. I was getting dizzy, and
wrapped my arms around his shoulders and inhaled his already
so familiar smell.

"Got you, lovers!"

Sudden annoying light crashed an illusion of intimacy and
both of us turned in the direction of the source – like two deer in
the headlights. Paul, Milo's friend and roommate from Slovakia,
got so close to us, an outsider might have thought there were

three of us kissing. He was holding a huge professional camera and was stupidly smiling at us. Paul happened to be extremely fond of photography. He was also pretty fond of me about two weeks ago, but I turned him down – I was engaged, for Christ's sake!

"Now I have a proof!" He waved the camera in front of us. "For your fiancé." He winked, grinned – quite nastily, I might say – and disappeared into the crowd.

"I hope I'll be eaten by an alligator tomorrow." I sighed and closed my eyes. We were planning to head out to Okefenokee Swamp the next morning, one of the trips that Chris had planned for all of us.

"Elena," Chris dreamily picked up a stray lock of my hair with his finger and whispered in my ear. "You have already been eaten by one. You just haven't realized it yet."

I looked around the room and saw that pretty much everybody had already left. I felt nauseous and guilty.

"I need to go to bed. Good night, Chris!" I turned around and glided to my bedroom. As I landed in the coziness of my bed, the objects started floating around me and I fell into a deep warm forgiving swamp of dreams.

***

"Chris, are you sure we'll find our way out of this swamp?" I asked.

"Of course! We'll be fine. I've been here multiple times. Plus, we have the map!" Chris happily waved the colorful brochure in front of my face.

I wasn't convinced. In fact, I was not quite sure as to how and why I had gotten where I was in the first place. Have you ever been at a swamp? At a real enormously plush green swamp filled with 10-foot alligators? On a tiny little boat with an engine that looked like it was about to fall off and hit one of those dreary heads with eerie citrine eyes?

"They're going to eat us, I know it..." Diana shot a quick look at the ice tea river underneath and shifted closer to the center of the boat.

"Oh, Banana, watch out, you're about to piss in your pants." Sonia took her camera out of the case and said, "Vera, try to get over to the front of the boat. I'll take a picture of you."

"Are you fucking crazy?" I couldn't believe my ears. "We're in the middle of gatorville, and you still have pictures on your mind!"

"They'd be posing in a war zone in front of a bomb that's about to explode," murmured Diana.

"I think that would be a very cool backdrop for a picture," declared Chris. He was sitting at the back of the boat and steering. "Come on, Elena, get your arse over there and get your picture taken!"

The scenery was indeed breathtaking. The scorching hot Georgia sun glistened in the tawny mirror of the river, and the only sound we could hear was a high-pitched buzz of mosquitoes. The river was enclosed in the cozy embrace of thick vegetation that came into perfect contrast with the wide open turquoise sky. If you looked closely enough, you could almost spot an Indian hiding behind the protective wall of flora. Well, if you had as rich imagination as I did.

"Okay." I shrugged. "I'll do it!"

With apprehension, I slowly moved towards the tip of the boat and finally sat down, leaning backwards on my elbows.

"Yesss! Elena, you look AMAZING!" yelled Sonia. "Let's take another one just in case."

My Hollywood posing in the midst of the jungle wilderness was interrupted by a sudden loud noise and a rude splash of the swamp water in my face.

"Hey, people! We've already been all around Okefenokee and back, and you're still stuck here!" The Slovak boat with Captain Milo in charge abruptly stopped next to ours.

"Milo!" laughed Chris. "Are you still wasted from yesterday? Don't drive the boat that fast – you'll disturb the gators!"

"Oh! Look at that whiny Brit with his Russian dolls. You're just jealous we're ahead of you, that's all. Admit it!"

"Milo," hissed Monika, who looked quite pissed off. "Slow the boat down! I'm too young to die in the middle of nowhere AND be eaten by alligators."

"Aghh, whatever!" Milo rolled his eyes. "You guys are so boring."

"Listen, why don't we all park the boats here and get out on the shore for a while?" said Chris. "This place looks perfect for a picnic."

"Okay, okay, you just don't want to race and lose all over again. I understand," laughed Milo.

It took us good twenty minutes to safely climb up the shore and situate ourselves on a small sandy patch surrounded by the wall of greenery.

"Guys!" announced Vera. "I got us some yogurts from Winn Dixie. Would you like some? We don't have any spoons though... We'll have to use our fingers."

"Yogurts?" Chris's face contorted in disgust. "We've been out on the swamp for at least two hours. I'm sure the yogurts have gone bad. Why would you buy yogurts for a trip to the swamp in the first place?"

"They were on big sale," smiled Vera.

"Oh, God!" exclaimed Diana. "Vera and Sonia love the bargain so much, they can spend a couple hundred dollars on a load of shit and be over the moon about it. And then come back home and wonder – what did I buy this crap for again?"

"That's not true," pouted Sonia. "We're trying to save us some money, that's all."

"Greedy Russians!" giggled Milo. "Anyone wants some potato chips?"

"Yes please!" Chris grabbed the bag of chips from Milo and added, "I've already donated some toilet paper. I hope that will help out our Russian refugee convention."

"Is Elena going to pay for that toilet paper, Chris?" asked Paul and once again gave me one of the nastiest smiles I'd ever seen.

"Guys!" yelled Sonia, who was at that point already positioned at the edge of the shore, her hands clutching the bag of chips. "This gator is not moving! Let's throw a chip at him – maybe that'll help!"

"Oh, wow, let's do it!" Vera rushed towards the water edge.

"You can't do that!" Chris sounded quite serious all of a sudden, "Gators can run pretty fast you know."

"Oh, you Americans are so afraid of everything," snorted Paul. "I'll do it!"

"Go ahead, Paul the Brave Heart! We'll remember you just like that – sunburned and covered in mosquito bites," I laughed.

"Elena, I really need to pee," whispered Monika. "Can you come with me?"

"Sure, you know I'm always ready to pee."

"Can I go too? I'll just look, I swear." Chris lifted his hands up as if in self-defense.

"Why is it that you guys are so fascinated about even an imaginative possibility of a lesbian relationship?" laughed Monika.

"And why are you chicks always going to the bathroom together?" asked Milo. "There must be a reason behind it."

"I want to go back to the Island!" said Diana and slapped her forearm, presumably killing an unfortunate bug. "I'm being eaten alive!"

"AAAAHH! It's hissing, it's hissing! The alligator is MAD at us!!!" Sonia was jumping up and down in utter excitement.

"Monika," I whispered and took Monika aside. "I really think it's time to go back. If none of us gets eaten by gators, I might just as well murder Paul, or Diana will kill Sonia, or Chris will throw all of us in the river – judging by his facial expression, at least."

Monika followed my gaze and snorted with laughter.

"You're right! This outing is about to turn into a disaster. Let's pee and go back home. Hey, guys! Let's go back. I'm already sunburned and exhausted!"

Naturally, we couldn't go that far for the fear of being attacked by swamp creatures who surely were lurking just around the bushes.

"I just hope I won't be stung by a poisonous snake." I squatted and looked around to make sure there were no gators behind me. "It would be pretty sad, you know. 'She died at the age of twenty, a month before her twenty-first birthday, after being bitten by a snake while pissing in the Georgia swamp.'"

"Yes, that sounds quite ridiculous," giggled Monika. "Honestly, it's probably the worst way to go I've ever heard of."

"Oh, no, I've already thought of the worst one – in the toilet on the airplane. I mean, that would be beyond horrible. I'd imagine that actually happened to some people..."

"Oh, God, that's just sad! Elena!" Monika looked at me half accusingly, half-jokingly. "Why on Earth are we discussing this depressing subject?"

"I'm sorry... I have these thoughts sometimes." I paused for a while as we were walking back to our picnic site. "I guess I'm trying to fight the unavoidable morbid reflections by mocking them. Some people think it's freaky."

"It is freaky! You ARE a freak – no wonder Chris is attracted to you so much."

I was about to ask Monika if she really thought Chris was that attracted to me, when we suddenly heard a loud shriek. We quickly looked at each other and ran towards the site. Everybody was already in the boats, but Sonia and Paul looked as pale as the first snow in December. And the bag of potato chips was floating in the river.

"What happened?" I managed to say.

"Paul wanted to give the gator another chip before we went." Chris was laughing so hard, it was impossible not to smile when looking at him (or was it just me?). "So Sonia kindly agreed to pass him the bag. Well, the gator apparently wanted to bid a memorable farewell to its tormentors. It slightly lifted its head above the water and let out quite a distinguishing sound. The kind of sound that nearly sent Sonia flying out of the boat."

"Oh gosh," exclaimed Monika and started slowly descending into the boat. "I thought somebody was being attacked."

"They kind of were." Chris nodded, "The moral of the story is – don't mess with the natural way of things." I felt his eyes on my neck as I was sitting down on the boat bench. "And don't mess with gators."

***

I wonder sometimes – what happens in the atmosphere, in the air around us that makes us pulsate with sheer excitement? You can see no obvious reason for it, but the result is there – pleasant anxiety that makes you want to dance, sing, scream, get wasted, smoke a pack of cigarettes at one go. Do you remember this feeling? I believe we find ourselves less and less often in this amusing state as we get older. I think this feeling is an unavoidable attribute of youth. You can sense endless possibilities the world can offer you, and it's intoxicating.

"It's been such an interesting day!" I exclaimed and swam towards the opposite edge of the pool.

The sun was just setting down, and Chris, Vera, and I were relaxing at the pool. The water was amazingly refreshing after the hot day at the swamp, and the air was warm, transparent, and sweetly aromatic.

"Elena, look, I got the flower for you as well." Vera descended down the pool steps, and put a big red flower behind my ear.

"Beautiful wild orchids," beamed Chris. "Maybe you two should kiss each other..."

"Oh, Chris!" laughed Vera. "You're such a perv!"

"I think he's aware of that. We'll – let it go. Thank you very much. I believe you know where you could go with this request – it would be easily satisfied, I'm sure." I tried to sound as careless as possible, but judging by Vera's surprised expression and an amused flicker in Chris's eyes I failed miserably.

"If I wanted to go elsewhere, I'd be there right now," said Chris in a low voice and halfway disappeared under the water, his eyes are still staring at mine. He slowly moved towards me, grabbed me by the leg, and jumped out on the surface. "Aaa! Alligator got you – you won't run away now!"

"But I will!" announced Vera as she was getting out of the pool and drying her hair with a towel. "I'll see you back at the apartment. Sex and the City is about to come on. Bye, guys!" And off she went.

"I'll be there in a sec!" I yelled and tried to pull myself up on the edge of the pool.

"Where do you think you're going?" Chris grabbed me by the waist and pulled me back down in the water, his body firmly pressed against my back. "I think we're not finished here yet," he whispered in my ear.

At that moment I felt so much, I couldn't move for a few long, long seconds. I was paralyzed with painful excitement.

Twenty-year-old Elena had never wanted a human being that much until then. But I was proud. Proud and confused. I spun around and looked up at him, my hands pressed against his chest in a pretty useless attempt to keep him further away.

"You know it's not going anywhere, Chris. Plus, it never works if you are aiming at more than one target." I squinted my eyes at him. And before he had a chance to come up with one of his smart-ass "I just had sex with two girls about two weeks ago" remarks, I quickly added, "Not if you are aiming at REAL targets."

"Hmmm..." Chris looked down at me and reflectively ran his fingers through my wet hair. "And I thought it's not going to work out because you're engaged."

"Well, yes. That would be the main reason." I clicked my tongue to show how extremely irritated I was and once again tried to pull away.

"Oi, quit it! I think you should take all these silly thoughts out of your head and stay a little bit longer."

He moved even closer to me and leaned down to kiss me. Warm evening air was caressing my bare arms, and the feeling that the kiss brought was so unbearably powerful, that I got curiously dizzy. The buildings around us could have easily collapsed, and the whole universe could have shattered, and I wouldn't have paid a slightest attention. We opened our eyes when we heard a sudden splash and an explosion of children's laughter somewhere very close by. I blushed as I saw a disapproving face of a woman hovering at the edge of the pool. She cast us a quick "you filthy bastards" glance and hurried her kids to the opposite side of the pool grounds.

"I think we got in trouble," whispered Chris.

"I think so too." I smiled. "We'd better go. I'm getting hungry."

"Burger King? I can pick us something up and meet you back at the apartment."

"I can come with you!" I declared somewhat desperately.

"Hmm, the thing is – I don't think I can get out of the pool just yet. I'll just hang out here for little a while longer."

In response to the question in my eyes, Chris looked down and then nodded in the direction of the kids.

"What? Why not?" I stared back at him, blinking incomprehensively.

Chris got just a touch closer to me and I blushed.

"Oh!" I laughed. "Really, Chris? Just one kiss?"

"Not funny." Chris was trying not to laugh.

"Oh, it's VERY funny!" I jumped out of the pool and wrapped a towel around my chest. "I'll see you back at the apartment then – after you cool off," I giggled. "It's been such a hot day."

"Indeed it was," Chris nodded and proceeded to swim alongside the pool, his face all stern and serious.

"And don't forget the burgers!" I said at last and disappeared through the gate.

As I briskly walked towards the apartment, my mood started to change. The high spirits were replaced by a distant gnawing feeling of guilt. I didn't want Chris to stay behind, because as soon as I was alone, I couldn't help but face my conscience – and it wasn't pleasant. I heard the voices around the corner by the steps, and realized that they belonged to Milo, Paul, and Monika.

"Look at this one. Sonia is SO wasted here, it's hilarious," laughed Monika.

"What are you guys doing?" I smiled and peeked over their shoulders.

"Checking out the pictures from last night. Look, Russian, they're so funny," said Milo.

He pressed the next button on the laptop and there I was, making out with the guy who wasn't my fiancé, with no shame or forethought. I quickly turned my eyes away. Doing something is one thing. Seeing oneself doing it on the screen of a laptop is a totally different cup of tea. It makes events more visual and thus unexplainably more real.

"Your boyfriend would love this," gloated Paul. "Would you like me to make him an extra copy? Or maybe an e-mail? It would be so much faster!"

"No, thanks." I felt extremely dizzy. It actually seemed as if the ground was slipping away from under my feet. "I think I need to make a phone call. Bye!" I managed a week smile.

"Are you okay?" Monika looked at me with sincere concern.

"I'm fine. Totally!" I started heading over in the direction of the pay phone.

"Russian! Are you going to walk all the way there in a towel?" Milo was trying to be funny, but I could tell that he was also worried.

"Yeah, it's just around the corner." I smiled at Milo and Monika and walked away.

Paul's words still ringing in my ears, I reached the phone booth and dialed the familiar number.

"Hmm... hello?" Alex sounded sleepy.

"Hi there!" I attempted to add some cheer to my voice.

"Elena? Are you all right?"

"Of course I'm all right! Why would I not be all right?"

"Because you're calling at six in the morning." Alex yawned and added, "How are you doing, darling? How's America treating you?"

"Oh it's fine... I miss you though. I wish you were here."

"In two months we'll be back together again – don't worry. Damn, I'm really tired. Tell me something to wake me up, something exciting."

The sardonic nature of mine happily suggested an honest answer: "Oh nothing, just finished making out with this English guy in the pool. He got so excited he actually got a boner from the kiss. Can you believe it?"

"Nothing exciting, you know, work... We're waking up so early I can't remember what I've been doing half of the time."

Paul's photo quickly flashed in my mind: my hair all disheveled, Chris's hand on the back of my neck, my hands pressed passionately against his shoulders.

"Listen, Elena. You don't really have to call me every day – if everything is fine. I understand. I know that you miss me. I miss you too, but right now I miss my pillow even more."

"Oh, okay. Go back to bed then."

"Good night!"

"Hey, Alex..."

"What?" He suppressed another yawn.

"I love you very, very much!"

"Damn, Elena if I didn't know you that well, I'd be convinced you're boning someone else and feeling extremely guilty right now! Ha ha!! Bye! Kiss you."

"Kiss you too."

I placed the receiver back in its place and stared at it as if it was about to turn into a poisonous snake and bite me on the hand. What the fuck had I gotten myself into?

CHAPTER TEN

Turkish Delight

I leaned against the back of a pool chair, straightened my legs, and lit a second cigarette. After talking to Alex I couldn't bring myself to face Chris again. I had to pull myself together and develop an elaborate defense strategy. I was obviously losing my head, and it had only happened to me once before. It actually never happened, but... does it count if you wanted it to happen?

My mind traveled two years back. I had just returned from a two-week trip to Germany. It was also a student exchange program of sorts, and I made a lot of international friends there: an extremely intelligent left-leaning Beatles-loving long-haired Italian boy named Marco, a sweet and almost fairy-tale beautiful Macedonian girl named Ana, a rock 'n' roll-obsessed progressive chick from South Korea named Uni, and Ozer. Ozer was from Turkey and he was breathtakingly handsome. I believe it is true that Turkish men and Russian women have something for each other, some kind of genetically programmed chemistry. Ozer and I liked each other right away. Nothing happened – I had Alex waiting for me at home and I was just as devoted and faithful as I'd always been. We had some very good times, all of us. We explored magically medieval town of Marburg, drank a lot of quality German beer and experienced an unforgettable weekend trip to Amsterdam. When I returned home, Alex and I had presumably passionate sex, and Alex – as guys tend to do – happily dozed off on the couch next to me. As I was lazily flicking through TV channels, it suddenly occurred to me that I wanted to get dressed, write Alex a goodbye note, walk out, and never come back. The atrocity of this rebellious thought that had come out of nowhere left me frozen for a few seconds. I quickly filed it in the back pocket of my subconscious and had never returned to it until that evening by the Island Retreat pool.

I exhaled the smoke of the third cigarette. I couldn't do it again. Alex was my friend and my first and only lover. I knew he'd always love me and would never betray me. And I was planning on having a family with him. I couldn't throw it all away for the sake of a silly summer fling. So many girls who went to school with me had gotten back from the U.S. and boasted about their American love adventures. They had a few boyfriends during the summer and then happily got back to their Russian boys. I'd always disapproved of that – and how harsh I was with my words and my judgment. One might have thought the words were coming out of Mother Teresa's mouth. I sighed and wiped the tears off with the back of my hand. Well, if it taught me anything, I would never be judgmental again. Never. I kicked back and closed my eyes.

"Elena! What are you doing here?"

"Oh, shit!" I jumped up and stared at Vera. "I must have lost ten years of my life just now. Don't be surprised if you notice some gray in my hair tomorrow. Why are you here?"

"Why am I here?" Vera laughed a bit nervously. "Well, Chris is on our couch, with the food he'd picked up for you. He's been there for at least two hours and he refuses to leave. He doesn't know where you are. For some reason, I had a feeling you were here... What's going on?"

"Oh, Vera!" I moaned. "I can't be possibly coming back to the apartment. Every time I see him, I'm doing something stupid. I can't be doing anything stupid anymore, I just can't."

"Maybe it's not stupid?" Vera gave me a tentative look.

"What do you mean?"

"I mean, if you want something so much, why should you be resisting?"

"No." I shook my head. "It's all just wrong. It must be some kind of a test. If I fail it, I don't deserve real love."

"I don't know about that." Vera shrugged. "The only test you have passed so far is the abstinence test. Sonia said that if you don't have sex with Chris until the end of the trip, she'll build a statue in your honor back in Voronezh and will call it Memorial to the Iron-Clad Vagina."

"Did she really say that?" I laughed. "Well, that, at least, makes me feel less slutty."

"Let's go, Elena. You can't be sleeping by the pool."

"Okay, okay. If you say so..."

I saw him the moment we walked in the door of our apartment. The lights were out, and the TV was quietly flashing with repetitive infomercials. Chris was curled up on the couch clutching a Burger King paper bag. He was fast asleep.

"Are you going to be all right?" asked Vera.

"Yeah, I'll be fine." I nodded. "Go to bed. I'll be quick."

I sat down on the couch next to him and gently moved the paper bag aside. I was watching him sleep, his freckled face so serene and somehow still funny. I touched his cheek and thought about how much I'd like to curl up next to him and wake up together in the morning. There it was – Turkish Delight number two. The British dessert I apparently couldn't have.

"Got ya!" I gave a startled jump as Chris quickly grabbed my wrist and pulled me towards him. "Just what do you think you're doing, young lady?"

"Chris, I came here to tell you that we've got to stop." I suspected that my serious tone sounded rather ridiculous considering I was sprawled on top of him.

"Stop? We haven't even started yet." Chris laughed and touched my neck with his finger. "What has to stop is you tickling my face with your hair."

I pulled away, sat up and looked him straight in the eye.

"Chris."

"Hmm?"

"We both know we like each other."

"Go on. That's the most honest thing you've said so far."

"But we can't go on. We've got to stop here. In two and a half months, on September 29th, to be exact, I'll be going back home. To my family, to Alex – to my life. I will probably never see you after that."

"Are you really leaving on September 29th?"

"Are you trying to confuse me again?"

"No." He shook his head and a sad smile touched his lips. "You're leaving on my birthday... And your birthday is July 31st – that's my mom's birthday. Talk about strange synchronicity..."

"Is September 29th really your birthday?"

Chris took his wallet, pulled out his driver's license and presented it to me with a sigh. I looked at it and my heart once again performed a dangerous summersault.

"In any case... We have to stop. You've got to go."

"Elena... I've been in a lot of relationships before, at least three of them were quite serious. But I've never had such chemistry with anyone." Chris got closer to me. "When we kiss... it just makes me delirious, makes me dizzy. I can't be the only one. You must be feeling the same."

"I do." I nodded. "But it's all irrelevant."

"Irrelevant?" Chris suddenly pulled away.

"Yes. I'll be leaving and you'll find somebody else."

"I don't think so."

"Well, at least you'll have your threesomes to come back to."

"That's a different thing." Chris smiled faintly. "Don't be like that. You know it's a different thing."

"I'm just trying to cheer you up." I smiled back at him and touched his cheek again. "I've got to go to bed. I'll need to be getting up in like... three hours. And you've got to go home."

"Can we at least sleep together? Just sleep – no sex, I promise – here on the couch?"

"No. Bye, Chris!"

"Bye." Chris got up with a sigh and opened the door. "I'll see you later, Elena the Paina."

***

I was positioned by one of the tea stations at the Beach Club Dining Room: the tray in my hands, the five-star smile on my face, the posture alert and proper. To the guests dining at the Beach Club that afternoon I must have presented a picture-perfect sample of the high-quality service. In reality, I was staring beyond the wide window at the endless and calm ocean. The sight of water had always managed to strangely calm me down. Not this time, though. I was utterly and completely lost. My thoughts kept persistently coming back to Chris. Chris kissing me on the couch, Chris kissing me at the party, Chris kissing me in the pool. What surprised me the most was the combination of mental and physical sensations that flooded me from inside out every time I thought about us. I wondered if it actually would be better if I did have sex with him and got over it. Maybe I wanted him so badly because I couldn't have him? And then I could happily come back to Russia – just like so many of my girlfriends had done – and be totally content with Alex. Hmm... no, I didn't think it was the right decision. I was too honest. I wouldn't be able to live with myself. What a shame. I wished I was cruder.

"Elena!"

I turned my head and saw Diana standing right in front of me. Oops, she looked quite annoyed.

"What?"

"Is that your table over there?" She discreetly pointed in the direction of a two-top by the window – a very nice elderly couple from Atlanta.

"Yes. Why?"

"They've been waving at you for the last ten minutes!"

"No! Really?" *Damn it. They must be thinking I'm a blind idiot! For all that they know, I've been staring at them all along and didn't even acknowledge their presence!*

I rushed towards the table and put an apologetic smile on my face. "I'm so sorry!! Is there anything I can help you with?"

"That's okay!" The lady smiled. "You were probably daydreaming about someone really handsome, weren't you, honey?"

"Oh, yeah!" I laughed and wondered if my secret thoughts were indeed that obvious.

"Dear, may we order a bottle of Dom Pérignon?" asked the gentleman.

"Absolutely!" I proactively nodded and added, "Just a minute. I'll be right back."

"Take your time, honey!"

Could it possibly get any worse? I couldn't open a bottle of champagne. Or a bottle of wine for that matter. Well, if I was at a party and I needed to get to it – yes, I certainly could. I'd crack it open with my teeth if need be. But here I was supposed to be following all the rules of the service etiquette: hold a bottle in one hand, a wine key in another hand, and open the bottle without actually placing it on the table. I still couldn't believe people were capable of pulling it off. Never had I managed to conquer a single wine bottle without messing up a cork, or spilling some of the precious drink, or dropping the whole damn thing on the floor. I was definitely not going to open up a $400 bottle of Dom Pérignon! I looked around in panic. Vera! She was better at it than I was.

"Hey! Vera!"

"Elena, I've got a lot to do. What do you need?"

"Can you open a bottle of Dom Pérignon for my table?"

"What? Somebody ordered a Dom Pérignon? Oh, wow! You'll be getting a chunk of change from that table!"

"Oh, I don't care!" I whined. "I won't be able to open it without screwing it up! Can you help me?"

"Hmmm, no, I don't think so. I'm not that confident in my sommelier abilities – and that would be a very expensive mistake! What? Don't look at me like that!"

"Like what?"

"I don't know! Like a sheep about to be slaughtered! We should be able to think of something..." Vera brought her index finger against her top lip and thought for a while. "Ah! I know what you should do! Chris is working in the Ocean Room. He'll open it for you!"

"No, I don't want to ask Chris to do anything for me... Maybe I should tell Ms. Laura?"

"DON'T tell Ms. Laura anything!! We're about to take a test to work dinner shifts. If any of them finds out we're not capable of opening a bottle of champagne, we'll be stuck on breakfast and lunch shifts forever."

"But I..."

"Elena! Go get Chris!"

I'd always wanted to believe that if you let things take their natural course, you will eventually end up in the best possible scenario. Fatalistic or not, it had always seemed to be working out for me. I seriously started to doubt my theory during that summer in the USA. I was practically cheating on my fiancé, my hair was curly, and now I was about to reveal to everyone at the Beach Club that I couldn't open a bottle of champagne!

I couldn't have possibly walked to the Ocean Room more slowly. It seemed like a few years had passed until I finally reached the elegant-in-their-simplicity double doors of the most beautiful Beach Club room. I stood on my tiptoes and peeked through the clear glass window into the dining room. Chris was zooming back and forth, placing the plates and drinks on the enormous table of at least thirty people. His movements were swift, effortless, and immaculately coordinated. At that moment, he reminded me of a jaguar: he was aggressive, confident and radiant with positive energy. I had never imagined that the table serving process could possibly turn me on, but there it was. I was officially going insane. I bit the corner of my lower lip, quickly exhaled to get rid of ever growing excitement inside, and walked in. I was immediately dazzled by the brilliant sparkles of sunshine reflecting in the French doors. The Ocean Room didn't actually have walls; it had a number of French doors around its perimeter. The right side of the room offered a view of the pool filled with laughing kids and happily boozing adults, and the left side opened up into the ocean. White and green striped beach umbrellas that glinted above the peach-colored dunes made me secretly wish I was out there – soaking up the sun and sipping on a cocktail. I caught a glimpse of red hair as Chris swooshed by me in the direction of the servers' station. Had his smile just faded away or was it a game of my inflamed imagination? I hurried after him and pushed the heavy door inside.

"Chris! I need your help!"

"I'm busy, Elena."

That was the only thing I heard before he disappeared once again. I stood there for probably five seconds at most and here he was already back inside, placing the rest of the plates on the tray.

"Chris, please!" I begged. "Don't be like that! I really need your help. With a table," I whispered as I noticed Farrah standing by the Micros.

"Why are you whispering?" Chris gave me an inquisitive look.

"I don't want anybody else to know about it."

"About what?"

"Well, can you come with me?"

"Elena, you've been out there, right? Have you seen that crowd? Do you know that it's pretty much impossible to wait on the table of this size alone? I can't leave."

"Please!"

I must have looked horrified, because after a moment of silence, Chris eventually drew a heavy sigh and said:

"Okay, let's go. But just ONE minute."

"Thank you thank you thank you!" I grabbed him by the elbow and we rushed towards the main dining room. "I need you to open a bottle of Dom Pérignon for me."

"Oh, Elena!! Don't tell me you dragged me out of there just for that!"

"Please!"

"Aghh... Let's do it fast."

We got the precious bottle from the bar and hurried over towards my table.

"Goodness, honey. Have you gone all the way to France to get it?" exclaimed the lady. "Hey there, Chris! Good to see you again. Do you not trust Elena with champagne?"

"Ha ha!" I laughed nervously and quickly tried to come up with an explanation of why I wasn't opening the bottle myself.

"Mr. and Mrs. Wilson, good afternoon! You know those Russians, so greedy for liquor."

Everybody laughed, including me. I was perfectly fine with being portrayed as an alcoholic – as long as there were no other questions to follow.

"But really." Mr. Wilson tilted his head. "Why Chris?"

"That's a very good question," I thought. Why Chris? Take this, for example. I was supposed to be nervous and upset about the whole situation, but instead my entire being was singing in his presence. I entered the state of utterly happy stupidity, just because he was standing by my side. I could feel the warmth of his elbow slightly touching my waist, and I swear to you, my darling reader, I felt as if I could stand there like that all my life long and be absolutely, one hundred percent, HAPPY.

"Elena asked me to help her, because she can't open a champagne bottle."

He didn't just say that. I gave Chris a mortified glare from under my eyelashes and wondered what I was going to do next.

"Oh no!" laughed Mrs. Wilson. "Come on, Elena. Just do it! You'll be fine."

"No, no!" I shook my head and savored a thought of strangling Chris in the middle of the dining room.

"Yes, Elena. Do it!" insisted Mr. Wilson.

I looked at Chris holding the exquisite bottle in his outstretched hand and considered it for a second.

"No, I don't think so." I shook my head and smiled meekly.

"Oh, Elena!" Mrs. Wilson gave me a look or reproach and gently patted my arm. "In life, you sometimes have to just do it. Otherwise, you can miss out on a lot of sweet things."

***

I energetically waved to Ozer from my bus seat and silently articulated: "See you later, motherfucka" with my lips. We both started laughing – how strange it was that we were relating on such a wacked subject as verbal offence – and I thought that I had actually just now lied to both of us. I wasn't sure we would see each other. In fact, I was quite positive we were never going to meet again. How would I explain it to Alex? "I've made A LOT of friends in Germany. By the way, this gorgeous dude from Turkey is coming over to stay with me next week". Hmm... No. I didn't see it happening. But why did I feel this weird excitement in every particle of my body? Each molecule was singing and there was no explanation. The bus started slowly moving and Ozer's face began to fade away. The inner excitement gave way, and the molecule song morphed into an eerie hoot resonating in my ears. I had to catch it. It was disappearing and I would never be able to grasp it again. The humming was so loud now that I was afraid I'd go deaf. I had to do something to stop it. I knew what I had to do.

"Stop the bus! Can't you hear me, driver? Stop the bus! I'm not going back to Russia."

"But you can't, Elena!" The driver looked at me and clicked his tongue in reproach. "Your mom is waiting for you in Moscow."

"Oh, that's right... Mom. Hold on... How do you know about it? How do you even know my name?"

I got on my tiptoes and looked into the window. Ozer was gone. As was Germany. We were already in Russia. How come? I thought it would take us at least two days to drive to Moscow. Baffled, I stared back at the driver. To my utter astonishment, Alex was now driving the bus.

"Alex? I didn't know you were going to drive me back home!"

"I saw you trying to get off the bus." He looked over his shoulder and shrugged, "Excitement eventually goes away, but commitment will stay forever."

"Forever? But what about the sweetness?"

"Sweets are bad for you."

"Ha. That makes sense."

"You don't want to be alone, Elena, do you? You might get cold."

"I AM cold! Why am I so cold?! What the..."

"Ha ha ha! Elena! You've got to get out of the sun. You're having some weird-ass dreams!" Sonia was looming above and splashing cold water all over me.

"Don't say words like "*weird-ass*", Sonia! It's very rude."

I sat up and looked around. I had totally forgotten we were on the beach. The sun was annoyingly bright and burning hot. I had to shut my eyes for a second.

"Oh, come on, Liz! It's just a word."

"No, Sonia! In this country, we don't swear in public."

That's right. I'm remembering now. Liz took us to the beach.
Liz was Monika's roommate. Her parents were some kind of big
wigs from Washington, D.C., and Chris had always called her
Mother Superior. And that always pissed Liz off, because she
was always trying extremely hard to act cool.

"Well, then you probably will have to re-think your plans
about visiting us in Russia next summer," said Sonia.

"Why is that?"

"Because in our country, everybody swears!"

"That's not true." I croaked and lit up a cigarette. "My mom
doesn't swear."

"I wonder who you took after then." Sonia chuckled. "Liz! If
you want to hear a person curse, come on over to our place at
five in the morning and watch Elena get ready for work."

"Whatever." I smiled and shook my hair.

It was so nice to feel the hot breeze on my skin. I inhaled the
salty ocean air and was about to say something funny to Sonia,
when I suddenly saw him. Chris was walking towards us, the
wind playing with his red hair, with nothing on but his
swimming shorts. Naturally. We were on the beach, after all. He
looked so handsome and happy that I couldn't help but smile
back. Plus – imagine that: hot sun, fresh air, summery wind, and
a man you have hots for is walking towards you. Wouldn't you
smile? But hold on... Fairy tales don't typically cover tall,
slender, curly-haired blonds in bikinis jumping on your prince
and wrapping her legs around his waist!

"Who is that?" muttered Sonia.

"Pff... Perhaps one of the million chicks Chris banged,"
snorted Liz.

"Elena. Have another cigarette." Sonia thoughtfully passed me the pack.

"Thanks," I mumbled and quickly glanced at Chris from under my eyelashes.

"Hello, my ladies!" Chris finally reached us. Without the damn bombshell, thank God. She apparently detached herself on the way. "How is it going?"

"Chris, how many women on St. Simons have you had sexual relationships with?" said Liz and gave him a contemptuous smile.

"This month?" The corner of his mouth twitched and I quickly tried to imagine something horrific that would prevent me from laughing.

"Oh, you are such a pervert!"

"Whatever you say, Mother Superior, whatever you say. So!" He sat next to me on the towel. "Are we going to St. Augustine on Wednesday?"

"Yes!" exclaimed Sonia. "We all got the days off! Chris, will you take us to Jacksonville Mall, too?"

"But of course! Elena, why are you so grim? What's wrong?" Chris slightly nudged me on the shoulder.

"Nothing. Just craving something sweet."

"Don't we all? I have a lot of sweets at my house." His smile was boyish and dashing.

"Oh, I'm sure you do. But I think I'll pass."

"Is it a Mother Superior convention I'm attending?"

"Yep." I nodded. "You are free to leave whenever you like, though. Just don't get attacked by hopping chimpanzees roaming through the beach."

"Ouch, that WAS bitter," laughed Chris. "Just make up your mind." He got really close to my face and whispered, "What is it that you really want?"

I picked up another cigarette from the box and turned away from him to face the ocean.

"I'll see you on Wednesday then. At McDonald's at 8:00 am. Sharp!" said Chris and walked off.

"St. Augustine, here we come!" yelled Sonia. "Cheer up, Elena – everything   is   going   to   be   SWEET!"

CHAPTER ELEVEN

Fountain of Youth

"So, it occurred to me this morning when I was washing my face, that one day I'll be old."

"What a genius realization!" snorted Milo.

"No. I mean, really. I imagined that my face – this face – will one day be covered in wrinkles. And I'll have age spots on these hands, and my abs and ass and boobs will droop and drag on the ground."

"Yikes! I'm not sure I like this conversation," Milo winced.

"You don't have boobs," mumbled nasty Paul.

"These days, you can load your picture up into a software program on the net and see what you'll look like in fifty years," drawled Thomas. Paul's quiet and geeky Slovak roommate. Thomas was one of those people whose presence you could easily fail to notice for hours to come – and then later on find out he was a genius who finally found the panacea for cancer. Or a vicious man-eating serial killer.

"That would be horrible!' exclaimed Monika and shook her head in disapproval.

"Hmm... I'm not sure I'd have guts to do that either," I reflectively rolled my eyes and took a bite of an Egg McMuffin.

We were enjoying our McDonald's breakfast at one of the outdoor tables next to the kiddy playground. Everybody showed up on time, but then Vera realized that she'd left her yogurts back at the apartment, at which point both she and Sonia decided to return to the Island Retreat and retrieve the beloved milk produce from the fridge. When Sonia and Vera were missing for the first twenty minutes, Diana announced that she was having a Moscow déjà vu and the girls "were about to miss this train as well" and set off in search of our lost friends. When all three of them didn't show up forty minutes after, Chris demonstrated that he was also capable of turning to the dark side of the moon, jumped in the car, and drove to the Island Retreat, infuriated.

So here we were – Milo, Monika, Paul, myself, and Hooper. Hooper's real name was Christine, and I had definitely never met a human being fuller of themselves than her. She was lucky to have a very attractive figure that made most guys turn their heads and subsequently walk into unfortunate objects, but her face kept persistently reminding me of a tanned hound dog. She was not at all familiar with the filtering process that defines, which thoughts leave our minds and which get to safely hide in the deep crevices of the brain. She simply said whatever she thought. Hooper also always did whatever she desired. Even now she was perched up on the table bench outside McDonalds, one of her feet positioned on top of the bench, and was applying polish on her toenails.

"Ugh, Hooper! Never mind that we're eating," drawled Milo and gave her a sideways glance.

"I don't want to think about getting old. Old people make me sick." Hooper completely ignored Milo's remark and went on. "Come to think of it, I'd rather die young than ever see myself all wrinkly. Eww, disgusting."

Youth and vanity go hand in hand. We all suffer from it. You remember who you wanted to become when you were a kid? An astronaut, an actress, a world famous scientist, an Olympic champion? What do these professions have in common? That is right – young people want to conquer the world. Even now, when I am writing, I am, relatively speaking, still very young. I imagine that one day, my memoir will see the world, and people will woo me, and my creation will be translated into hundreds of languages. And I will be invited to the Letterman show. And I can dye my hair blue. And Hollywood studios will be fighting for the rights to make a movie based on my novel. And my book will have one of those stickers that say, "Now a Major Motion Picture." And I'll win the Oscar for the best written book and will walk down the red carpet (hold on – do they actually give Oscars to book writers? – never mind, in my imagination, they do). And mom and dad will be so proud of me. Hmm... we always tend to come back to that one – or is it just me? Somehow, I was quite positive that people like Hooper didn't need anybody's approval. They were so sure they were the oracles of the truth, they wouldn't believe otherwise even if all gods descended Mount Olympus to teach them a lesson. No, I couldn't imagine

Hooper as an elderly person. Young vain people make sense; old vain people are quite a paradoxical picture indeed.

"And why are we going to St. Augustine again? I mean, the mall there is all right. Shit! My nail is ruined! What was I saying? Anyhow, Jacksonville malls are much better."

"I think Chris was planning on going to the historic district first," said Monika, somewhat apologetically.

Monika really liked hanging out with Hooper. They always went shopping together, and watched silly girly movies together, and discussed... I'm actually not sure what exactly they talked about. We all knew that we'd asked Hooper to come with us, because we needed a second car. Obviously, Hooper was not aware of our reasons.

"What? I'm not going to waste my time on those worthless ruins! I'll tell you what – let's go shopping and let them do their dorky thing."

I coughed a little bit in a useless attempt to let Hooper know that "them" was actually present and sitting at the same table with her.

"Elena, you really need to quit smoking. You are coughing all the time. My grandfather and great-grandfather died of lung cancer. You don't want that, do you?" Hooper said.

At that particular moment, I would have rather gone for the lung cancer alternative as opposed to spending the rest of the day in Hooper's company, but instead, I stuck to a cowardly decision to nod and remain silent. That's what I tend to do in my life. When somebody hurts me or abuses me in any way, I will practice hot philosophical debates in front of the mirror for hours – and I will inevitably win the argument with my offender retreating shamefully and fervently asking me for forgiveness.

But when it comes to actually facing the music, I'd always choose the non-confrontational strategy and eventually cave in. Except for when I'm PMSing, but that doesn't really count, does it? In my teens, I attempted to act more aggressive and ruthless, following the role model of the cool chicks on the block, but in my early twenties, I realized that the only person I was kidding was myself. I've always been as soft and sweet as cotton candy – what can you do about it? So, coming back to the story, I just nodded to Hooper and took another drag of the cigarette. Hooper gave me the look that clearly stated how childish and pathetic my behavior was in her humble opinion and turned away – apparently to take her precious attention elsewhere, away from my bleak persona. I followed her gaze, and my jaw dropped and painfully hit my knees. The girls were drenched and seemed to be covered in white foam. What in the world?

***

Another inevitable companion of youth is judgment. I used to be extremely judgmental until one day I read a very smart self-help book (yes, I've read those, too). The book stated that any judgment that we cast on people around us, even silently, is a projection on our own personality. So in actuality, when judging others, you are judging yourself. What a genius simplicity! What an eye-opener! This No Judgment Strategy helped me get rid of the most in-built insecurities that had been torturing me forever. But this would happen later. Now we are in 2004, and I am strict and unforgiving to myself and everybody around me. I looked behind at the girls seated in the back of the car and burst out into annoying giggles for the tenth time in the last minute.

"Would you just shut it, Elena?" Sonia hissed at me and turned away to face the road.

We were on the I-95 heading south towards St. Augustine, Florida. All four of us were trying to sneak the peek at the scenery behind the window, but all we could see was a boring road. A few beautiful palm trees here and there, but other than that, just the road.

"Chris!" I turned to my left and playfully touched his shoulder.

"Yes, mom!"

Ever since the Okefenokee trip this had been our inside joke. Chris and I were dad and mom and the girls were the kids – simply because I was always riding up front, and the girls were in the back.

"How come we're not passing any picturesque villages or little quirky towns or something? This road is pretty boring."

"Well, it's the I-95, the highway. We could have taken a more scenic route, if Sonia hadn't flooded the apartment." Chris couldn't help himself and chuckled. "But since we've lost quite some time on wiping the foam off your couch and stove, we've got to take the shortest route now."

"Chris!" exclaimed Sonia. "Stop it! I didn't know. We don't have dishwashers in Russia."

I looked back at Vera and Diana and saw that they were barely hanging on. Laughter was trying to escape through their eyes, chins, and body language. Poor things – at least I could turn away from Sonia and laugh my ass off here without deeply offending her.

Okay, let's start from the beginning. It is actually true that most Russian households don't have dishwashers. And when I say "most households," I mean that I had never been to a Russian house that had one. I am still quite baffled by the mystery as to why this is so. Contrary to the common belief in the West, Russia is not stuck in the Stone Age. I can already see some people smirking as they are reading this. Yeah, right! We saw it on TV – how you were lining up for food stamps in the Soviet Union. And that is correct. We were, in the late eighties-early nineties. If you visit Russia now, you would probably be blown away by the technological progress – in some areas of life even more so than in the States. But the dishwasher – no. Don't have them. With you, my darling reader, as a witness, I solemnly swear to look into this mystery, which has been bugging me for a while, and find the elusive answer. Anyhow, since we had never seen a dishwasher, we didn't have any idea what it looked like. We lived in our apartment for more than a month until one day Chris asked us why we were washing the dishes by hand. When he pointed out that we had a dishwasher, we just stared at it like four little chimpanzees getting familiar with a new toy – with curiosity and complete incomprehension.

"And we always thought it was just a cabinet for stacking plates," mumbled Vera.

"Yes! I thought so as well!" I exclaimed.

"Is there any hidden purpose also for this drain that always seems to stink?" asked Diana.

Chris's facial expression could have been described as a combination of cautiousness and comic despair. He came up to the sink and flipped one of the light switches up. The loud grinding noise, akin to the ones you might hear in that part of a horror movie when everybody gets demolished by a chainsaw, made all of us jump up.

"It's a garbage disposer," said Chris slowly. "It disposes of garbage. Are you seriously trying to tell me you've had food chunks in here for the last month?"

"I've been wondering about the stink," said Sonia. "I thought one of the girls was silently giving out very evil farts."

As you can see, we had a very short introduction to the modern American household appliances. This could possibly explain why Sonia, prior to our departure from the apartment earlier this morning, loaded the dishwasher with the regular detergent. The one that you would use to wash your clothes with. Have you ever tried to do that? Well, don't.

When Chris drove to the Island Retreat to chew the girls out for being so late, he found all three of them completely covered in bubbly foam that seemed to be coming out of the dishwasher. The dishwasher actually looked like one of those kiddy bubble machines that kept perpetually generating the glittery foam. According to Chris, the apartment resembled the streets of Montreal in January: snow-white foam piles were covering the stove, the couch, and most of the floor, and the whole scene was somewhat reminiscent of a bad porn flick – three girls covered in foam and jumping around all over the place in an attempt to shake it off. The worst thing was that even though the dishwasher was off, the foam kept stubbornly coming out of it. Chris said that he could not remember laughing that much in his entire life. Oh, I so wished I could have seen it with my own two eyes.

"Look, sistas! Jacksonville skyline! Look at those office buildings! One day I'll work here." Sonia seemed to have completely forgotten about the dishwasher incident and was happily glued to the car window.

"Yeah! Wouldn't that be cool?" said Vera dreamily.

Skyscrapers no doubt symbolize America for everybody in the world. Skylines of American cities are synonymous to the new world, the new dream and the new achievement. They represent a young nation that is literally attempting to reach the skies and is actually succeeding in doing so. Youth, so amazing and so beautiful in its naivety and its stubborn strive for idealism, is actually capable of achieving goals that are deemed utopian by skeptics. If young people didn't dream and didn't dare to fly, where would we be right now?

"Yes, you will work there!" added Diana. "Just don't do their dishes."

That was too much. All of us, including Sonia, couldn't stop the laughter invasion. Sparkles of laughter flooded Chris's Ford Explorer just like the dishwasher foam earlier this morning flooded our apartment.

Yes, we are very judgmental when we are young. A similar dishwasher situation – but worse – would happen to me exactly a year and a half after that St. Augustine day trip and I would look back and think: "And you laughed at Sonia because of the dishwasher!" Call it karma or perhaps just a natural order of things in the universe, but what goes around comes around. I would yet have to learn that.

***

St. Augustine is originally a Spanish town founded in 1565 on the site of a Timucuan Indian village, and it is considered the oldest continuously-occupied European settlement in the continental United States. Apart from the fact that the town gives you an impression that you have been drugged up, transported across the ocean in the state of a deep comatose sleep, and blissfully thrown out into the very heart of Spain, St. Augustine is associated with a few quite tantalizing myths. My favorite one is about the Fountain of Youth. Legend has it that Spanish explorer Ponce de Leon set off to Florida in quest of the mythical land of Bimini, the land of wealth, prosperity, and the fountain of youth. The legend also claims that Ponce de Leon was looking for the fountain to cure his impotence. Whether Mr. de Leon managed to drink the elixir of life and regain his manhood powers or whether he simply liked Florida so much that he figured he might just as well settle down here for the time being (and who would blame him for that?), the Fountain of Youth Archeological Park stays one of the main St. Augustine attractions up to this moment.

The idea of eternal youth has always excited me. Mortality is our main weakness. Plus, who wouldn't want to stay forever young? Sensible people say that we have to follow the natural circle of life – be born, grow old, die. That does make perfect sense simply due to the fact that we don't have a more attractive alternative we could go for. But what if we did? Imagine just for one second, that you could always feel that wet electric excitement in the tips of your fingers! Imagine that you could make amazingly brave and magnificent-in-their-grandeur plans for the future forever! Imagine that ability to completely isolate yourself from the whole world and build your existence, your life based on how you, and only you, feel about the universe. I want it! Yes, the older I get, the more I realize that I don't want to grow up. Herein I declare – and please, if I ever break my promise, please shove my face into this very page of this book and remind me of this declaration – that Elena will never, ever grow up.

"What. Are we doing here again?"

This was not a case of incorrect punctuation. This was how Hooper really said it. With a pause and a full stop after the question word.

"Enjoying the view of the Castillo de San Marcos. It is the oldest fort in the United States, Hooper. Are you ever interested in anything else but yourself?" laughed Chris.

"The past and its ruins don't present any interest to me whatsoever." Hooper shrugged. "Fuck! My nail is ruined again. Elena, do you know where my nail polish is?"

Chris and I exchanged understanding glances over Hooper's shoulder, and I had to quickly turn away to hide my amusement. I stretched my legs along the edge of the stone balustrade I was sitting on and lit a cigarette. I closed my eyes and felt warm orange sun spots kissing my eyelids. I smiled, and when I reopened my eyes, the magnificent Castillo de San Marcos set against the blue glamour of the Matanzas River jumped out at me as if superimposed against the backdrop of dull reality. I stared at the old wise walls and wondered what exactly they had witnessed. I closed my eyes again and tried to interpret the tales of foregone passions that the hot summer wind was whispering in my ears. Everything as we know it, even ourselves, eventually goes away, disappears into the abyss of peaceful eternity; people we once knew wave us their bittersweet farewell, and new people are born into this world – brave and daring – but these amazing stones – or in this case, coquina shell walls – will always remain the silent spectators of our dreams, fears, and desires. Even now, the imposing walls of the fort were probably thinking, "Jesus! Another one with problems in her love life! How exquisitely boring!"

"The fort is haunted, you know?" said Chris as if in response to my inner monologue.

He sat down right next to me on the balustrade, his side slightly touching the side of my leg.

"Legend has it that long, long time ago one of the colonels of the Fort, Colonel Garcia, found out that his wife Dolores and Captain Abella were enjoying a passionate quickie on the side. He didn't particularly like it – obviously. So he killed them."

"How did he kill them?" asked Hooper.

"Nobody knows. He actually said that Dolores got back home to Mexico, and Captain Abella was sent back to Spain. But years later, unidentified bones and ashes were found in the hidden room in the dungeon. People say that when they toured that room they could feel sudden cold spots and could smell the sweet perfume that poor Dolores used to wear."

"Well, how do they know they were their ashes? Did they run any tests on them or something?" asked Hooper nervously.

"Hooper! Have you tried to audition for CSI Miami? You'd be brilliant!"

"Whatever, asshole. Listen, don't even think about touring the damn fort. I'm not going there!"

"Shit! I thought we'd get lucky and you'd be taken by the ghosts during the tour."

This time, I couldn't help laughing. Chris turned to face me, his red hair glittering in the sun.

"Would you like to tour the fort, madam?"

"But of course! I love ruins."

"Elena, what's all this flirting about? Don't you have a fiancé or something?" Hooper rolled her eyes in irritation and flipped her cell phone open. "Hunter? Where were you this morning? I called you like ten times!"

"The only things that Hunter will be able to hunt if he marries this girl will be his lost dreams," mumbled Chris under his breath. "One morning, he'll wake up and think to himself, 'How the fuck did I get here?' "

"Wouldn't that be awful?" I frowned.

"You won't let that happen to you, will you, Elena?"

I knew that he knew me. I didn't have to explain. We didn't have to talk. Psychological intimacy is much harder to fight than physical one. You can't just shake it off. Plus, you are never quite sure if anything ever happened.

"Guys!" Vera ran toward us, happily skipping from one foot onto another. "We took so many COOL pictures of the fort."

"Wow, I got some awesome pics!" Milo was glued to the little screen of his camera.

"And I didn't take a single one! I'm so bad at taking pictures." I took my camera out and focused it on the Castillo.

"Russian! Do you not have digital cameras in your great motherland?"

"Whatever..." I blushed. "I don't have a camera at all. Alex lent me this one. I'll buy a new one after the summer is over. When I earn enough money. And what do you have against my country?"

"He he, nothing, nothing... Easy, Russian, don't get all defensive. I'm just joking."

"Maybe the fact that you brought your tanks to Prague in 1968?" I swear I could hear Thomas grind his teeth.

"I didn't bring anything anywhere in 1968 – I wasn't born yet!"

"Okay then! Who's for going inside of the fort?" Chris quickly jumped up from the balustrade and smiled at all of us.

"Good one, Chris," I thought to myself, " *You should consider working for the Peace Corps."*

"I'm not touring the fucking fort. I already told you!" hissed Hooper.

"Chriiiis!" yelled Sonia. "Please, let's go shopping. Let's not go to the fort!"

"Chris," Monika added softly, "maybe we should check out those pretty stores down the street and have some ice cream?"

"NO! I've planned this trip and we ARE going inside! What's wrong with you, people?"

***

"So... the fort was already closed. It's a shame." I gave Chris a careful look from under my eyelashes.

"Why would they close that early?" Chris was still pouting. "If not for that bloody dishwasher accident!"

"It's okay, Chris. There's plenty to see here. Just look around."

We were walking down quaint St. Augustine streets dotted with charming little shops, cafes, and old-world street lamps. Even street signs, curvy and romantic in their curviness, made me believe for one happy moment that I was Catherine Zeta-Jones from the Zorro movie. Everybody else was walking behind us, in twos and threes, chatting away and gawking around. Through the soft hum of the street noise and a pleasant serenade of the wind, you couldn't help but hear Hooper whining and perpetually asking when we were going to drive to the mall. I think miserable people should be sent off to The Miserable Fuckersland. Over there, they can complain to each other, poison their lives with unnecessary drama, gossip, and ignorance, and quite possibly, be one-hundred percent happy. Because that's what makes them happy. On the other hand, another half of humanity (I honestly want to believe that another half is actually much larger than a half – perhaps three quarters?) could also enjoy the precious moments we get to spend on the planet Earth without gnawing frustration of having to deal with the miserable fuckers. I mean, it doesn't have to be Siberia or anything. Maybe an atoll in the middle of the Pacific?

"Oh look, guys! What's that?" Diana paused and brought our attention to the building across the street.

Actually, I was quite surprised we hadn't already noticed it. It looked like a miniature castle from a fairy tale, but – how can I describe it? There was something sinister about it. I couldn't put my finger on it; the building was beautiful, with curiously shaped window frames, tastefully ornamented arches and medieval-infused balustrades, but under the picture-perfect skin of innocuousness there was something else lurking in the hallways of what used to be known as Castle Warden.

"That's Ripley's Believe It or Not!" exclaimed Chris. "It totally slipped my mind. Let's go there, shall we?"

"What is it?" asked Monika, apprehensive glitter in her eyes.

"It's a stupid fucking museum of stupid fucking things!" exploded Hooper.

"Interpreted from Hooper's language of self-misery, it means that this is a museum of extraordinary things from all over the world," laughed Chris.

"I've heard about it!" said Milo. "That's the one that has shrunken human heads! Let's go!"

"Yep." I nodded. "The building definitely has the vibe of one that has human heads in there. Well, that sounds interesting. I'm up for it!"

I looked at Vera, Sonia and Diana and realized that they were on the fence. They were torn between morbid curiosity and love for shopping. And that's a tough one.

"I heard the gift shop there is amazing," mumbled Chris.

You've got to love him. Don't you?

"I think we'll go to the museum," said Vera. "What do you think, girls?"

"Sounds like a good idea! Let's go!" Sonia was already crossing the street.

"Okay, guys! Hooper and I will check out the shops. Will see you here in like... an hour?" asked Monika, a bit apologetically.

"Are you sure you don't want to go?" smiled Chris. "Perhaps we can talk to the staff members about exhibiting Hooper as one of their artifacts? The most superficial and ignorant creature of the 21st century?"

With the corner of my eye, I caught the sight of Hooper furiously flipping Chris off. But we didn't care. We were already on our way into the wackily amazing world of Robert Ripley.

***

I was stuck on the bridge of the swirling tunnel and I couldn't move. Multicolored waves of weirdness created an impression of falling, and it was apparently driving me insane.

"Come on, Russian! Just go!" laughed Milo. "You're so sissy."

However hard I tried, I just couldn't unzip myself from the side of the bridge. My fingers turned pale-white from clasping onto the railing, and I just couldn't let go. I looked up and realized that I was in my dream. I was falling upwards. It was actually happening. I gulped for air, and my head started spinning in an unnaturally zigzag-shaped pattern.

"Elena! Remember – it's just an illusion. You can step out of there. Just let go."

My eyes mercifully became capable of focusing on Chris's outstretched hand. I grabbed it and stepped out of the psychedelic rainbow madness. When I looked around, I realized that everybody was already gone. Milo, Thomas, and Paul had moved on to the next exhibit, and the girls were nowhere to be seen. We were surrounded by warm and plush darkness – Chris and I – in that corner of the museum where nobody goes, because they are in a hurry to move on and see what's there next to be seen.

"While you were stuck in limbo, I was reading about Robert Ripley's life," whispered Chris.

"Oh really? And what did you find out?" I whispered back.

"He was a notorious ladies' man. There are rumors that sometimes, he had up to five live-in girlfriends in the same house."

"Sounds horribly familiar."

"He was a world traveler."

"Can't blame him for that one."

"He's known to have said, 'I have traveled in 201 countries and the strangest thing I saw was man.' " Chris got breathtakingly close to me.

I exhaled and dissolved into weirdness. The desire for the man standing next to me was so overpowering, that my brain didn't even register the moment when I decided to respond to Chris's kiss. I just did it. The warm darkness that surrounded us filled every cell of poor little Elena, and I got feeble and meek in Chris's arms. He could have made play-dough shapes out of me if he wanted to. I didn't even know who I was. I could have been that six-legged cow exhibited in the previous room for all that I knew. The Elena that I had always known disappeared for a moment in the dark halls of Castle Warden. And even though it was the wackiest occurrence in my entire life, it felt almost normal. When the boundaries between normality and weirdness vanish, you know that something has changed forever.

"We've got to stop right now," whispered Chris. "No PDE in Ripley's Museum."

"What's PDE?"

"Public Display of Erection."

"You're such a dumbass!–" I laughed and nervously pulled the edge of my pink skirt.

"Come on. I wanted you to see something."

He took my hand and we walked out into the main exhibition room with a gigantic wheel as its centerpiece. People – young couples, groups of students, families with kids – were all over the museum. I felt the hot flash of shame color my face as I remembered what I'd been doing just a few moments ago around that very corner.

"Check this out!" Chris pushed heavy, burgundy draperies aside and pulled me into a tiny little cabin.

"I'm claustrophobic!" I panicked.

"Oh, come on, Elena the Paina! Are there any phobias that don't possess your sexy Russian body?"

"Hmm..." I thought about it for a while. "I'm not afraid of heights!" I exclaimed with almost hysterical excitement. *Finally, there was something that I wasn't scared of.*

"I don't see how that can be true. You're afraid of falling in your dream."

"Yes, I am," I was puzzled. "But in reality I'm not afraid of heights. I love roller coasters!"

"You do?" Chris seemed doubtful. "I absolutely hate them!"

"See? We're not compatible!" I smiled and bit the corner of my lip. "So... what are we doing in this tuna can anyway?"

"I thought we might take a picture. Look – the machine takes a photo, and then processes it to look as if it was created by famous artists. There is Renoir and Van Gough, Rembrandt and Leonardo."

"Let's do it!"

"Okay! Ready? One, two, three – cheese!"

"Cool! Which artist should we go for?"

"Let's do Leonardo? "

"Why Leonardo?"

"I don't know. Just feels right," Chris shrugged and winked at me in a way that made me wish we were on an uninhabited island instead of a museum. Naked and free from all inhibitions. "Ok, let's see. What do we have here?"

***

"It looks like you guys are a famous Hollywood couple on their honeymoon or something! Wow! I love it!" said Vera.

We were lazily lounging in the rocking chairs on the porch of the museum. I was enjoying my late afternoon cigarette, and Vera wouldn't quit rambling on about the picture. I just wished everybody else would hurry back from the gift shop so that we could move on from the topic. But no. Even Chris was stuck in there buying God knows what.

Okay, so the Leonardo picture didn't turn out to be exactly what I thought it would be. In fact, I didn't expect it to be anything. It was just a photo! My eyes apprehensively traveled to the picture in Vera's hands and I exhaled with frustration. Ha. Definitely couldn't show it to Alex. I wasn't quite sure where it had gone wrong, but when I was looking at this photo touched up to look like a Leonardo drawing, I saw a couple in love. I saw a couple so deeply connected, I was blinded by the sparks flying through the paper into the world of actual reality and painfully hitting me on the forehead. The strangest thing was that we were not even touching each other. I was looking a little bit sideways, my face unusually sad and nostalgic (I had never seen myself nostalgic – ever). Chris was leaning towards me slightly, and his eyes were directed straight at the camera. That was it.

"We DON'T look like a couple," I insisted and stubbornly lifted my chin up in the air, like a little pouting kid.

"You're delusional..." sang Vera in a very annoying musical show voice. "Just in case you decide to be in denial forever, at least now you'll have a proof of the fact that you're fucking wrong! Just look at it – this picture is a masterpiece. You've got to frame it."

"Oh, okay then! I'll frame it and put it on the wall above Alex's bed. He will love it!" I retorted. "You know? I'll probably just throw it out." I stretched my arm out and took the actual proof of my virtual infidelity from Vera.

"Don't you dare!" Vera snatched the picture back from me. "I'm sure Chris would love to keep it."

"I'd love to keep what?" mumbled Chris, his mouth full of jelly beans (judging by a half-empty jelly bean bag in his hands) as he emerged from the museum, followed by the rest of our international crew.

"Nothing..." I mumbled back. "Are we going to get on the trolley or what? We've been waiting for you guys forever!"

"Easy, psycho!" laughed Chris and stuffed his mouth with another portion of what looked like fifty multicolored jelly beans.

"Whatever!" I snapped. "It's just that we've paid for the tickets and I'd hate to lose twenty bucks, that's all!"

"Oh, wow! I didn't realize you were so greedy, Paina," announced Chris. He then got a bit closer to me and nonchalantly whispered in my ear, "Greedy girls are the best in bed."

"Guys!" exclaimed Sonia. "Look, the trolley is here. Let's run."

Still torn somewhere between strangling Chris with my bare hands and grabbing his hand and taking him to the nearest motel room, I ran to the trolley. I ran as if I was running for my life, trying to get rid of all that physical and psychological tension, attempting to leave all this heavy, stuffy pressure in Castle Warden.

I probably wouldn't have survived if I was really running for my life, since I was the last one to hop on the trolley. I quickly scanned the seating situation and realized that there was an empty seat next to Chris, and there was one vacant bench across from him. I lowered my eyes and landed my exhausted sweaty self on the empty bench. I heavily exhaled, licked my lips and was just about to relax and soak in the view of the elegant St. Augustine streets, when it suddenly occurred to me that I was feeling uneasy. I turned into the direction of the source of this inconvenient uneasiness that happened to be seated opposite from me, and raised my eyebrows in question, "What?"

"That's just not going to work, Elena!"

"What?" I repeated, subconsciously realizing that I knew the answer.

Chris quickly got up from his seat and plunged down next to me.

"I'm taking you all the way to romantic St. Augustine and you deliberately avoid sitting next to me?"

"I didn't realize you'd be affected by this that much." I blinked a few times like a stupid cow from a cartoon and stared down at my bright-pink toenails.

"Oh, yeah? Well, it's our trip and it's my time. And we WILL sit together."

Chris's behavior might seem just a touch wacko to you, my darling reader, but I couldn't help but smile inside. My inner smile was the one of pure superficial female satisfaction. *Ha. Got him.* I finally took my eyes off my wedge sandals – very beautiful, I might add, but still not deserving five minutes of undivided attention – and slowly said, "Okay then."

Chris discreetly took my hand in his, and we both turned our heads to the open window of the trolley. We passed the opulent Flagler College with its Rapunzel towers, the spectacular Lightner Museum with an open palm Spanish Renaissance courtyard. Tiny romantic streets with an old love story around every corner were flashing past us like a photo slideshow. I closed my eyes and imagined my whole life passing by me just like that – like a kaleidoscope of bright bitter-sweet memories. When you are old and about to kick it, wouldn't you want to sit in the rocking chair, have a glass of wine, and actually remember those pictures? How upsetting would that be to sit in that chair and realize that you don't really remember anything in particular? Just a dull boring road – like the I-95. Wouldn't it make sense to sometimes follow some off-roads? Maybe even get lost from time to time, but nevertheless have fun trying to find the way back? I looked at the Leonardo picture on my lap and suddenly realized that I would never be able to throw it out. I would probably take it to that rocking chair with me. When I'm old and wrinkly, I will look at myself, young, beautiful (sorry for the lack of modesty, but I did turn out all right there) and despite whatever I might be thinking now, so madly in love, and I will smile. I'll be a woman with a secret, like in the Titanic. I squeezed Chris's hand and turned to face him.

"Everybody keeps telling me: you are so young, your life is a clean slate, everything is ahead of you, you're so lucky. Don't people realize that this scares me? There are so many possibilities, I'm afraid I might go mad! It's so challenging to be young."

"You just have to do what you like. That's the only filter that you can use." Chris shrugged and squeezed my hand back.

I remember that feeling painfully well. As we grow older, we tend to know better what we want or which way we want to go. Or perhaps we simply don't have as many choices as we become limited by responsibilities: family, work, friends. I still sometimes feel at loss; should I buy a new laptop, an iPad, or and iPhone? As I'm stuck on the crossroads of the amazing technological advances, I feel like I'm back in my teens again. My head is spinning from future opportunities and I can't help but take a step back just to remember who the hell I am and why I needed a laptop/iPad/iPhone in the first place.

I think we don't give enough credit to young people. We grow old and naturally start looking down on the youth, teaching them, preaching at them, and totally forgetting that once we were in their shoes and knew some things that today fly past us, bleak and unnoticed. There must be a good reason for why humanity has always been in constant quest of eternal youth. My darling reader, don't underestimate young people. Learn from them, it will do you good.

"Look, guys!" exclaimed Vera. "The brochure says that if we get off at this stop, we can go wine tasting for free."

"Wow! That's cool. Let's do it!" said Sonia.

"We can't do wine tasting," I said. "We're underage here, remember?"

Plus, under the influence of wine, I might do something I would regret afterwards, I thought, but, of course, failed to voice my shameful reflections to the audience. I glanced sideways at Chris, who was still discreetly holding my hand in his, and recognized the familiar glitter in his eyes. Damn it. He had read my thoughts again.

***

Finally, Hooper quit nagging; we arrived in the Jacksonville Mall, and she and Monika blissfully disappeared in the monotonous jungle of jeans, T-shirts, and sneakers. I have always been able to relate more to the sistas' fashion than the one of the white girls in America. It just seems that African-American women are ready to improvise and dare to wear seemingly incompatible pieces together. And it works! And they always wear high heels! Even though I will always have the deepest respect to all American girls who have the guts to get out there, in 110-degree heat, squeezed into impossibly tight jeans. Even the sight of them makes me sweat all over! Fashion definitely requires sacrifice – in any country and perhaps on any planet. I already started to imagine alien female entities with elongated heads attempting to put straw hats a la mode despite their elf-like banana ears being persistently in the way of otherworldly fashion, when I stumbled onto the store that attracted my attention and snapped me back to planet Earth. We all had decided to split up, snoop around the mall on our own, and meet back up in an hour. I quickly glanced at my watch – I still had ten minutes to spare. I wish I hadn't! In that case, I wouldn't be stuck in the zombified mode in front of the changing room mirror performing scary budget calculations in my mind. I really wanted to buy two items, light-pink cotton Capri pants with black polka-dot underlining and cool pair of summer turquoise shorts. But I couldn't afford both of them. Oh, what torture! It has always been excruciatingly difficult for me to part with a clothing item that I've fallen in love with. Yes, don't laugh! How else can one describe this sensation of utter fascination, when your whole being – your eyes, your thoughts, your soul, your hands – are focused on one and only one goal – the ultimate purchase of that particular item.

"Elena, are you all right?"

I jumped up in surprise and stuck my head out from behind the changing room curtain.

"How long have you been stalking me here?" I whispered.

"I haven't been stalking you!" pouted Chris. "But honestly, I feel offended. You could have invited me to help you zip up a dress or something."

"There's been no need," I laughed. "I can't decide if I should buy a pair of pants or a pair of shorts! I've already bought my birthday dress."

"I'll tell you what, madam – no need to torture yourself. I'll buy you one of the items as a gift for your 21st."

"Oh no, Chris, you can't do that!"

"Elena, you could have at least tried to sound sincere. That glitter of a hopeless shopaholic in your eyes gives you away. And come on out of there, your naked shoulder makes me think dirty thoughts."

"Anything would make you think dirty!" I giggled. "Where have you been in the last hour anyways? Oh, hold on, let me guess. Looking for porn DVDs?"

"Ah, yeah. You got me! I bought one just for you," said Chris and handed me a little white and black shopping bag.

"Hmm, great... I don't really watch porn, I was just joking," I hesitated.

"Elena, just take it."

I shot Chris an apprehensive look and peeked inside. There it was. A dictionary. A Japanese-English dictionary to be more exact.

"Wow! Thank you, Chris..."

That was all I could say. I knew people around the store started casting at us "check out those two fucking weirdoes" looks (and who could blame them? Who else would have a lengthy discussion of absolutely nothing with your head stuck from behind the changing room curtain?), but I really couldn't care less. I was too busy trying to shake off the thought that Alex had never cared about my love for languages. He actually would make fun of me. "Oh, now we're picking up Japanese? Ms. Know-It-All! What's going on next week then? Brazilian?" I would typically be too mortified to even mention that they speak Portuguese in Brazil... Had I gone terribly wrong somewhere? I helplessly stared at Chris and suddenly realized that I was extremely thirsty.

"Give me those pants, Elena-san!" announced Chris. "We'll pay up and go home."

And then there was a long drive back to St. Simons Island. We were surrounded by the infinite darkness of the hot southern night, and everybody in the car was asleep. I also started dozing off to la-la land, but then it occurred to me that I didn't want to leave Chris all alone. I opened the window, and the sweet swampy smell of the marsh flooded the car. An unexpected thought struck me. I wasn't afraid of getting old. I thought that it would actually be unbelievably cool to start noticing wrinkles on my face. It would mean that I had lived my life, experienced its sometimes paradoxical twists and turns; it would mean that I had laughed, cried, and loved. It would mean that if I suddenly dropped dead, it wouldn't be that bad. I caught a quick glimpse of enormous white magnolias looming in the dark and once again realized how ridiculously happy I was. Youth comes with so many unexplored opportunities, one can't help but wonder which direction they have to go for. I could be working for the United Nations one day – perhaps spend some time in Africa, and then move to New York or Geneva and interpret at international and very important conferences; I could become a flight attendant, be as free as a bird, and fly all over this amazing and fascinating globe; I could become an astronaut and see other planets (which would be difficult to pull off, since I'm claustrophobic); I could become a Russian housewife, have kids with Alex, and never change anything in my present life. What? It sounds attractively painless and familiar. Or I could tell Chris that he could stay tonight and enjoy this painfully sweet present moment. As if in a movie, the car stereo – or rather Liam Gallagher of Oasis – telepathically sang:

So what do you say?
You can't give me the dreams that are mine anyway
You're half the world away
Half the world away
Half the world away
I've been lost I've been found but I don't feel down.

I silently stared at the stereo in utter disbelief – I had songs speaking to me now, for goodness' sake! What would be next? Some days are so strange, I could have sworn I wouldn't have been surprised if a gigantic space ship had landed on the road in front of us. I looked at Chris and smiled. Life has so many choices: do we always have to have the answer?

CHAPTER TWELVE

Dedication to the Parking Lot

The Ocean Isle parking lot was an extremely secluded place. In fact, it made me recall the times when I used to hide in the fort back when I was a kid. Remember? That feeling of sweet isolation, of being out of everybody's eyesight... It's not like you were up to no good. It's the possibility of doing something absolutely and out-of-hand naughty. Ocean Isle's parking lot had always made me feel that way. The space was enormous, with four separate shuttle stops and parking places for a few hundred cars, and it was surrounded by lush subtropical vegetation that made you believe you were lost in the midst of a Floridian forest. In reality, there was quite a busy shopping center just across the street with the characteristic hustle and bustle of an exquisite boutique mall for the rich and powerful. It seemed to me that the parking lot would be there forever. Like a paradoxical constant that, despite the inevitable law of the universe, will never change. But one day, it will change. There could even be Zaxby's or something like that at the same very place I was sitting right now. Civilization will burst in, uninvited, but still impossible to avoid, and despite our mixed feelings about the matter, we will still go there and buy a fried chicken sandwich. By this time, my darling reader, you are probably thinking that I have gone completely nuts. But no. I'm just whining. One day, I'll make a great old person – I'll be able to lament about the past times on and on and on, and my future grandkids will roll their eyes in understandable irritation and mumble, "Oh, not grandma with her stories again."

"Yes, I do indeed suffer from the worst case of blue balls known to mankind!"

I looked at Chris, who was laughing in that bubbly manner of his – with his head tilted backwards and the smile that could have melted glaciers – and thought that I was about to melt myself if the shuttle didn't arrive in the next two seconds. Wearing the Beach Club Dining Room monkey suit that boasted thick long navy-colored pants didn't particularly help in 100-degree heat either.

"Oh come on, Chris. Be for real. Are you tagging that ass or what?" whispered Justin as he was trying to turn away from me.

Did he really think I couldn't hear him? Honestly?

"No, Justin. I'm not tagging this ass," announced Chris loudly as he whopped on the bench next to me. "And even if I was, I wouldn't have told you."

Justin was your typical all-American cutie. Everybody loved him, he was engaged to the typical all-American princess with shiny chestnut hair and a fabulous row of white teeth, and he was going to school to be a pharmacist. Meanwhile, he was working with us at the Beach Club. He also had something going on with Vera. Nobody was quite sure what exactly was happening between them.

"Justin, he couldn't be possibly tagging my ass. I'm engaged."

"Me too!" He laughed. "But cheating doesn't count if you're outside of the area code when the actual act occurs. In your case, it's even better – you're half the world away!"

"Hmm..." I pondered and quizzically placed my index finger on my top lip, "I've never heard that before. It sounds outrageously ridiculous."

"You might consider it, though," Justin shrugged.

I gave him a sideways glance of disbelief and with the corner of my eye noticed that Chris was almost falling over laughing.

"Justin, this theory sucks! I have nothing left but to laugh about it."

"Why, man?"

"Because it's not about whether she finds out or not. It's about what really happened. *You* will always know that you've pissed on that flower!"

"So what?"

I was already not paying attention to Justin – I was too puzzled by the fact that the physical incarnation of my potential infidelity was obviously quite strongly opposed to infidelity.

"Finally! The Shuttle! Madam, your carriage has arrived," announced Chris in a mocking manner. "The parking lot is now behind us."

After I hopped in and situated myself in the seat by the window, I got to thinking about time. Time... this capricious beautiful woman who changes her hairstyle ever so often, never stops, but essentially stays the same. I will ride this shuttle multiple times in the near future, and I will always get caught up in a philosophical mousetrap of unavoidable thoughts about the past. And who could blame me for it? When you are going down this winding road and looking at the magnificent pink, yellow and orange palette of the sky trimmed by the sawgrass frame of marsh, oaks and palm trees, you inevitably start imagining people, who were going down the same road on their journey to the famous hotel for the rich and powerful. Ocean Isle was founded in 1927, and pretty much immediately became the place to be. Ever since then, vacationing here has been a status symbol, a notary stamp on the document of your life that powerfully attested: "You have made it in this world! Congratulations!" I could picture young girls wearing audacious flapper dresses and bold cloche hats, riding in a ridiculously expensive Rolls Royce Twenty and babbling and giggling about boys, dancing, and what to wear that evening. They were thinking what I am thinking, they were feeling what I am feeling, they were enjoying the same breathtaking view, they were inhaling the same marshy aroma of Glynn. What happened to all of them? Where did they all go?

***

The lunch shift was a beast. It seemed to me that by the middle of the summer, vacationers finally realized that the fall was just around the corner and it was about time to get down and party. So they took hordes of their kids, friends, and relatives and set off to the beach. After half a day of soaking up the iridescent Georgia sun, splashing in the hot waves and rolling in the sand, they would get hungry to the point of starvation and attack the closest location – in our case, the Beach Club. They were typically extremely impatient, underdressed, and accompanied by a deafening concerto of wailing kids. By the time I finished resetting my tables and made it, barely, to the employee cafeteria, I was exhausted beyond human comprehension. My temples were pulsating from running in the heat (yes, I did work outside), and my eyes were watering from chronic lack of sleep. I waved to the Beach Club crew who were seated at the long table and got myself a glass of my favorite pink lemonade.

"Come on, Elena! I saved the place for you," said Monika and picked up her purse from the seat next to her. "Grab yourself a bite to eat. You look tired."

"Tired? I'm surprised I don't look dead," I sighed and plopped down on the chair. "I'm not even hungry..."

"A rough day, huh?" smiled Monika.

"I'm telling you, I'm not sure how I'm going to survive the dinner shift."

"Where are you working tonight?"

"Ocean Room. With Chris and Farrah."

"Lucky you!" Monika giggled and took a bite off her chicken salad sandwich. "Is Chris still after you or what?"

Apart from his other superhuman abilities (e.g. reading my mind), Chris was probably also gifted with the long-distance hearing talent. As soon as Monika asked me the question, he quickly turned away from Farrah and stared at us. And he was at the other end of the table! Engaged in a lively (too lively, if you ask me) conversation with Farrah, and there were at least ten people between us and him – talking and laughing. Honestly... I didn't even know he had noticed that I was there.

"Yeah," I said in a quiet voice and lowered my eyes. "On Tuesday evening, after we got back from Jacksonville..."

"Yeah? What happened?" Monika apprehensively glanced at Chris and moved closer to me.

"Well, he dropped us off, and the girls went to bed..."

"And? Come on, Elena! Quit egging me on!"

"No, nothing like that," I whispered and cut myself a piece of Monika's sandwich.

"Chris bought lottery tickets and we scratched them off. And then we made out for like... an hour." I gave Monika a look of a rabbit about to be slaughtered and nodded. "I know, I'm absolutely nuts..."

"Well, are you guys dating now?" Monika's eyes flickered as she shifted in her chair with excitement.

"Shh! No! We're not dating," I whispered again and tried for the tenth time in the last two minutes to ignore Chris staring at me. "Of course not! I'm marrying Alex next summer. End of story."

Before Monika had a chance to reply, I heard a loud pounding and jumped up in my chair. To my horror, I saw Chris jokingly hitting the table with his fist, turning his head in my direction and shouting to an astonishment of all thirty people in the cafeteria.

"Elena! I fucking love you!"

I could feel thirty pairs of eyes drilling a hole in my face. It was akin to that nightmare that is always there in scary movies – when a protagonist is at the head of the table, and then something happens, and everybody alongside that table turns and looks at them. I could swear my face resembled a ripe pomegranate at that moment. My heart was beating so fast, I was afraid everybody could hear it. I didn't know what to do. I caught a quick flash of annoyance on Farrah's face. I noticed an excitement of a new gossip opportunity in Hooper's eyes. I was amused by the bewildered expressions of Vera, Diana, and Sonia. But most of all, I was mortified by how happy I was. At that particular moment, I realized that when I was gone, just like those imaginary girls in the Rolls Royce, whatever would be left of me – my soul, my spirit, or perhaps simply nothing really, just the transparent memory of me – that memory would be soaring lightly in the atmosphere, hopping from one cloud to another and smiling upon all the mortals down on the adventurous Earth, singing her song of love.

***

Ghostly raindrops were lightly tapping on the window. I turned over in the bed and opened my eyes. Alex was sound asleep on the pillow next to me, and the TV was peacefully mumbling away in the living room. I sat up and stretched. My back muscles hurt with that dull achy feeling that one might end up with after spending too much time in the same position. How long had we been here? I got up and slowly walked up to the window. The thick pine-tree forest across the street was almost invisible under the powerful crystal wall of sky water. Strange... I'd never seen rain like that in Voronezh before. Typically, it just drizzled all day long, especially in fall. The drumming sound was getting more intense and overpoweringly loud. I couldn't hear the news reporter on the TV anymore. I closed my eyes and touched the window with my forehead. It was soothingly cold. Why was I feeling guilty? What was that constricted knot in my chest that grew bigger and bigger? I could easily suffocate like that! Everything is okay, right? I'm at home. Alex is at home. We're together. This rain seems almost subtropical. I've never been in the subtropics... Or have I? Hold on. I remember seeing the ocean. It's so different from the sea, much more powerful and vast. Where could I have seen the ocean? Oh no! I quickly turned around, terrified, as the memory wave of reality swallowed my entire being. And right in there – in Alex's bed out of all places – happily snoozed Chris. I closed my ears to block the sound of this rain that was trying to wash away everything and everyone I ever knew and loved. Stop it!

"Elena, you really need to quit drinking."

"Yeah. I've heard that alcoholics suffer from really bad nightmares."

With my head still on the pillow, I looked around the room. Vera, Sonia and Diana were towering over me like gigantic hobbits with big heads.

"I think her conscience is bothering her," murmured Diana.

"Diana..." I drawled. "Don't think too much. It's usually not to your advantage."

"Well, if you're being such a bitch, I'm not gonna go to the movies with you and Chris."

Fuck. Movies.

"I think I'll pass as well," added Vera apologetically. "Sorry, Elena. The rain's coming down like crazy, and I'm sleepy."

"Yeah, I'll give it a miss, too," said Sonia and quickly disappeared in the kitchen.

I couldn't believe it. Earlier today, Chris had invited all of us to go to the movies and see King Arthur. I wouldn't have agreed if these three heifers hadn't been that enthusiastic about the idea. I glanced at the clock on the bedside table. Great. Chris was supposed to be there any minute. I didn't even have time to call and cancel.

"Traitors!" I hissed and threw a pillow at Vera and Diana. "What am I going to do now?"

"Elena," smiled Vera, "the question is – what are you NOT going to do now? Right? You're not going to do anything. Just watch a historic movie."

"You're such a bitch!" I growled. "You're setting me up for disaster!"

"Elena!" announced Sonia from around the kitchen door. "We're not here to guard your vagina, okay? You're a big girl. You can easily take care of yourself."

"I'm not sure about that." I propped myself up on the pillow and sighed. "I just wasn't prepared for a real date." I helplessly stared at the girls. "I mean, what would Alex say?"

"Why would he say anything?" Diana shrugged. "He's not going to know. Unless you tell him..." She paused and looked at me with that deep knowledge of life and universe that only a nineteen-year-old girl can pull off.

"I don't understand! Why is the modern society promoting cheating? When did it become fashionable to be a lying bitch?" I covered my eyes with my hands in exasperation and quickly turned away from Alex's picture on my bedside table.

"Elena, the society doesn't have anything to do with it. YOU are being a lying, selfish bitch, and we're trying to make you feel better, because you're our friend. A bit hypocritical, but still a friend."

Yes. You're right, my darling reader. I wanted to murder Diana. At that particular moment, truth wasn't what I ordered off the menu. I was in the mood for denial. Perhaps some self-pity for dessert.

I had taken a quick hot shower that rejuvenated my body, if not my exhausted mind, and was stuck in the closet. My female readers have probably already guessed what had happened here. I was stuck in horrible, horrible limbo. I didn't know what to wear. Like any normal vain twenty-year-old, I wanted to look stunning. I wanted guys, who went past me to turn around and I wanted their girlfriends to hiss at them in irritation. (Just an FYI – I'm not a big fan of the young superficial Elena, but I've evolved since then, I swear; plus, I promised myself to be perfectly honest when writing this novel, so...) Thankfully, inside of the self-devouring Gorgon of insecurity already lived a tiny little seedling of a more conscious and compassionate human being. To my astonishment, the seedling beeped, "If you don't want anything to happen, why show off then?" I winced. I was already hearing Diana's voice in my head and that couldn't possibly be any good. I went for my pink patterned Sisley skirt that was barely covering my knees and a suede-colored top with spaghetti straps that showed off my belly button. Something in between a bitch and a seedling. I was also wearing extremely high wedge sandals. The sandals screamed, "I'll fuck your brains out." I was satisfied with the way I looked; my appearance reflected exactly how confused I was on the inside.

As I was scrutinizing my image in the bathroom mirror, I heard a confident knock on the door. I quickly applied peach-colored lipstick and fluffed my hair. To my horror, I looked horny. I didn't have time to do anything about it, and I had no idea how I'd get down to getting rid of that problem, so I briskly walked through the musty smelling living room and swung the door open.

Fresh drops of rain landed on my bare arms, and magnolia-scented air burst inside of our apartment. He was standing in the doorway. At that moment, I realized that Chris and I had never seen each other when it was raining. Ever since we met, the weather had been perfectly sunny, clear, and hot. His hair was particularly red on the backdrop of the gloomy sky, and he was wearing a funny multicolored leather jacket that made him look like a rock star from the sixties. I smiled.

"What's the deal with the jacket?"

"It's my dad's. He wore it when he took my mom out for their first date."

"Nice," I grinned, "Do you say the same thing to all of your potential lays?"

"Yes," He nodded.

"Well, I've got to watch out then. It looks like it's just you and me tonight."

***

I couldn't help but notice that in life, everybody is kissing somebody's ass, to this or that extent, perhaps not all life long, just a few times, to get in here or there. You know what I'm talking about! I dare to bet you that 99% of the human population at some point of their lives kissed somebody's ass. You might have not admitted it to yourselves, but you've done it! And then some of us decide that it's not our cup of tea and the taste of some strange person's arse isn't that great after all, and some of us continue with the sad practice regularly on the day-to-day basis and, unfortunately, typically prove to be quite successful in their careers.

King Arthur didn't kiss anybody's ass. He was a rock star of his century and he definitely didn't deserve to be betrayed. The exemplar of medieval chivalry and the legendary proponent of round table equality, he with no doubt deserved a loyal woman who would stay by his side until he drew his last breath. But no. The woman follows the unavoidable animalistic instincts and gets it on with the hot stud Lancelot. I used to judge Guinevere without mercy. I used to think of her as a heartless slut who undermined the idea of true love, friendship, and integrity, and was now doomed to represent the opposite of graceful romance for eternity.

At that point in time though, in the dark movie theater hall on the rainy July evening in 2004, I realized that I could relate to Guinevere. As I was watching Keira Knightley tormented by the horrendous dilemma, it suddenly dawned on me that the legend of Arthur, Guinevere, and Lancelot was quite possibly the only fairy tale out there that wasn't deceptive or misleading in any way. Perhaps because it was based on the real story. When you are reading a fairy tale or watching a romantic movie, everything is crystal clear. Everything is classified into the defined areas of black and white. There is a good guy, and there is a bad guy – the girl would really have to be a dumb twat to go for the baddie! People's actions are strictly categorized into either good or evil, and the moral compass of a protagonist is never fucked up. Whereas in reality – and how grateful I was at that moment that we chose to go and see King Arthur that night – the whole vast horizon in front of you is colored in all shades of gray. Oh, how I wished that characters of the play called "Elena's Life" would be a bit less ambiguous. Wouldn't that be nice, if they came with labels on their foreheads? I glanced at Chris secretly hoping that he will demonstrate a label on his forehead, but – alas – it wasn't there.

We didn't say a word to each other all movie long. He was holding my hand and my heart was singing so loud, I was half expecting people from the row in front of us to turn around and tell me to hush. We were surrounded by people, but we were alone. Chris squeezed my hand and I squeezed it back. Lancelot kissed Guinevere. Yikes. She gave in.

***

There is something wrong with us, women. The majority of us are for some mysterious reason looking for a bad guy. We don't want to be cheated on, we don't want to be lied to, and in the be-all-end-all, we want be that only fair-haired Rapunzel happily reigning over her conquered and head-over-heals-in-love Prince. But... it would always be nicer if the Prince had been hanging out with the evil folks before he changed his path and ended up with you, right? It would always feel much more rewarding if the Prince had broken a few princesses' hearts and then... and then he met you, and his entire world exploded. And then the Prince would become gentle, romantic and domesticated. And then you would totally forget that one day you wanted a bad boy and any of the Prince's actions that didn't fit in your picture of ideal togetherness would cause a mini storm in the typically calm and surpassingly undramatic waters of your marital union. So, what's wrong with us, women?

These somewhat sad thoughts were crossing my mind as I was staring at the moldy ceiling of our apartment and listening to Chris's Boy Scout stories. We were lying on the carpeted floor of our living room, and the rain that seemed to have become even more intense in the last two hours was drumming on the windows. The room was dark, except for the shadows of TV infomercials dancing on the walls and silvery moon light peeking through the drawn blinds. We were fully clothed and, no, we did not have sex. We got back from the movies, scratched off a few lottery tickets (Chris would get me hooked on the lottery, I swear!), and then sat down on the floor and started chatting. Here's the thing: Chris and I could talk forever. We would never run out of topics for discussions, and we never made fun of each other if one of us would get too much into philosophizing about life. That was rare for me. I was always afraid to get stoned, since I was usually told that I think and speak as if I was already baked out of my mind. Well, talking with Chris felt good. It felt normal.

"So, my brother Tony and I were the only two boys who got kicked out from the Boy Scouts in the history of Glynn County," laughed Chris.

"Well, at least now I know what can get somebody kicked out of the Boy Scouts." I smiled. "Stealing a World War II flag from a museum. That's quite an offense! How did they find out?"

"They called our mom!" Chris couldn't stop laughing. "And told her that they suspected that her sons had stolen an extremely precious item from the museum. Mom said that her boys would never do such a thing, but still went and checked our bedroom. And there it was, hanging over our beds!" Chris was laughing so hard, I thought he'd start hiccupping any minute. And I was no better!

"Why...?" I managed to utter as I was fighting the stubborn giggles. "Why did you even do that?"

"I didn't!" exclaimed Chris. "It was Tony! It's always been like that – he's the main instigator extraordinaire! I was simply the one that was easily convinced."

"Yeah, right!" I gave Chris a look that clearly expressed my doubt and smiled. "Something tells me it's a lie!"

"It's not a lie, but I'm not going to try to convince you otherwise. Every girl wants a bad boy."

As I was contemplating this sad statement, I let my guard down for a second and didn't notice Chris spinning around until he was miraculously on top of me. It was not good.

"Chris..." I tried to push him away, but he caught my hands, pinned them to the floor, and started kissing my neck. My hands still firmly in his, he slowly went down and kissed my breasts through the fabric of the damned beige top (I knew it would get me in trouble!). He attempted to go lower, but then suddenly stopped and looked at me.

Time stopped. I imagined how many women before me were in the same situation – some of them many, many centuries ago. Take Guinevere! And what if some of them decided to go an honest route and follow their moral compass? What then? Where were they now? Well, wherever they were, I'm pretty sure they couldn't be feeling as good as I was feeling at that moment. What if I let this moment of pure intense pleasure go? Sonia might build the monument to my iron-clad vagina, as she had kindly promised, and millions of yet to be born women of high morale will stare at it and say in pure awe: "I'll follow Elena's route! I'll give up pleasure for my principles!" I winced. If I ever wanted to be remembered by future generations, that wasn't something I wanted to be remembered for. As I was about to nod and fall into that painfully attractive canyon, I caught a glimpse of the modest golden band on my hand.

It was New Year's Eve, 2002. I was invited to celebrate the beginning of the new year at Alex's parents' apartment. We were all sitting at a traditional Russian celebratory table with the generous spread of exquisite meals that were cooked specifically for that night. President Putin was giving a usual New Year speech to the citizens of Russia, and the Red Square clock was about to announce the beginning of the new era. Everything was illuminating fresh hope and the sunrise of new dreams. I knew what was going to happen. As we raised our champagne flutes to say farewell to the past year, Alex reached into his pocket and took out a tiny, silk, heart-shaped red box. My heart jumped up and painfully hit my ribs.

"Elena." He paused and smiled with his usual mischievous grin. _"Right now, in front of my parents and in front of Vladimir_ –" He nodded in the direction of the TV and I chuckled nervously, _"I would like to ask you to marry me."_

I swiftly got up from the floor and sat on the couch. I looked at Chris, and I was pretty sure my eyes were glistening in the dark. He got up off the floor and walked out. The sound of the shut door came as a relief.

CHAPTER THIRTEEN

Confusion Central

There are two things I will never – ever! – learn to do in my life. One is driving a car (How do people even do that? I mean – you have to be able to use your feet, hands, eyes and brain at the same time! That's far beyond my poor abilities), and two is opening a bottle of wine in front of guests. Yes, we were already approaching the end of July, and I was still hopeless. That night, Chris was my trainer. We were getting ready to serve a large private party in the Ocean Room, and guess what? Farrah was working with us as well. Not exactly my dream-come-true situation. At that point, I would have preferred to spend a few hours in the company of hyped-up guerilla warriors. But no. I was sentenced by the ruthless rule of the fair Mother Universe to work all evening long with Chris, who had gotten even more aggressive with his attempts to get in my pants, and Farrah who... Hmm... What could I say about Farrah? She didn't necessarily dislike me, but I was pretty sure she wouldn't have minded if one day I simply disappeared off the face of the Earth.

Silent wars between women are a very interesting phenomenon. We can smile at one another, we can make each other coffee, we can chit-chat about new fashion and make-up trends, and – get that! – we can even giggle about guys, but deep down, in the volatile realm of vanity, we hate each other's guts. In fact, if you carefully listen to a conversation of rivaling women, you will find out that they *never* mean what they say. Come to think of it, it is an amazing art form of speaking in riddles that only female creatures can interpret and master.

"Your hair looks really pretty today, Elena!" Farrah smiled and placed a polished wine glass on the counter with the distinct and victorious clink.

"Oh, yes? Thanks!" I self-consciously touched the back of my head. My hair had never looked worse. It was frizzy, salty from swimming in the ocean the night before, and the split ends were absolutely horrible.

"Oh yes, and by the way, I absolutely love the top you were wearing the other day! The turquoise one with spaghetti straps? I wish I could wear tops like that – you're so skinny." She sighed and picked up another glass from the rack.

I painfully bit my lip and pretended I was placing an order in the Micros to hide my irritation. Farrah's voluptuous breasts made me feel like I was a flat-chested orangutan roaming through the vast plains of native Africa. *Spaghetti-strapped top, my ass.* I completed my "order", briskly turned around from the Micros with the most sincere and wide smile that would convince anybody that I was 100% honest, and said:

"What are you talking about? You're beautiful!"

"Oh, no. I need to lose about ten pounds. Still working on it."

"Quit that!" I giggled and gloatingly thought to myself that her badonkadonk could indeed lose a few pounds.

"What are my girls up to here?" exclaimed Chris as he burst inside on his way from the Ocean Room, an enormous tray full of dirty dishes on his shoulder.

"Nothing, just chatting," smiled Farrah.

His girls. A wave of annoyance reached an overflow mark inside of poor little Elena. If I had any breasts, they would have been going up and down in demonstration of how disgusted I was by the fact that he dared to address us as one. But I didn't have breasts. Nor did I have any right to be upset about anything. So I did the last thing I wanted to do at the moment. I smiled and said, "Yeah, just chatting, us, girls," and turned away from both of them before my face transformed into one of a fire-spitting, tongue-thrusting old hag.

"What are you doing, Elena?" Chris apparently didn't realize I needed some time to travel back from the evil side of my versatile personality and nonchalantly approached me from behind.

"I'm trying to practice opening a bottle of wine," I whined. "I'm about to be tested next week and I'd hate to fail it."

"Come on, Elena!" chuckled Farrah. "It's easy. You can do it!"

I quietly ground my teeth once again and hoped that she wasn't going to bring up the fact that I also couldn't drive a car. I felt like we had already had this conversation at some point in time that summer, and everybody in the room treated me like a paralyzed, half-witted baby cow simply because I said that I didn't have a driver's license. Thankfully, Hooper stuck her head in the door and announced that she needed Farrah for something and it was extremely urgent. Well, at least they would humiliate me in my absence – that was indeed a relief. We watched as Farrah triumphantly glided out of the room and the door slammed shut behind her.

"Okay, Paina," whispered Chris and took the bottle of wine out of my hands. "Give this to me. You're looking at it as if it's an explosive device about to rip your head off. Relax. I'll show you."

I watched Chris as he was talking me through the process and was honestly trying to concentrate on the topic. Instead, I couldn't help but wonder why he wasn't mad at me. Last time I saw him, he left me in the middle of my living room – distressed, disheveled, and absurdly horny. Any other man scorned would have been giving me the cold treatment right now. But he wasn't.

"Come on. Your turn now."

I stared at the bottle of wine.

"If you're trying to cast a spell on it, it's not going to work – I can tell you right now," laughed Chris. "Come on then!"

I cast him a rebellious look, grabbed the bottle, and started a mock presentation. I described what kind of wine it was and which winery it originated from, and proceeded to the extremely difficult part of trying to cut the foil with the wine key knife. As I was fumbling with the stubborn bottle, I realized that Chris wasn't looking at it at all. I looked up and saw him watching me silently and intently.

"What?" I mumbled.

"Nothing." He shook his head. "I was just imagining how these little hands would feel on my..."

"Enough," I squeaked. "I think I got the idea. Thanks."

Honestly. It's been about ten years since that moment and I'm yet to open a bottle of wine without picturing... you know. I like to refer to it as my wine-bottle post-traumatic syndrome. I wanted to laugh – a lot – but I couldn't. I just couldn't let Chris realize that I was capable of appreciating dirty jokes, because if we both bonded over that one, the escape route for the faithful Elena would have been closed forever. I had to pretend to be more prim and proper than I was. That was my plan.

"You are a dirty man, Chris Harrison."

"Thanks!" He bowed his head and I had to turn away so that he wouldn't see me giggle.

The evening was going by extremely fast. I found myself running from the Ocean Room to the Dining Room to the Loggia Bar and back to the Ocean Room at least ten times. My leg muscles were exhausted and I wouldn't have been surprised if I'd fallen over, breathless and rippled by convulsions, in front of all the astonished but nevertheless sated diners. That would have been really funny! Everybody would have been worried senseless – what happened to that Russian girl? Is she all right? And Chris would run up to me, pale-faced from painful concern, drop down to his knees, and start kissing my face. Okay, a bit over the top, I know. But this was my fantasy world, so... why not? I pushed the door to the Ocean Room service station open with my bum, carefully holding a tray with eleven full water glasses, turned my head around, and froze. Here they were – Chris and Farrah. She was meticulously cleaning the counter of all the dirty dishes, and he was just as meticulously grabbing her ass. She pushed his hand away in annoyance. That surprised me, but I was too hurt to register my astonishment. Afraid they were going to spot my awkward presence any second, I stepped forward and the door swung hard and sent me flying out into the Beach Club hallway. I landed on my arse and just kept on sitting there, in the middle of the busy restaurant, the tray with glasses still miraculously in my lap. A few little kids gathered around me, silent questions poised in their large, wide-open eyes. I smiled with quite possibly the saddest smile these kids had ever seen and blew a stray lock of hair off my eyes.

"Ma'am, are you all right?" A girl with a curly pink-bowed pony tail carefully touched my hand and quickly stepped away, as if scared that a crazy waitress would bite her and run off.

"I'm fine." I smiled and tried to wink away the stubborn tears. "I'm fine, really."

***

I wasn't fine. In fact, I spent half-night long staring at the ceiling and thinking what a bloody idiot I had made of myself. I also couldn't believe I was suddenly so jealous. Jealousy is a curious feeling. It's an inevitable nagging companion of attachment, and it only shows its face when you are under the illusion that the person you have feelings for has become your property, and any hint of possible trespassing sends you off the rocker. I groaned and assumed a comfy and safe embryo position in my bed as this thought crossed my mind. I didn't like the phrase "have feelings for someone." It made it sound like I had feelings for Chris, and it definitely wasn't a part of my grand plan. I wasn't ready to be jealous of Chris – I wasn't even with Chris! How much more confusion could this summer trip possibly bring? I tried to close my eyes and fall asleep, but I kept zapping out of the safe dreamland realm back into illogical and complicated reality. I sat up and looked at the framed picture of Alex on my bedside table. The photo actually was a close-up shot of him holding a framed close-up shot of me. Cheesy. I smiled and picked up the photo. Only people who are head-over-heals in love dare to do such cheesy things and are still not ashamed of demonstrating it. We were in love. Right? I mean, how else would we be able to explain three and a half years of laughing, smiling, and crying together? Of walking down dark lilac-scented streets and holding hands? Of blood-pressure-elevating make-out sessions in movie theaters? Of dreaming about a future family we were going to have together? All this couldn't just dissolve into nothingness overnight. I closed my eyes and all of a sudden, it felt right. *I was safe. In fact, I was taking a shower at our old apartment. Mom and dad were at work, and my Nan was aspiringly working on her next culinary creation. It would more than likely turn out to be another fiasco, but my parents and I would still have to put our best Academy Award faces on and consume everything on the plate. And we would definitely have to emphasize how delicious everything had turned out to be. I smiled and lathered aromatic fruity shampoo in my hair. Everything would have been perfect on that sunny summer day in 2002, except... Alex and I'd had a really bad fight the night before. Like a really bad one. I tried to focus on the homely aroma of baked goods that was sneaking through the crack underneath the bathroom door (perhaps this time Nan was really making something tasty for a change!), but to no avail. The nasty memories of last night kept persistently coming back and were making themselves feel at home inside my disturbed mind. It was our first fight, and it was ugly. It was also useless, because no matter how hard I tried, I couldn't recall what we were arguing about in the first place! So, apart from being upset, I also couldn't help but feel absolutely stupid. The hot water coming down my face instantly acquired familiar salty taste, and I desperately tried to think of something funny to help me snap back to the happy-go-lucky Elena. And then I heard the doorbell ring. My heart leaped into a very impressive summersault and nearly jumped out of my rib cage. He was there! I knew it was him. Mom and dad were at work – it could be nobody else but him! I froze and attempted to listen to the voices in the hallway through the annoying shield of the running water. It WAS him. Him and Dima, Alex's best friend and my former classmate. Judging by their voices, they were heading into the kitchen. I carefully got on my tiptoes and tried to peek through the small rectangular glass window into the kitchen (yes, our old apartment indeed had a window from the bathroom into the kitchen; it was mysteriously located above the bathtub up top – I'm assuming it was there for the purpose of letting the natural light into the bathroom, but lo and behold – what a curious concept!). I was really good at spying through that window ever since I was a kid – and nobody ever caught me red-handed. But Alex knew me too well. To my utter astonishment, the only thing I managed to see was a gorgeous bouquet of bright yellow, orange, and red flowers. Flowers were everywhere. That was the happiest moment of my entire life. I laughed through my tears and pretended to be sniffing the flowers through the glass. And right there, between the multicolored petals and splashes of sunlight, I caught his eye. And everything was right.*

I closed my eyes to wink away my tears. When I opened them again, there was complete darkness. It was nighttime and I was peeking through the window. It wasn't my Nan's bathroom window and there were no flowers. I was staring at the moon, and I could swear I saw a witch flying astride her broomstick towards the orange of the moon. Or perhaps it wasn't a witch. Perhaps it was the old me, and I was – quite obviously – departing into the unknown.

***

"Why are you pouting, Paina? Is it that time of the month again?"

"I'm not pouting," I pouted and pretended to be distracted by something of supposedly extraordinary interest behind the car window.

Chris and the girls gave me suspicious looks, and who could blame them – there was nothing but the highway behind that window. They carried on having a very engaging conversation of supposedly extraordinary interesting content. Something about dogs and pooping in the street. I watched trees fly past me and was doing my absolute best not to cry. I was jealous. I was *so* jealous of what had happened the night before, it seemed as if my chest had an enormous cement block resting in its center. It was heavy and extremely uncomfortable. The only way to get rid of it would have been to burst into tears, but I was too proud. I would die first before I'd mention the reason for my upset feelings. I'd have preferred to be eaten by furious cannibals with yellow razor-sharp, drooling teeth to ever spilling a single word about that incident. I would never in my life mention to him what I saw. Ever. My cheeks flushed in indignation and I fervently wished I was on a different planet. Or better in a different galaxy. I hated myself for being so fucking stupid and trusting. I also hated myself for feeling what I was feeling. And most of all, I hated myself for knowing that I had no right to feel that way. We were not dating. We didn't have sex. I kept rejecting him on a regular daily basis. Why should he not try and make a move on somebody else? My vision blurred and I started blinking as fast as I could in an attempt to chase a rebellious tear back into my eyeball.

"Elena! Are you having a facial spasm or something?"

I turned over my shoulder and stared at Diana's face through the space between my chair and the car wall. I slowly shook my head and silently pleaded with her to shut up. She understood and sat back in her seat, an expression of worry on her face.

Confusion is the most dominant memory of that summer. Confusion ruled every aspect of my life back then. Love, friendship, dirty laundry. My room was a mess, and my life was a total fucking mess. My closest friends were the girls whose names I could barely remember before we got on the plane in Moscow, I felt like I'd been cheated on by a guy who I wasn't even dating, and my room in Island Retreat looked like a second-hand clothing store after a nuclear blast. I sighed and tried to gather my senses. I would be fine. Everything was where it was supposed to have been in the first place. Chris was with Farrah. They had the chemistry everybody in the Beach Club was talking about and they'd already had sex. Where was I supposed to be fitting in? Definitely not as a guest in a threesome... Or perhaps this was how I was looked at to start with? What was I thinking? Anyway, Chris and Farrah could set sails to the happy land of endless ménage à trois and partner swapping, and I'd come back to the warm and loving coziness of safe relationship with Alex. How could I even be fooled into seeing the scenario differently? My bitter mental diarrhea was rudely interrupted by the feel of Chris's hand on my knee. He'd always do that while we were driving. It would make me laugh just because it was so absurd. He was acting as if we were a couple in a long-lasting, stable relationship. There was no horniness in that gesture... just a tender touch that whispered: "Hey, I'm here, and I always will be." At least that's what the stupid cow Elena used to think. I wanted to turn around and punch him in the face. I wanted to scream at him and tell him to go and grope Farrah's knee. I wanted to tell him that I detested his touch. But I couldn't afford the luxury of any of the above-mentioned actions. Punching him in the face might have caused us to have a car accident. And - the worst of all! - I loved his hand on my knee... because whatever happened yesterday, his hand was still persistently saying, "Hey, I'm here, and I will always be." I aggressively took his hand off my leg, and my knee immediately felt lonely. I looked him in the eye and saw a sad question. He didn't understand. He was confused.

***

Savannah was also confused. Considering it was supposed to be a town well-known for its irresistible beauty – hell, even Sherman didn't burn it on his infamous route of destruction and subsequently presented it to President Lincoln as a Christmas gift – it was... well... strange. Savannah houses, amazing in their ornamental beauty and architectural variety, were peeking through the Spanish moss, and their flirty windows were glinting in hot and steamy sunshine. Each house was different and each one of them was a masterpiece of an eccentric genius, but yet all of them combined were strategically distributed in a perfect and repetitive pattern of neat squares. The geometrical perfection of Savannah was as aesthetically pleasing as it was disturbing. Typically, when visiting a historic town, you'd expect to take a walk down the memory lane. Cobbled streets whisper the old tales of yesterday, and with every step you take you can see how the town grew and changed and eventually became what it is. Savannah looked as if one day a bunch of dudes got together and decided that they were going to create the most gorgeous settlement in the entire world. They created the plan, got a few great architectural minds together and abra kadabra – Savannah was born. Savannah was a European town in a different dimension – in the perfect dimension where teenagers don't have zits, spouses don't cheat on one another, and the sun never sets. At least it was supposed to be that way. Yet time will always find a way to play its dirty tricks. The jewel of the Savannah Historic district, River Street, was maliciously adorned by the ugliest chimney a human mind could imagine. Everywhere I turned, there it was, silent and solemn, a sad reminder that perfection was a utopian concept that could never survive in the rough waters of pragmatic reality. I squinted at the chimney and frowned. River Street with its endless shops, pubs, and sidewalk cafes would have been absolutely charming if not for this annoying chimney! Come to think of it, the statement precisely describes the way we feel every single day of our lives. I'd be the happiest person in the world, if only I could get this job... Everything would be hunky-dory, if only my boyfriend would propose... I wouldn't ask for anything else, if only I could go on vacation next week. If only, if only, if only... Why can't we just be happy with what we have? Why can't we focus our attention on the precious things that *are* there, instead of the ones that aren't? Fuck this chimney! Just look around, Elena! Look at these magic little shops that lure a gawking passerby in with artsy trinkets and rainbow-splashed sugar candy. Look at these restaurants and pubs – so full of unique character and charisma and so full of leisurely tourists enjoying a warm, yet cloudy day of people-watching. Look at the Savannah River with its gray palette of colors and gloomy skies reflecting in its wise waters. What a beauty!

"What a beauty..." I whispered and gently stroked a decorative saucer with the famous picture of Vivien Leigh as Scarlett O'Hara – the one with the fabulous green dress that boasted the bold décolleté and the straw hat with the ribbon to match the dress.

"What a stare! These eyes look like they can shoot you down in a moment's time."

"Chris, you just have to quit sneaking up on me like that. It's really nerve-wrecking."

"Easy, mama! If you are trying to mimic her gaze, you're on it. And what's wrong with you anyway? Are you mad at me?"

"It's the second time you've said something along these lines in the last two hours," I sighed. "What makes you say that?"

"Have you seen yourself in the mirror? You look just like Charlotte, but three times meaner."

"Who's Charlotte?"

"Her." Chris nodded in the direction of my teenage idol and rolled his eyes.

"Her name is Scarlett." I hissed through my clenched teeth, turned around and marched out of the shop.

A salty, refreshing breeze wrapped around my face and soothed my dry and tired skin. I quickly crossed the trolley rails and angrily landed on the bench overlooking the river. A ferry boat with the traditional Southern tri-colored flag was almost blocking the entire view, but I didn't care. I blindly searched for a pack of cigarettes in my purse and was rudely stopped in my tracks with Chris's hand suddenly covering mine.

"I thought you wanted to visit Savannah. What happened?"

I did my best not to look him in the eye. I focused all my attention on that tri-colored flag waving in the wind and silently promised myself not to give in.

"It's beautiful, Chris, thank you." I managed to say.

He squeezed my hand and kicked back on the bench, his face looking up into the gloomy sky.

"Have you noticed how pretty the balconies are here?"

"What?"

"The ironwork on the balconies? Very impressive, so much detail... Living in one of these apartments must be really nice."

I looked up and noticed rows of fuchsia-colored window flowers on the background of silvery clouds. No matter how hard I wanted to disagree, I simply couldn't.

"Yes, it must be really nice." I nodded and lit a cigarette.

"You know what I want to do one day?"

"What?"

"I want to wake up early in the morning in of these apartments. I want to turn around in my bed and feel your naked back on my skin. I want to come up to the balcony and see Savannah River in morning sunshine."

I wasn't looking at him, but I was listening, and my stupid heart started to react to the words that I knew for a fact were nothing but a mousetrap.

"What I want to know is what you would do if the people saw you on the balcony..." I mumbled. "You're obviously planning to be naked – what if they call the police?"

"They would be so impressed by my morning wood, they'd be lost for words and for actions. They would just stare..." he added somewhat dreamily and snorted with laughter.

"Chris, you're disgusting."

"Well, that's why you love me." His fingers tiptoed across the bench and found my hand.

"Oh, what a surprise! I guess I wasn't informed. I had no idea I declared my love for you at some point this summer." I snapped and took away my hand.

"You did. You just didn't notice."

"You know what, Chris?" I quickly turned to face him and at the same time moved away further from him on the bench. "I'm so sick and tired of your fucking arrogance! Why don't you just leave me alone? I don't like you, I don't like your jokes, and I don't imagine why I'd end up naked in one of these apartments with your ass by my side. Plus, I'd find exposing yourself in front of poor tourists rude and absolutely retarded!"

"And I think you'd laugh about it."

"Well, you're wrong. You don't know anything about me, and – with all due respect – I don't know anything about you. So, please, let's not jump to conclusions, okay?"

"Are you all right?" Chris finally got up from his reclined position and looked me in the eye.

"I'm perfectly fine," I glanced down at my wrist. "Where are the girls? I thought we were meeting up at 2:30."

"Elena."

"What?"

"You don't even have a wrist watch."

"What are you trying to say?"

"I'm trying to say, quit being an arsehole and quit changing the subject. Have I done something wrong?"

"No, you haven't." I shrugged. "You've done nothing wrong." *I only wished I knew from the beginning what you were about*, I wanted to add. Wouldn't it be easier, if we just accepted people for who they were and quit making up false concepts about their personalities? Chris had done nothing wrong. I, on the other hand, created a person who never really existed, and now was feeling disillusioned simply because of my own foolish expectations.

"Chris!" Sonia surprised us by placing her hands on our shoulders from behind. "Let's hurry! We still need to make it to the mall."

I quickly caught the glimpse of Chris's face and squeaked with suppressed laughter.

"Well, Chris Harrison, if you have done anything wrong, you're paying for your sins right now," I whispered in his ear, grabbed his hand and stood up. "Come on, my friend, let's do it. We NEED to make it to the mall."

***

After a few exhausting hours of hopping from one store to another, we finally found ourselves back in the car. It was getting late, and the deep-red reflections of tired sunshine were dancing on the walls and windows of our Ford Explorer. The girls were giggling in the back and showing each other the lucky bargains they'd managed to find in the mall. I closed my eyes and drifted away into the happy land of primrose flashes of light on my eye-lids and "Breakfast in America" by Supertramp. Chris was a womanizing asshole, but he definitely had good taste in music. To be honest with you, my darling reader, I was ready to head back to St. Simons and plunge into my cozy bed. But no, we had Napoleonic plans! We were first going on a famous carriage-drawn ghost tour of Historic Savannah, followed by a night-time stroll down River Street. I couldn't possibly picture myself doing any of that, but the tickets for the tour had been already purchased and Chris was extremely adamant about the fact that we needed to see Savannah by night. I moaned and rubbed my eyes.

"Elena! Check this out – isn't this absolutely gorgeous?"

I opened my eyes and saw a silky violet fusion of a kimono-influenced top shoved in my face.

"Can you believe it was just five bucks?" Vera sounded so enthusiastic, I felt guilty for being such a droopy old bore.

"It's very cool. Elegant but sexy." I smiled and touched the smooth fabric. "Justin will love you in it."

"You think? Perhaps he'll change his mind about getting married after seeing me in this? What do you think?" Vera got so excited, she didn't even notice she was repeating herself.

I laughed and was about to move on to one of Sonia's treasures, when I suddenly noticed a top part of the African continent floating in the sky.

"Hold on, Chris," I said. "What is THAT?"

And right there, soaring in the silvery clouds of Savannah, was an impressively large globe. You could see all the continents quite clearly, and even what looked like a hurricane formation in the Atlantic moving towards Savannah. This man-made Earth was so surreal, so mysterious as to the reason of its presence in the residential part of the town, it almost made no sense whatsoever.

"Wow! I've never seen it before," exclaimed Chris. "Let's pull over and take a closer look at it."

As we walked out onto the sidewalk and stared up at the dominating spherical structure, I couldn't shake off the weird feeling that this monument was some sort of premonition. I didn't know what I was supposed to get out of it, but there was some kind of message.

"Guys, say "Cheese," yelled Vera, who had already somehow managed to run across to the other side of the street. "I'll take a picture of you."

"Smile, Elena," said Chris and protectively placed his arm on my waist.

The flash blinded me for a split second, I smiled, somewhat nervously – perhaps too late for the picture – and started to slowly retreat back to the car. I could hear the girls laughing away and clicking their newly purchased digital cameras, and the swooshing hum of the cars going by, but all these sounds of foreground reality seemed to have been traveling through the tunnel. I zoned out for a little while and couldn't even understand where I was and why I was there. I sat up in the passenger seat of the car and stared at the globe in front of me. Radiant glints of the last sunshine bounced off the toy Earth and made me squint. I turned to my left and saw Chris sitting next to me. He leaned forward and started kissing me. And I kissed him back. I kissed him back as if I'd never been kissed before. I kissed him back as if Alex, Farrah, and the whole world the way we had known it before never existed. I kissed him back as if I didn't care if they ever existed. I kissed him back as if we had our own little world, just for ourselves. The sound tunnel only delivered our heavy breathing weaved into the notes of the Supertramp song. I could feel his hands on my face, my neck, my shoulders. I could give anything, even my newly purchased fashion romper, just to be able to have him right there, in that car seat, to have him all for myself. I was so happy, I wanted to cry. I grabbed his face in my hands and looked at him. I saw the globe reflect in his gray eyes. I heard the first shy rain drops touch the window. This was officially the moment when I gave up thinking.

***

Why does proximity to danger put us into a romantic mood? Have you ever thought about it? There must be a reason why couples go to watch horror movies together, and girls who typically detest even the slightest hint of violence, scream in oxymoronic delight at the sight of a blood-thirsty zombie ripping a poor mortal's head off and consuming their brain. And then they cling to their date, so male and strong in his ability to wrap his arm around her back and patronizingly kiss her forehead. It's not like he'd protect her from the zombie if it decided to step out from the movie screen and have its slaughterous fun with the spectators. And yet she likes it.

I was no exception. I was sitting on the back bench of a horse-drawn carriage, getting ready to set off on a thrilling, nerve-rattling ghost tour of Savannah. Our guide was a chipper middle-aged lady named Paula, with the softest Southern accent and an enormous black hat that seemed to be a part of her uniform. She was currently engaged in a lively conversation with a family from the Midwest, who were visiting Georgia for a few weeks in the summer. Their tiny daughter, who couldn't have been older than five or six, was desperately clutching onto her worn and fluffy teddy bear and, judging by the look in her innocent blue eyes, was not at all looking forward to this tour. The girls were perched on the bench in front of us. Vera and Diana were chatting away, laughing just a touch nervously in anticipation of the scary tour, and Sonia was quietly complaining about the cost of the tickets. I wasn't sure who she was complaining to, since Diana and Vera were busy talking to one another and I was behind her and couldn't have possibly been engaged in the dialogue. She was speaking Russian.

"Sonia," I whispered and touched her shoulder. "Just chill out. You'll make up for the money tomorrow – you'll be working a triple shift!"

"Elena! I need to pay my mom back in September!" exploded Sonia.

"Shh!" I whispered and gave a few people who turned around to check on what was going on at the back of the carriage a comforting "we'll be just fine" smile. "Twenty bucks isn't gonna kill ya."

"Twenty bucks here, twenty bucks there," Sonia kept whining. "Elena, you never save any money and I'm not going to take any advice from you."

The statement was cruel, but truthful, so I decided to tactfully give up on any attempts to console my friend and kicked back in my seat. Having done that, I surprisingly landed into the cozy arch of Chris arm, his lips dangerously close to my ear.

"Are you ready for the romantic ride, Paina?"

I swear I must have two G-spots. And both of them are in my ears. How else could I explain this close-to-orgasmic sensation at any distant possibility of an ear-lobe kiss? Barely having recovered from the ear-whisper attack, I turned away from him and looked up into the dark starry sky. The night was simply perfect. Magnolia blooms were floating in the silver waves of moonlight, and the air was so sweet and light, it almost made me want to lick my lips and taste the floral aroma in my mouth. I was a bit scared – the possible presence of supernatural entities had always made me just a touch self-conscious – but having Chris by my side made me curiously exhilarated. On the other hand, the potential involvement of ghosts and evil spirits made me feel less guilty, as if the risk of being confronted or attacked by one of them justified the fact that I was cuddling with the guy who didn't happen to be my fiancé. But as I have said before, by that moment I had already given up thinking, and this analysis of my strange behavior is the result of all the thinking I'd have to do afterwards... After the summer of 2004.

"Okay, my gals and ghouls!" wailed Paula the tour guide, making all of us jump up in unison. "Let us commence our ride, shall we?"

"I'm already terrified," snorted Chris. "I can feel the blood freeze in my veins."

"Shh!" I hissed. "You're being rude!"

"Okay, okay... I just don't want you to be too afraid."

"I'm not afraid!"

The sarcastic question in his eyes implied that he didn't believe me in the least, but he tactfully remained silent.

"Before we go anywhere, my dears, let me tell you a few interesting stories about this very square..." Paula meaningfully widened her eyes and paused for a more dramatic effect. "As many of you might already know, the multiple squares of historic Savannah are adorned by the famous Spanish moss. You can spot the moss on every single oak in our beloved town, except for in Wright Square, where we happen to be at this very moment."

She paused for a few more seconds to let this curious fact sink in and then continued her story.

"A coastal Georgia legend claims that Spanish moss will not grow where the blood of the innocent was spilled. You can believe it or not – it's up to you – but I have to tell you what happened on this cursed square."

Before Paula even finished the last sentence, I already felt traitorous goose bumps tiptoeing all over my arms and legs. I instinctually got closer to Chris and squeezed his hand.

"Alice Riley and her beloved husband, Robert, were loyal and diligent workers of William Wise, notorious for his cruelty and promiscuity. People said he used to rape poor Alice on a regular basis and beat her husband up with inhuman ruthlessness. So one day, the couple decided that they'd had enough and came to the horrible decision. They decided to murder their lord."

"No wonder..." mumbled Diana. "I mean, how many times should a woman be raped before she decides to murder the old fuck?"

"Diana," I gently ventured. "I thought you didn't use profanity in public..."

"I'm outraged," she said. "I consider situations like these an exception to the general rule."

"A–hh," I drawled and shot Vera, Sonia, and Chris a look that clearly stated that I was about to laugh my ass off.

"Excuse me, belles and beaus in the back! I would like to ask you to respect the foregone spirits of the past," whispered Paula, her eyes glaring in the dark. "You never know how they might surprise us tonight, should they sense disrespect."

I obediently kicked back in my seat and bit my lower lip. I felt like I was back in high school and was about to be kicked out from my biology class for the extremely loud act of flirtation with boys.

"So... one day Alice was helping the evil man with his bath, and then her husband ran in and they drowned Wise by forcing his head under water. Unfortunately for the love birds, they were caught by an angry search mob on the Isle of Hope and thrown into prison. Alice had to watch her husband die on the gallows right here, on this very square. The poor gal wept and thrashed and flailed as she was witnessing the horrible and unjust death of her beloved."

The story created a very deep impression on everybody in the carriage: the silence was almost palpable, interrupted slightly here and there by Paula's heavy breathing, and even Sonia stopped whining about money and stared at the dark ominous square in front of us. I moved even closer to Chris, because no matter how hard I tried, I couldn't brush off the anticipation of being grabbed by some apparitional bony green hand and dragged out of the carriage.

"But Alice wasn't executed that day," solemnly announced the tour guide. "When her turn came, she announced that she was pregnant. She was then sent back to prison to wait for the baby's arrival. Eight months following the baby's birth, Alice was taken back to the gallows and hung by the neck. The poor woman was screaming and pleading to be forgiven – she wanted to be with her newborn – but the officials were ruthless. Alice was left hanging on Wright Square for three more days as a warning for people of Savannah that justice would be indeed carried out in the town."

"Justice my ass," hissed Sonia. "How horrible is that?"

"Many times each year, people still see a young woman dressed in rags running through the Wright Square and wailing for her baby..."

"I thought this was supposed to be a romantic ride," I whispered through my clenched teeth and slid down in my seat, further away from the end of the carriage.

"Why? Don't you think it's romantic?" Chris smiled and pressed me even closer to his shoulder.

"Hmmm, let me think – gallows, death, babies left without their mothers – no, definitely not my definition of romantic."

"But there's love involved. Love doesn't always imply happy ending."

"What do you mean?" I looked up at him and for one short-lived moment forgot that we weren't alone.

"I mean, you make your own luck. You don't have to be a martyr."

"But Alice didn't have a choice," I retorted. "Had she told the officials about William Wise and his cruel habits, they would have never believed her!"

"I'm not talking about Alice," Chris whispered in my ear and I had to hold on to the railing. You know what the G-spots are like.

With all the intensity of our conversation, I didn't notice that we had apparently started moving. The carriage was maneuvering through the narrow cobbled streets of Savannah and heavy strands of Spanish moss were dangling from the oak trees. Apparently, we were back in the safe zone, where no innocent blood was spilled. At least, I wanted to think so. As we approached a tall and impressive gate with very exquisite ironwork, the carriage stopped and Paula extended her arm in the direction of the entrance.

"Ladies and gentlemen!" she announced with enviable aplomb. "Welcome to the Bonaventure Cemetery, one of the most beautiful and scenic places in Savannah – yet, one of the most haunted ones as well."

"Great," I exhaled. "Now we are at a cemetery."

Don't get me wrong, my darling readers... I'm a very adventurous person. However, visiting old graveyards in the middle of the night is not what I would typically describe as my usual kind of adventure.

"If you carefully look to your right, straight through the ironwork flower of the gate," said Paula, "you'll see a statue of Gracie Watson, a little six-year old girl who, to the greatest distress of her loving parents, succumbed to pneumonia."

"It's just getting better and better, innit?" whispered Chris sarcastically. "Now we have to listen to stories about dying children."

"People still bring gifts and toys for Gracie and leave them by her statue. They say that if any of the gifts are stolen, Gracie starts crying with tears of blood. Listen!" The guide suddenly raised her index finger up in the air and mystifyingly stared in the direction of the gate. "If you listen very carefully, you will hear her cry..."

I scooted even closer to Chris, if that was at all possible – the next step would be jumping in his lap – and focused all my senses on the sounds of the night. And oh my God! I could indeed hear something. The sound of running water. A bit too much water for a ghost of a six-year-old, if you ask me, but the sound was unmistakably there! People were gasping and wowing and looking around in transcendental awe. I knew something was wrong when I glanced sideways at Chris and saw him laughing uncontrollably with his face buried in his hands. At that moment, I realized that the sound of running water wasn't coming from the eerie cemetery gate – it was coming from underneath us. Or from under one of the horses, to be more exact.

"Chris, is that what I'm thinking it is?"

"Yes, I believe so." Chris finally lifted his head up and looked at me, his boyish smile so wide and infectious, it sent bright yellow daisies swimming all around my chest and made me feel warm, fuzzy, and safe.

"Chris!" Sonia turned around, almost hiccupping from laughter. "Is our horse taking a piss or am I dreaming it?"

"Sonia, I'd love to say that you have a sick imagination, but I'm afraid you're right – our horse is indeed taking a piss. And a very long piss, I should say. I believe it's been at least two full minutes."

"Guys!" Vera giggled, her red curls bouncing around her face. "The horse must have gotten so scared, it literally couldn't hold it anymore."

"The guide told us the ghosts would surprise us," mumbled Diana, the corner of her mouth twitching sardonically. "They surprised us, all right. The spirits of Savannah seem to have quite a funny sense of humor."

"Okay, ladies and gentlemen!" Paula waved her hands nervously and tried to raise her voice in order to overcome the growing hum of excited tourists. "Let's just continue our tour, shall we? Our next stop will be the Pirate House..."

"I don't understand. Why is the poor lady so embarrassed?" whispered Sonia. "It's not like she was the one who's just relieved herself out in the open!"

"Shh!" Chris leaned forward toward the girls. "Be nice. Judging by her reaction, it doesn't happen too often. Must be something in the air."

"Something that stinks like very pungent horse piss," snorted Diana.

"Yeah, that one, and perhaps something else as well..."

"What?" asked Sonia.

"I don't know." Chris shrugged. "Maybe the spirits are trying to tell us to take it easy and try to look at life a bit more humorously. Go with the flow?"

"If I could go with the flow, I would have joined the horsey," I muttered. "I wanna pee so badly! When is the tour going to be over?"

"Oh, Elena! Not again!"

"Elena, really?"

"Oh, come on!"

"Paina, how many times do you pee a day, I wonder?"

"Well, Chris, if you feel like we're bound to be together, you'll just have to learn to put up with that." I smirked and patted his shoulder.

"Hmm..." He rubbed his chin in mock reluctance and chuckled. "I think I can handle it."

***

Since I wasn't a horse, I couldn't take a pee right off the carriage. Which was quite a pity. My bladder was about to pop any minute, and nothing Paula was telling us scared me even in a tiny little way. When overpowered by simple physiological needs, we tend to become much more fearless and perhaps even reckless. For instance, at that particular moment, I didn't care about where I could pee. I just had to pee. I know you know what I'm talking about – you must have been there at some point in your lives. As soon as the carriage pulled over back at the Wright Square, I jumped off it and pleadingly stared at Chris.

"Please!"

"What?"

"I really need to go! Where can I pee?"

"Well, let's go back to the car, find the nearest gas station, and then you can pee."

"Chris!" I hissed, "I don't think you understand the seriousness of the situation. If I can't find a place to pee in the next sixty seconds, I will squat right here!"

"Really?" Chris smiled and eyed me up and down, "I wouldn't mind that."

I would have loved to have a mirror at that very minute. Apparently my face – or my facial spasm – spoke louder than any words of any language, because Chris quickly looked around and pointed at the dark statue by the river.

"How about there? You can hide behind the statue."

"Oh, I don't care," I added grumpily and almost flew behind the statue.

At this point, my dear reader, you probably can't help but wonder – why does she dedicate a good portion of her book to the topic of peeing? Let me explain myself. I can justify that, I swear. Wanting to go to the bathroom at unexpected and inconvenient moments, and feeling mortifyingly shameful about it, are things that I've had to deal with my entire life. That's who I am! If only I could recall all embarrassing moments when I had to tiptoe out of the room full of people casting me looks of disgrace and poorly disguised contempt. One instance I remember particularly well. I was in my sophomore year, and our college was visited by a well-known professor of linguistics from Oxford. The academician kindly agreed to give one – and one only! – lecture, and the room was packed with professors and students to such an extent, it made a rush hour in Tokyo subway seem like the Serengeti plains. As everybody was gawking at the lecturer, almost afraid to breathe for the fear of distracting the genius from his enlightening monologue, I – to my utmost distress and horror – felt the familiar tingling sensation down below. If there are Olympian gods, they must have decided one day that they were going to fuck with Elena by constantly making her want to pee in the most ridiculous circumstances. I could hear them laugh at me back then, pointing their translucent divine fingers at me and covering their mouths with mockery and derision in anticipation of a scene they had already witnessed on multiple occasions. I realized that I couldn't do it. I'd rather have peed right there in the room, than experience those degrading glares from the people I had to deal with on a daily basis. But then I remembered what my mom had told me once. "Don't worry where you are, my darling, or who you are with – if you have to go, just leave. It's your body and you don't have to ask for anyone's permission." I exhaled, victoriously glanced up at the smirking gods, and walked out of the room, with my chin up and everything. I could see the same mortifying looks. I noticed that my academic advisor almost fainted at the sight of me departing the room. And when I looked up at the gods, they were watching me quietly and... was it respect that I spotted in their dreamy eyes?

"It takes you a while, doesn't it, Paina?" Chris stuck his head out from behind the statue and I almost fell over in my attempt to quickly get up and pull my pants up.

"Shouldn't you ask first if I'm done or something like that?"

"I should. But I chose not to."

I scowled at him and started walking towards the embankment.

"Where are the girls?"

"Guess."

"At that candy store at the corner?"

"Good girl."

"Well," I laughed and shrugged. "That's the only store within walking distance that happens to be open."

I leaned across the railing of the embankment, cupped my chin, and stared at the silent, dark river beneath us. Whatever was going on with me, with Chris, with any of us, the river was still flowing. It was a comforting thought. As if in grateful answer to my compliment, the river sent a refreshing salty breeze that covered my neck and arms with ticklish goose bumps. I felt Chris's firm arms go around me. He grabbed the railing, in that relaxed "It's not really an intimate hug, and yet somehow it's the sexiest thing ever" way and gently kissed my shoulder. I turned around to face him and immediately tried to think about something extremely gruesome, just to distract me from this ridiculously romantic moment and the gnawing necessity to make out, right there and for a very long period of time. Perhaps for eternity. Thankfully, the Olympian gods were gracious to me that day. Something in the indigo dark of the night attracted my attention and helped me snap out of this movie-perfect realm.

"What is that, Chris?"

"Hmm, how old are you? A week from turning 21? You should know what it is by now, young lady," murmured Chris in my ear.

"No, you dirty bastard! I'm not talking about this." I laughed and thanked the universe for the fact it was nighttime and he couldn't see me blush. "I didn't realize it was a statue of a girl."

"Well, it's a bit hard to notice what the statue is like from a squatting position, don't you think?" chuckled Chris and lightly pecked my neck.

"What is she doing? Is she waving?" I gently pushed Chris away and walked up to the monument.

"You haven't heard about it? It's the statue of the Waving Girl. I believe her name was Florence Martus – people say she'd fallen in love with a sailor and spent her entire life waiting for him and waving at every single ship that arrived for or departed from Savannah for 44 years – day and night."

"Did he ever come back?"

"I don't know. You're always interested in the final result, aren't you, Elena?"

"What do you mean?"

"I mean you've got to enjoy the road as well as the destination. Don't rush. The end is the same for everyone."

"Oh, don't be a smartass." I waved him off and handed him my camera. "Can you take a picture, please?"

I sat down next to the dog that was the part of the statue ensemble and smiled at the camera. The flash lasted for just a second,   and   then   it   was   gone.

CHAPTER FOURTEEN

Twenty-One and Counting

"So, as you can imagine, we were so young back then. Gosh! It was THREE years ago. Right, honey?" Inessa gently but firmly patted her husband's hand and took a graceful and careful sip of her hot coffee.

The girls met Inessa, a petite stunner from Belarus, as they were working a function on Rainbow Island. The function was called Plantation Supper and entailed – as you can probably imagine – lots of fried Southern food and an overkill of Bluegrass music. When I worked Plantation Supper for the first time, the uniqueness and charisma of the famed Southern hospitality mixed with upbeat notes of bluegrass made me want to dance, jump, smile, and greedily consume what seemed to have been at least two dozen delicious hush puppies. Come to think of it, anything would taste delicious if you haven't eaten for ten hours, but oh well – I had fun, and in the end, that's what matters, right? Unfortunately, there are just so many smiles that one can give out and so many hush puppies that one can digest. Eventually, everybody will get tired of working triple shifts and will succumb to a much more attractive idea of burying her head under the pillow and drifting off to dreamland. At least I did. And it so happened, that that particular evening, when lazy Elena decided to give the famous Plantation Supper a miss and go home instead, the girls met Inessa.

Inessa worked as a baby-sitter for one of the Ocean Isle members and was extremely excited to get to know four Russian waitresses. She exchanged phone numbers with the girls, and they agreed to meet for a coffee at some point. So here we were, drinking coffee in the Books-a-Million coffee shop and attentively listening to each other's life stories. Inessa and Z were already dating back in Belarus. Four years ago, Z won a grant and went to the United States to live with a host family in Georgia and study computer science. Inessa came to visit him the next summer on the Work & Travel program – just like us. They were so madly in love, Inessa couldn't bear to leave at the end of the summer, so they ended up getting married and staying together to live in Brunswick happily ever after.

"So how is it? The married life?" I asked in a fakely excited manner and shifted in my chair just a little bit to prove that I indeed was excited.

"You know, it's a marriage," sighed Inessa somewhat dishearteningly and tidied her blond bob by placing a stray lock of hair behind her ear. "We're not newlyweds anymore, don't have too many illusions if you know what I mean, but we have our fun." She laughed and took another careful sip of her coffee.

I didn't know what she meant, but I could totally agree with her that I had no illusions about stability in any relationships. I thought that perhaps she was absolutely right. Once the honeymoon is over, there is no need to lament the electricity of the newborn relationship. The more years people spend together, the less wattage is involved. There are no more sparks, just slightly warm coals of almost non-existent fire. The ones you can use for baking potatoes when camping. Have you tried that? It works! Those coals make for really savory potatoes with the faint smoky notes of forest fire. Many, many years after we turn twenty-one, I guess that's all we have to enjoy. When we find out that there is nothing we want to talk, laugh, or cry about together. When we find out that we actually don't even want to see each other. And then we will lower our eyes and will munch on those baked potatoes in silence, except for when you need to ask him to pass you some salt.

"So... Are you dating anyone back at home?" asked Inessa and mysteriously nodded in the direction of Chris, who was standing by the travel section aisle and studying a book on Greece. "Are you working both fronts?"

"What do you mean?" I blinked a few times and desperately tried to pretend I had no idea what she was talking about.

"You think I can't see the way he's looking at you?" Inessa laughed in that amazingly melodic way that only very confident girls can pull off. "Or the way you're looking at him?"

"Oh, no! It's just... nothing." I tried to wave the idea off as if it was an annoying fly that kept persistently buzzing in my ear even though I was under the impression that I had already killed it at least five times. "He likes me, I think... but I have a fiancé back home, so... there's nothing between us. Nothing at all."

"Okaay," drawled Inessa and kicked back in the chair, her slender arms placed across her tiny little waist. "Just be careful. Z's sister Julia came over to visit us last year. This American guy who goes to school with Z was head over heels in love with her. Promised her manna from heaven. Told her that he wanted to propose and all that stuff. And what do you think?" Inessa paused and looked at me in that strict-first-grade-teacher way that made me recoil in my seat.

"What?" I murmured, afraid to come up with suggestions of any kind.

"He backed out," she whispered, her eyes glaring victoriously at the thought that such a thing could never happen to her, because she wouldn't be trusting enough to take such silly chances. "And I'd told her so!"

"Hmm." I pondered and dared a sideways glance at Chris who was still completely entranced by the Greece book – he was probably already mentally sailing away by the turquoise coast of Mykonos. "Nothing I should be worried about, really... I don't have any plans on staying with Chris or staying in America. I'm going back to Russia," I added in a pitiful attempt to chase off slideshow images of Chris and I swimming in the Mediterranean... Chris and I hiking in the Alps... Chris and I on top of the Eiffel Tower...

"Oh, okay then," said Inessa and gave me a warm, motherly smile. "I just thought you should know, that's all."

"You guys should come to my birthday party. It's this Tuesday," I changed the topic, secretly hoping to save my sanity from an unwelcome photo collage of Mr. and Mrs. Jet-Set Harrison.

"Happy Birthday!" exclaimed Inessa. "How old are you going to be?"

"Twenty-one," I said and smiled. "I'll officially be able to drink in America. Yay!"

"Oh! You are just a baby! My younger sister has just turned twenty-one."

"How old are you?" I asked, half-expecting Inessa to announce she was eighty-four and just happened to look so young thanks to this amazing French moisturizer made of Zimbabwean monkey testicles.

"Twenty-three," said Inessa and finished off her coffee with an aggressive gulp. "Where is everyone?" She looked around the store, her lips pursed in slight irritation. "Z needs to get up early tomorrow – you know he has to drive to Savannah every day?"

"Oh," I muttered and thought that I didn't really fancy baked potatoes. I was rather in the mood for Greece.

***

I specifically remember the moment when I found out that I was not going to live forever. I am not exactly sure how we came about to discuss such a philosophical matter, but it happened as my mom and I were walking to my Pre-K school. It is one of my earliest memories and – as all earliest memories tend to be – it's just a touch blurry. I believe it was fall – or maybe spring – and we have just crossed this major street and then I heard the words. "One day, everyone goes where your Granddad went."

"Even me?"

I recall that mom was quite taken aback. She obviously hadn't expected this question from me, a normal parental reaction to the sudden realization that the creature you gave birth to is capable of thinking deep thoughts and questioning existential concepts.

"Everyone does, Elena."

We walked a little longer, away from the hustle and bustle of the congested intersection into the quieter and older part of the town sheltered by the shade of tall and powerful poplars.

"But I don't want to go away," I broke the silence.

"You have a lot of time before it happens."

"How much time?"

"A hundred years. At least."

You've got to give my mom credit here. From that moment on, I firmly believed that I was going to live a minimum of up to a hundred years of age. Plus, I snapped back to the typical excited toddler mood, because a hundred years back then was equivalent to eternity.

"I don't want to go away." Amateur philosophers always like to come back at that one with their usual, "You wouldn't want to live forever, would you?" Hmm, let me think about that one. Of course I would! Why would I want to leave this world? There is so much to see and do – so much to explore! How can I willingly give up the first primrose-pink of the rising sun and zealous anticipation of a new day to eternal darkness and uncertainty? They say that when you get older, you just get tired and are ready to fall asleep for good. I think they say that because there is no alternative. You know you are ready to kick it, so you do what you have been doing most of your life when things were not going the way you planned – you convince yourself that everything is for the better and that is the way you wanted to go anyway. Voilà. Plus, you do not want to discourage young people by telling them, "Yes, actually, I'm scared shitless, I don't want to die, please help." That would just create a global panic and half of the world population would commit mass suicide or something.

That day, I turned twenty-one. I was on the shuttle coming back from the Beach Club as these psychopathic thoughts were roaming through my mind. The girls were happily chirping in the back seat. From the excerpts of their conversation I could tell they were discussing the upcoming party. We were expecting a lot of people – our parties have earned quite a reputation in the last month and a half – and we had to think ahead about all the preparations we had to take care of. What with booze and music and snacks, it was a lot to pull off in one day, so the girls were slightly panicking. Curiously, I didn't really care. A bit bizarre, considering it was my birthday celebration, but I honestly couldn't bother.

"Elena!" Hissed Diana and painfully pinched my arm. "Did you even hear what we just asked you?"

"Hmm... What?"

"Oh my fucking God! Do you even want this party or not?"

"Of course I want the party!" I protested. "Why are you screaming at me, mean woman?"

"Because you're lame, lame, lame! Vera just asked you, like, three times, if you and Chris could go to Winn Dixie and buy the snacks, and you completely ignored us!"

"Yes, you did," said Sonia grumpily. "You're acting like a dude who's so entranced by a soccer game, he only registers one third of what his poor wife is trying to tell his stupid arse."

"How do you know that?" I wondered.

"My mom has always said that male species is not capable of doing just one thing or concentrating on just one conversation. They're perpetually somewhere else. At first, you get annoyed by that almost to the point of hammering him on the head, but then the worst happens – you get used to it."

"Good to know." I frowned. "I still don't think I'd ever put up with that kind of behavior!"

"Oh yeah?" Vera laughed as she was getting off the bus. "And what are you going to do to punish your future husband? Lock your pussy up in the chastity belt like you're doing now with Chris?"

Since Vera was too busy laughing her ass off, she didn't notice that she'd walked in straight into Chris, who was getting ready to get on the shuttle.

"I didn't know there was a chastity belt involved." He smirked. "Perhaps that's why it's taking her so long."

I grinned at him and tried to quickly go past him to avoid any kind of extra interaction. Just an FYI, my dear reader, *any* extra interaction with Chris was not good for Elena. It paralyzed my mind and I started daydreaming about scenarios I'm too ashamed to talk about even though I am writing under a pseudonym. I failed miserably in my noble attempt. As I was swooshing by him, Chris quickly grabbed my elbow, spun me around and whispered, "Happy Birthday, beautiful!"

And disappeared into the oblivion of the shuttle.

"Let me guess." Diana's gloating face materialized in front of my tired blurry eyes. "You probably wish that chastity belt wasn't on, ha?"

"Diana! I'll do whatever you want me to do for the party. Just promise that you'll stay quiet for at least ten minutes, okay?"

"It's a deal!" Diana high-fived Vera and Sonia and triumphantly got on her bike. "Oh, by the way, have fun walking. It's about 150 degrees out here – a bit hot – but look on the bright side, you won't have to work out this week."

***

I am quite positive that the reason I didn't gain any weight that summer in America was because I had to do so much walking in the heat that could only be compared to the temperature at which you'd typically broil your well-done steak. I was sweating so badly, a leisurely passerby might have thought I'd taken a dip in the ocean and forgotten to use a towel. I looked pathetic and probably deserved it. As I crossed the intersection of Frederica and Demere Roads – courageously trying to ignore the glares drivers were giving me from their blissfully air-conditioned vehicles – I was stunned by a sudden mortifying thought. In fact, the thought pinned me to the ground, like a gigantic powerful nail, and I had to stop in my tracks and process the heavy conclusions that accompanied that thought. I realized that I didn't want to marry Alex. You are probably reading this and thinking, "Well, duh, you'd figure you already knew that after all the stuff with Chris." But I didn't! I'd still believed – with all my heart – that I was confused, young, and perhaps a bit too horny. Never had I even started to believe that I would not want to be with my fiancé. I got so used to the idea of us throwing an enormous wedding, eventually having a family together, and living happily ever after, I was astonished to detect that all of a sudden, I definitely didn't want any of that. It was akin to adoring chocolate all your life long and then one day realizing that even the sight of it is making you sick. I don't mean to be cruel in any way – this is the last of my intentions – but it precisely describes the nasty thought I was faced with that hot summer afternoon.

After recovering from the initial shock, I shook my head as if trying to throw the idea out of my cluttered mind and started slowly walking back to the apartment. As I was watching my black, ugly man boots pound the pavement, I was bombarded by an array of vivid images – Chris and I walking the dogs in the park, Chris and I kicked back on the couch after a tiring day of work and watching a movie, me driving a car (nonsense!) to Jacksonville Airport to pick up my mom and dad, who were coming to visit us, me wearing beachy flip-flops that American girls wear. I started walking faster and faster as if hoping that these images wouldn't survive high velocity and would vanish forever. I wanted to cry. But I loved this place so much! I loved Demere Road with the mouth-watering Del Taco. I loved that McDonalds with the pay phone booth. I loved our Island Retreat apartment. I couldn't go home. That afternoon, I realized that somehow – miraculously and with no warning whatsoever – I was already there.

I ran into the apartment and shut the door behind me. I wanted to stay there forever. I heard the girls laugh in one of the bedrooms and rushed there to see them. I needed to see them! I came in and there they were, drinking cheap strawberry chardonnay and singing along with Whitney Houston, "Beach Cluuuuuub, we'll aaaalways love youuuu." I wanted to close this time capsule up tight and stay there until my last moment on planet Earth. I plunged my sweaty self down on Vera's bed, picked up an empty and ridiculously enormous plastic cup, and extended my arm:

"Sonia, can I have some of that chardonnay goodness?"

"Of course, birthday girl, anything for you! I was just about to propose a toast."

"Pour her a full glass," mumbled Diana. "She looks like she was just visited by death herself. What's wrong with you today?"

"Getting old." I smiled, feebly and pathetically, and picked up the cup.

"Come on, Elena!" Vera was hugging me tight. "Your life is just about to begin!"

"Excuse me!" called Sonia and cleared her throat in an attempt to shut us all up. "I have a toast, remember?"

"Sure, sure, go ahead." I nodded apologetically and raised my cup.

"I would like to propose a toast to our friend, Elena. When I first saw you, I thought you were such a stuck-up, Miss-Know-It-All bitch with long legs and no soul, and I never thought we could be friends. But here we are – as close as we could ever be. We – and I am speaking on behalf of all of us – love you very much. We think you're amazing and, most importantly, we accept you as you are. No matter how confused, no matter, which path you choose to follow –" Sonia paused and gave me a heavy look, her eyes watering just a touch (how much wine could they had possibly drunk while I was gone?) " - we will always be by your side. To you, Elena."

"To you," laughed Vera. "You can even smoke inside today. Just one cigarette though," she quickly added as she caught a glimpse of hope in my eyes.

"To you, Elena. Even though you are always littering up the apartment and swearing like a sailor." Diana smiled and gave me a spontaneous hug.

And we drank that cheap wine, and it was so amazingly good – the sweetness of it was so tart and unpredictably head-spinning – it could only have been the flair of twenty-one. It could only have been youth and anticipation of the life ahead, all that exciting roller-coaster of life that made that headache in the bottle so inexplicably delicious.

As I was looking around the room, taking mental pictures of my friends with their red plastic cups and striped Beach Club uniform tops – just tops, mind you, my dear reader, no bottoms (heavy navy pants was the first thing that we would typically take off the moment we entered our apartment), I suddenly heard the front door slam:

"Girls! Heellouuu! Anybody home?"

"Oh my God, what's Chris doing here?" Diana jumped up and started running around the room in search of her pants or some sort of lower body cover.

"Elena, wasn't he supposed to be working? We just saw him getting on the shuttle!" Vera hopped over her bed and hid behind the pillows.

"Oh shit oh shit oh shit." Sonia was nervously zig-zagging across the room without any concrete plan whatsoever.

And before I was even able to crack a smile at the comic nature of what was about to take place, there he was, standing at the bedroom doorstep, a bouquet of red roses in his hands.

"Wowie-zowie! Birthday Beach Club orgy. Just what I ordered."

***

"So... Let me get this straight, Chris. You gave Elena six roses?" whispered Vera and let out a quiet crackling laugh.

"Just let it go, Vera, let it go," sighed Chris, a touch of frustration in his voice, as he kicked back in his seat.

"I can't let it go, she's only turning twenty-one and you're already trying to bury her," snorted Vera and threw a few pop corns in her mouth. "On her birthday!"

"Come on, he didn't know," I smiled and patted Chris on the shoulder.

"It's a stupid rule," pouted Chris.

"It's not really a rule," I shrugged, "It's just... alive people get an odd number of flowers and an even number is reserved for the dead ones."

"Yep. We might as well go to the closest cemetery and pick a spot for Elena," Vera was getting too much of a kick out of the situation.

"Quit that!" I hissed at her and tried to suppress the desire to laugh. "He didn't know! It's a Russian rule – I guess it doesn't apply in the States."

"Oh, Elena, I wish you could see your face when Chris handed you the flowers! You know what..."

"Quiet, Vera, we're in the movie theater after all. You've got to keep it down," Chris seemed to be getting madder and madder.

"Whatever," Vera giggled and hid behind the popcorn bucket of colossal proportions.

"It's okay, people, relax." I put one arm on Vera's shoulder and one on Chris's, since I was sitting between the two of them. "We're here to watch the best movie of the summer. Let's forget about that nuisance. Look! It's already started."

I hadn't realized that the Notebook was going to be such a tear-jerker. In a moment's time, all three of us forgot about the argument entirely and were almost entranced by the plot unraveling on the screen in front of us. I thanked all the gods I could possibly think of that Vera went with us. Otherwise, I'd have been watching the most romantic film of the century alone with Chris, in the intimate dark of the movie theater, when even the smell of popcorn – strange as it may sound - seemed to have the effect of an aphrodisiac. I watched Rachel McAdams trying to figure out, which one of the guys she should stick with and couldn't believe that she didn't know. Of course it should be Noah. Couldn't she see that? Noah was her destiny. I wished everything would be just as easy in real life. I wished I would be able to tell who my guy was just as quickly and painlessly as I had just picked the course of the heroine. Was it easier to see such things if you were an outsider? Was it why Sonia proposed her toast earlier this afternoon, with such a cunning expression in her eyes? Did they know? I quickly cast Vera an apprehensive glance and stuffed buttery popcorn in my mouth. As I was chewing it, fervently and hastily, it dawned on me that perhaps everybody else but me had the answer. I was the silly blind cow on the screen and they were the happy spectators – laughing, munching on their popcorn, and silently wondering where my eyes were.

"Chris!" I whispered and tugged at his sleeve.

"Shh, it's one of the most romantic scenes of the film. What is it?"

"Did you pick this movie on purpose?"

"What do you mean?" Chris blinked a few more times than a normal not-lying person would blink in three seconds, and I gasped in disbelief.

"The girl is forced to choose between her fiancé and the guy she met on her summer holiday, that's what I mean, you conniving bastard," I blurted out under my breath and buried both of my hands in the fatty bucket.

"You look very sexy right now," Chris whispered in my ear, "with all that grease around your lips."

"Shut up!"

"What?" he grinned. "I'm just trying to make the scenario less romantic – with you accusing me of all kinds of stuff."

I attempted to give him a look of spite – which I probably failed quite miserably at, since I loved every piece and bit of him at that particular moment – and stared back at the screen. Right there, Allie and Noah had just quietly slipped into the next world in each other's arms.

"See, that's what I'm talking about," I pointed out. "Alex is my soul mate. He's the guy, whose embrace I want to die in."

"Well, if you say so," Chris shrugged, "I'm personally more about living, but if you prefer to look so much ahead, more power to you." He smirked and gently kissed my cheek somewhere that seemed to be very close to yet another G-Spot.

"Don't repeat that to Vera," I smirked back at him, "She might have an uncontrollable laughter seizure and we'll have to call an ambulance that we can't afford."

"Hmm... You're even sexier when you're trying to be a smartass."

"You don't say."

"By the way," Chris turned away for a second and took something out of his jacket pocket, "this is a little something for your birthday. Nothing too special – just a CD with all the songs we've been listening to this summer – mainly Oasis and some Beatles – something for you to remember me by when you're back home."

The credits started playing and with the flash of light from the screen I read what was scribbled on the CD cover: "To Elena from Chris."

Sometimes not saying certain words or not naming certain notions or relations means so much more than any imaginable terms and descriptions. When I come back home, Alex might come across this CD and might nonchalantly ask me, "Who's Chris?" And I would probably say, "It's just a guy I worked with in America." And that would be that.

***

That evening humidity was wicked. Simply wicked. I had tried to straighten my hair for almost an hour, practically succeeded – perhaps with an exception of a few particularly stubborn strands – and then walked outside for a cigarette, and there they were, wavy, frizzy hair with absolutely no style or purpose whatsoever. You know how some girls still manage to look sexy even with frizzy, unruly hair? Bed hair, they call it. They have this I-just-rolled-out-of-bed-after-a-night-of-hot-sex look about them that makes me grind my teeth in furious psychopathic silence. Because I don't happen to be one of those girls. When my hair loses its shape, it looks absolutely and undoubtedly horrid. I sighed, stretched my back, and stared at the lilac-blue sky above me. It was that magic time of the day when the sun had not set yet, but you could already spot the moon. Small, ghostly, with blurry edges – but definitely there. Heavy and hot air was scented with magnolia blooms and was strangely still. Not a movement. Not a tiny little breeze. I put my head on my knees and swayed back and forth as if in prayer. It was kind of a prayer. I was addressing my inner god and was asking her (I was almost positive my inner self was a female) to tell me what the fuck was happening to my life. In about twenty minutes, approximately fifty people would come here to celebrate my birthday. I'd have to be polite and smiley, and in general act like I knew what I was doing. And for the first time in my life, I had no idea what I was doing. My own intentions were a complete mystery to me, I could never tell what I would do in the next few minutes, and I definitely didn't know what my future held. Prior to this summer, I was certain that my fate was in my hands. I blindly searched for the second cigarette in the pack as I was still busy chatting with my inner goddess – or my knees – whatever you want to call it. I hoped that the second cigarette would help me trash the memory of the previous night in the dark dumpster of my subconscious.

After we got back from the movies, Vera went straight to bed. As you would expect from a traitor. Chris and I spent over an hour, or what seemed to have been an hour – I honestly never knew how much time we spent together – discussing the movie. I could talk to Chris for ages. Nobody had ever really listened to what I had to say before. My parents and Nan kind of had, with that proud and yet a bit condescending and a bit distant glare in their eyes that is so characteristic of parents, like they were never entirely there. Parents assume that their kids know they mean the world to them. That's why parents can get distracted by something else, and they still believe with all their hearts and sincerity that their kids know how their mom and dad feel. Well, parents, get that – your kids don't know. And they won't know until they become parents. And when they do, they'll forget. Just like you did. Anyways... I got a bit sidetracked. Chris was winning me over with that intense attention to everything I was mentioning. He continued my most out-there speculations and conclusions and even took them to the next level.

"I can't believe you just got what I was trying to say!" I smiled faintly and wrapped my arms around my knees.

We were sitting in complete darkness on the living room floor, quietly whispering to each other to the heart-pinching notes of Chris's CD. He'd managed to record all my favorite songs of the summer. I could already imagine myself back in Voronezh, crying desperate tears in the quiet of the night, the Walkman in my ears, for the love that never happened half the world away in the Southeast Georgia.

"I've already known what you were trying to say," Chris whispered back and tried to kiss me.

"Whatever, mind reader," I whisper-giggled and moved away from him.

"You know I'm right," He moved closer to me and kissed my neck.

"Of course, you're always right, and all the women of the world are at your feet," I smiled and stood up, away from him, leaning against the wall.

"Oh, you know!" Chris waved his finger, quickly got up from the floor, and pressed me to the wall with his hands firmly around my back.

"Oh, please, not that," I mentally yelled for help. When Chris did that, I seemed to lose whatever was left of my brain and turned into a soft cookie dough with a stupid smile on my face. He started kissing me, and Let It Be started playing, and Elena started to depart into the land of wherever silly people in love tend to go. I wasn't sure what that land was called or where it was located, but it was pink, sparkly, and made me think about the third spare bedroom that happened to be just around the corner. Chris's warm hands were already on my lower back, under my shirt, I could hear his breath and the rhythm of his heartbeat, which was in tune with mine. I suddenly remembered that Alex's heartbeat was never in tune with mine. In fact, when we tried to fall asleep next to each other, it always took me a while, because we were always out of tune. It might seem weird to you, my darling reader, but sleeping next to someone while trying to synchronize your breathing rhythms is no joke. Chris

and I started slowly crumbling down the wall back on the floor. I hugged him tight, I wrapped my legs around his waist and...

"Elena, are you okay?"

I quickly lifted my face off my knees and stared at the people in front of me – Inessa, Z, and a young good-looking guy with an elegant flower bouquet in his hands.

"Oh yes, I'm great! Just, you know... nervous before the party," I managed a weak smile and quickly got up on my feet.

"You are nervous before the party," Inessa repeated slowly and narrowed her eyes in understandable disbelief.

"Yes. Very nervous," I attempted a lighthearted laugh, "You know, so many people wishing me happy birthday. Strange cute guys with flowers," I finally looked straight at the stranger, "Inessa, aren't you going to introduce us?"

"Oh, of course! I'm so sorry. Where are my manners? This is Vitalik. He lives here in Brunswick, but guess where he's actually from?"

"Where?" I smiled meekly and thought to myself that I honestly couldn't give a damn where he was from. He could have been a Prince of Persia for all that I cared.

"From Voronezh," smiled Vitalik. "I actually go to the same college your fiancé does. Inessa says he's a soccer referee?"

"Aaaaa..." I croaked and fumbled for yet another cigarette. "Really?"

Okay, this is it. I'm done for. The Atlantic Ocean had just disappeared and the two continents merged. Life is over.

"And this is for you – Happy Birthday!" Vitalik gave me the widest and cutest smile ever and handed me the flowers. "We have so much to talk about! We probably have lots of friends in common."

"Are you sure you're all right?" asked Inessa and placed her hand on my shoulder. "You're very pale. Are you not feeling well?"

"I'm fine," I added in a tiny little voice. "Just... a bit surprised at how small the world is."

"Indeed," said Vitalik. "Are we the first ones to arrive?"

"I think so," I nodded.

"I can't believe it! Have you already forgotten about me, Paina? I've been here for the last twenty hours! Helped you set up and everything."

Chris and Diana appeared in the doorway, multicolored balloons in their hands.

"Oh, Christopher!" Diana giggled. "You don't count as a guest – you stayed the night."

"He stayed the night?" Inessa tilted her head and quizzically looked at Chris.

"In the third bedroom," I added hastily. "He stayed in the third bedroom."

"Hopefully not for long," Chris smiled and gave me one of those hard stares that made it obvious for everyone who had at least one brain cell what exactly he intended to do to me once he moved out of that third bedroom.

"What do you mean?" asked Vitalik, a comical glare in his eyes.

"He's just joking," I waved my hand, "Those Brits and their witty jokes. By the way, Diana, Chris, this is Vitalik. He apparently goes to the same school as Alex does."

"You're kidding!" laughed Chris.

"Nope. He's not kidding," I smiled and shot Chris a look that clearly said, "Shut up, shut up, shut up, you WANKER!" "Why don't we go inside and have a drink?"

"What a great idea!" Chris smirked. "That's exactly what we all need right now – a big old drink."

***

"I don't need any more drinks," I winced and pushed the plastic cup filled with strange alcoholic substance away from me.

"Okay," announced Sonia and looked around the kitchen. "Bitchez, she's definitely not all right. If Elena refuses vodka, she needs to be sent for a physical check-up or something. She could be seriously sick!"

"Yeah, all right, take a piss, why don't you?" I pouted. "I've already told you I can't drink. Because when I drink, I get stupid and horny. And I end up doing things that I regret. And I can't afford it right now."

"When we have the Voronezh soccer guy at our party," added Diana in that annoying smartass tone of hers.

"Precisely. You nailed it. Congratulations."

"Well, if I were you, I'd have a drink," said Diana and nodded towards the living room that in the last few hours had been transformed into a night-club dance floor with dozens of partying people roaming through.

"Why? If you're trying to distract me with something stu –" I stopped in my tracks as I saw Chris sandwiched between two girls on the sofa. Farrah on one side and Kate on the other. Oh yes. Kate. I haven't told you about Kate, have I? Kate was blond, beautiful, and working for the Department of Natural Resources trying to save ocean bottom dwellers from the harmful influence of human interference. Or something noble along those lines. Something green and selfless enough to have made Chris fall in love with her and stay in love with her for the past year or so. I know, I know – you are thinking: "Don't believe the gossip, Elena, Chris is in love with you." But that came straight from Chris. He told me about how crazy in love he was with Kate and how she kept rejecting him. And now she was gently covering his hand with hers and bathing him in her reindeer-jingle-bell melodic laughter.

"Ok, I think I'll take one," I grabbed the drink from Diana without looking at her and slammed it down. "Oh my God! What's in there? Rubbing alcohol?"

"Almost," grinned Diana, "But look at the bright side, you're under the influence now and that definitely places you in the same category with Farrah."

I followed Diana's gaze and frowned. I couldn't agree with her more. Farrah seemed to be having lots of trouble coping with the Russian drinking techniques. Her speech slurred, her eyes glared with distant incomprehension, and, strangely enough, she seemed to be not leaving Chris's side even for a split second. I suddenly was struck by a genius realization – or perhaps that was the magnificent power of booze that always gives us an amazing insight into the hearts and minds of others – Farrah was in love with Chris. She was wearing a mask of a liberated bisexual party chick, but she actually was in love with Chris! This thought made me very sad. It made me want to sit down on the floor amidst all the drunken dancing people and cry. Why did everything have to be so complicated? Why did it have to involve hurting so many people? *Why is it always so easy in books and movies and so not easy at all in real life?* I thought that the world needed a committee that would regulate publishing books and releasing movies that contradicted reality. Imagine how many people would be much better off! Without any stupid fragile illusions, hopes, and dreams! I didn't even notice when I started to dance. One more magic power of booze. It keeps you going even if you don't want to move a muscle. I was jiggling and jumping and laughing and flailing my arms, and all of a sudden, I didn't care anymore. I didn't know what life would hold, but it was undoubtedly in front of me, with all its twists and turns and inconvenient circumstances. I was young, healthy, full of life and I was having fun! I caught a quick glimpse of a few astonished faces – let me tell you, my dancing moves can attract lots of attention when I really get into it. And I was into it. I was taking in this energy of fun, and I was loving every second of it. I saw Inessa's face, surprised at first, and then lit up by a flicker of recognition. Of course, I thought – she remembered herself back at home, in Belarus. She looked at me and remembered where she left her old self, and now her old self was coming back. And I liked her! Inessa joined me and the girls in the twirling reality of dance, and I saw Z and Vitalik grin. Yes, everybody was having fun. That's the only thing we can do while we are here on planet Earth. We could be confused, we could be bored, we could be burdened with gazillions of problems, but everything would be all right as long as we still could have fun. I opened my eyes and guess who was there right in front of me?

"Okay, you win."

"I don't understand what you mean, Chris," I smiled and twirled my body in an unpredictable dance move.

"Oh, you do," he laughed, "You win this contest of fired-up tigresses fighting for the attention of one single member of the male species."

"You're so full of yourself, I don't even want to talk to you," I turned around and started dancing away towards the snack table.

"Come on, Elena, I was joking. Wait," he grabbed my arm and stopped me in my tracks.

"I know you were joking," I said slowly, "It doesn't make you less full of yourself or revolting."

"I like it when you're using bookish words for ordinary conversations."

"That's because I'm speaking a foreign language and struggling for words. And don't change the subject," I hiccupped.

"Easy, mama," Chris caught my elbow and laughed, "Just exactly how much did you have to drink?"

"Just one drink, but who knows what Diana put in it," I mumbled, "But honestly, Chris, you've got to be more worried about what Farrah had to drink, since she is obviously getting ready to drive."

Farrah was laughing uncontrollably as she was standing in the open doorway and waving to all of us.

"Bye, you guys! Bye, Eleeeeeeeeeeeeena, it was FUN! But I need to go houuuu..."

"Farrah, Farrah!" Chris ran up to her. "You can't drive like that. You'll get into a car accident. You can barely walk."

"Oh, I'll be fiiiiine," Farrah's voice reached a totally different pitch level that can only be obtained in the state of intense intoxication.

"No, Farrah. You're not driving. I'll drive you home," said Chris.

"No!" exclaimed Farrah and gave Chris a very sober look that made even me recoil with fear. "You stay here!"

And off she went – or rather stumbled – in the direction of her car.

"Hey, Chris, man. I'll drive her. Don't worry," Z patted Chris on the shoulder.

"Oh, thanks, Z – that's very cool of you," said Chris, who seemed to be a little lost.

"Looks like your game that involves too many tigresses went a bit too far," I added as we watched Z drive Farrah off in her car.

"She said she didn't want anything to do with me. You know, after we had sex that one time."

"Yeah, the one with Emma."

"Yes, the one with Emma," smirked Chris.

"Obviously, very romantic. I wonder why she didn't announce her lifelong devotion to you right that second? Oh, wait – perhaps Emma was resting on your hip and happened to be in the way," I wrinkled my eyebrows in mock-thought and started walking back to the apartment.

"It bothers you, doesn't it?" Chris gave me yet another irritating smirk as he popped another beer open.

"What?"

"Me getting it on with two girls. You have a problem with that? Does it make you jealous?" He got dangerously close to me.

"Wake up, Christopher. I don't really care about you or your love life. Oops, hold on, sex life."

"Oh, I'm 'Christopher' now. Now you are being serious."

"Whatever. Kate looks like she wants to talk to you. Good luck with that!" I nodded in the direction of the sofa where Kate was sitting, looking all lonely and entirely focused on Chris.

"You should quit sweating small stuff, Elena."

"What do you mean?" I turned around to look at him as I was heading back to the dance floor.

"You know, you let small irrelevant stuff get to you. It's not worth it. You're wasting your precious time on worrying about stupid shit. You'll regret it later."

Yes, young people sweat small stuff. They also tend to be overly generous with their time. They can close their eyes each night and the only thing on their mind will be anticipation of the day ahead of them. Recently I've noticed that I got greedy with my time. Every evening I think to myself, "Well, shit, another day has gone by..." It's like that designer dress that you really want to buy, but when you finally buy it, you still feel bad that the money is gone. You can make more money. And time... well, that's an old one – you can't buy time. I look back at the twenty-one year old Elena and I want to be her forever. Yes, there are certain things – insecurity, jealousy, cigarette addiction – that I don't exactly miss, but I can't help myself but feel nostalgic about the times when the sight of a pretty girl would make me instantly insecure, when a tiny indication of my boyfriend's attention for another woman would send me off my rocker, and when I could wake up and smoke that cigarette – so delicious back then – and somehow manage not to think about the fact that it would more than likely cause me to have cancer in the near future. I want to be her forever. And yet I keep on changing.

CHAPTER FIFTEEN

The Journey to the Ocean

Okay, there are certain things that I definitely would not welcome back into my present life. Like brain-twisting, needle-prickling, eye-watering headaches that come with an after-party hangover. I tried to lift my head up off the pillow and immediately fell back on the nice and cuddly bed.

"I can't do this. I can't get up," I groaned and slowly opened one eye.

Alex stared straight at me from the picture.

"Fuck," I covered my eyes from the cruelly bright Georgia sunshine, "What have you done, Elena?"

"Elena, I know that your soul is beyond salvation – what's with all the drinking, smoking, swearing, and turning our room into a warzone – but talking to yourself? Really?"

I cracked another eye open and saw Diana sitting on her bed and skillfully applying yet another layer of makeup.

"What time is it?" I croaked.

"Too late," retorted Diana, "You'd better get up and get ready. We're going to Orlando today, remember?"

"Aaaghhhh... Is it today?"

"Yes, it's today. And – just in case you forgot that as well – we're in the United States of America and you're a moron."

"Thanks," I smiled faintly. Because you couldn't help but laugh at Diana's jokes.

"Oh, and by the way, Chris is already here."

"He is?" I jumped up in my bed, ignoring the angry scowling little gnomes pounding on my brain.

"Yes, he is in the living room," said Diana and applied the last little bit of mascara on her eyelashes.

After what seemed to be an eternity, I finally managed to dress myself. Even though it was just a pair of bright-turquoise shorts, a leopard-print backless top and a pair of flip-flops, it took me as much time as it did to get myself ready for my prom night. I slowly crawled out into the living room to see Chris, Sonia, and Vera chatting away on the sofa. The girls were extremely excited in anticipation of the imminent trip, and – oh man! – we were heading down to Disney, the land of our childhood dreams! I would also have been excited if I hadn't been so hung-over and suffocating with guilt. Chris was telling them about the different parks we could visit and things we could get up to. As I approached them and was about to sit my bum down, Chris suddenly got up, put his arm around my back, and kissed me on the lips.

"Good morning, darling. How are you feeling this morning?"

I stared at him in silence. Needless to say, my reaction was just a tad slower than normal. I gazed around the room. Vera and Sonia were quizzically looking me up and down, and Chris had the widest imaginable smile spread on his face.

"What are you doing?" I hissed through my clenched teeth.

"Just saying good morning to my girlfriend. What are *you* doing?"

I shot a look of fear and despair at the girls and growled, "When did I become your girlfriend? As far as I know, we're just friends."

"Friends?" Chris's face twitched – was it anger that I spotted? – and then immediately morphed back into his usual self-satisfied grin. "I don't think friends typically get up to what we did last night."

Okay, okay, my darling reader. So I owe you a bit of information. It's a touch too personal though – that's why I didn't go there at first. I wasn't planning to hide it from you forever, I promise.

The night before, after Farrah was gone and we got a word from Z that she got home all right, everybody resumed celebrating my birthday – even though I was quite positive that half of those people had no idea who I was. American party code is very intriguing indeed. Apparently, anybody could show up at your party – distant acquaintances of friends, second, third and fourth cousins of coworkers, and neighbors who you never met before. This was fine by me – the more the merrier. We just couldn't imagine that such a scenario would occur in Russia, where you were only allowed to attend a party if you, and only you, were specifically invited. In any case, all my guests, whoever they were, were enjoying themselves, and I was enjoying myself even more. A few hours had gone by in the sweet frenzy of dancing, laughing and drinking. Please, don't be too strict with me, my reader. Yes, drinking – I was turning twenty-one! With the last beats of "Let's Get It Started in Here," I heavily plunged down on the sofa and closed my eyes with a content sigh. What a night!

"Elena, can I talk to you for a second?"

I looked up and pondered at the blurry edges of Chris's face in front of me.

"Yes, sure, go right ahead."

"In private."

"Chris," I looked around the room, "I'm pretty positive that no one in here even knows what their own name is. It's the best privacy you can possibly get on the whole island."

"Please," he begged, "I really need to talk to you. Let's go to the third bedroom."

"Yeah, right," I rolled my eyes, "Let's go to the third bedroom, why don't we?"

"I'm not going to try to hit on you, I promise. I just..." He paused, "I really need to talk to you about something."

He looked so distraught and so sincere, I couldn't bring myself to say no. Plus, there were so many people around there, I was sure I was relatively safe.

"Okay, okay, let's go," I smiled and headed to the spare bedroom.

As soon as we entered the room, Chris pushed the door shut, locked it, and quickly flicked the lights off before I could even open my mouth to ask the inevitable and already so familiar question.

"Chris. What are you doing?"

"What do you think I'm doing?" He whispered in my ear and then gently kissed me on the neck.

"But you promised you were not going to do anything!"

"I lied," he laughed as he picked me up and laid me down on the bed.

"Chris!!! We can't be doing this!"

"We can, because you are not going to do anything," said Chris as he was sliding down from my face to... Well, you get the picture. Technically speaking, it wasn't my fault, because I honestly didn't do anything. Technically speaking. On top of that, we were very quickly interrupted by a loud knock on the door.

"Elena! Are you there? We're leaving." It was Inessa.

"Just let them go. Don't say anything," whispered Chris.

"I can't do that. I need to say good-bye," I sat up and hopped to the door.

"What if Vitalik is with her? I mean – I couldn't care less," laughed Chris. "I just worry for you."

"Oh, how nice of you to worry for my and Alex's relationship. You're so sweet," I retorted in a furious whisper.

"No, you're sweet," grinned Chris.

"Oh, shut up!" I threw a pillow at him and swung the door open.

"Elena? What are you doing here in complete darkness?"

"Vitalik," I let out a tiny psycho laugh, "I was just... resting."

"Resting?" Inessa smiled, narrowed her eyes, and got on her tiptoes trying to peak over my shoulder.

"Is that Chris on the bed?" asked Vitalik and shot me a comic quizzical look.

"Hey, man," said Chris and lifted his hands in dismay as he saw my face, which – and I'm quite positive about that one – carried more of a resemblance to a face of a vicious ogre than that of a twenty-one-year-old girl.

"Hey," Vitalik grinned, "Well, I just wanted to say, it was very good to meet all of you guys. We'll have to catch up later."

"Sure," I smiled as I started to pull myself back together, "We'll definitely need to meet up one more time – at least – before we go back home."

"Of course," said Vitalik, "Elena?"

"Yes? What is it?" I tilted my head politely and coquettishly.

"Your pants. They're unbuttoned."

I looked down in horror and felt the red hot flash of shame devour my entire being.

"Thanks," I swallowed and tried to glue a polite smile back onto my crimson-colored face. "Drive safe," I squeaked.

When Inessa and Vitalik finally left the cursed doorstep, I covered my face with my hands and groaned.

"If it helps any, I tried to tell you," Chris shrugged as he was leaving the room. "I'm actually very tired right now. I think I'll be going home. See you tomorrow morning!"

So, that's all that happened. Nothing really. Technically speaking. I didn't realize that it somehow upgraded me to the status of a girlfriend.

"Oh, okay," I smirked back at Chris trying to ignore the shocked looks on Vera's and Sonia's faces. "I thought "not friends" don't leave that abruptly."

"Is that why you're so upset?" Chris laughed. "I was just tired, that's all."

"Tired my ass," I thought to myself bitterly. Every single evening ever since we came to America, he'd been trying to get in my pants. And on the day that he actually manages to almost get there, he leaves me alone! I wasn't sure if I was mad at Chris for abandoning me, or at myself for having cheated – technically speaking – on my fiancé – and still being more bothered by Chris leaving me last night than by my act of infidelity. Go figure.

***

Disney has always been something unattainable and only distantly dreamable. Back in Russia every Sunday at 9:00 a.m., there was a Disney program on TV: two cartoons (Duck Tales and Chip and Dale) followed by a Disney parade special. When I was a little girl, I would get myself a warmly delicious cup of tea, curl up in my bed, and savor every moment of those pseudo-trips to the magic fantasy land. With the corner of my eye I would watch snowflakes slowly – as if in a dream – hydroplane on my window sill, and I and would imagine myself being one of those kids that were lucky enough to be standing next to Cinderella's Castle and greeting their favorite cartoon characters in person. My mom and dad would still be asleep – my parents love to sleep in in the mornings – and that Sunday hour from 9 till 10 was Elena's time. It was my fun zone when I could let myself perpetually dream on without any interruptions. Disney had always been so far away, it almost seemed unreal.

But here I was. In Orlando, Florida. I rolled the window down and closed my eyes in pleasure as the hot, subtropical wind kissed my face. I was ten years old all over again, but this time, I was going to actually witness everything for myself! I turned around in my seat to face the girls who seemed to be no less excited. Well, you can judge for yourselves.

"Aaaaaaaaahhhhhhh!" Sonia was screaming in delight. "Orlando, here we come!"

"Chris," meowed Vera, "do you think we can get inside of the castle and take a picture with Cinderella?"

"Crazy bitches," That was Milo. I could only see his feet rested against the trunk door, since Milo and Tom had to ride – yep, you're right – in the back of Chris's Ford Explorer. "Didn't we already decide we were going to the Universal, not the Magic Kingdom?"

"Yeah, Uncle Milo," laughed Chris, "we all came to this conclusion about half an hour ago."

"Well, can't we still walk to the castle?" proposed Diana, who kept on beaming all the way from Brunswick.

"No, Diana," Chris chuckled, "the parks are enormous. You can sometimes barely walk from one side of the park to the other side. I'm not even talking about walking from one park to another."

"Well, we're more used to walking in Russia than Americans are. I'm sure we can walk it."

"You know," added Chris to the sound of the low gurgling laughter from the back, "I wish I could bet on that. I could win lots of money that way, but I'd feel bad for you. You've worked so hard this summer, I'd hate for you to lose the moolah that was earned so diligently."

"Oh, whatever," Diana waved him off, "We'll give it a try. You'll see."

"Okay," Chris snorted with suppressed laughter and gave me a devastating wink.

I didn't care which park we went to. I was there and that was the only thing that mattered to me. I was watching the palm trees, which, in the last hour of our trip, had managed to turn more tropical-looking, fly by past me through the window and couldn't help but feel so head-spinningly happy, my whole being seemed to be singing. I glanced at Chris and realized that, if anything, I was very grateful to him. He was making my dream come true. He was making me feel like my ten-year-old, content self again, who was just happy to be herself – and I hadn't felt like that in a while.

"A one-day pass, please," I watched Chris pay for the parking and felt the tingles of excitement run down my back and make my stomach turn in tummy-aching anticipation.

The Charlatans on the stereo came on with their "You're so pretty, I'm so pretty" song as we were approaching the kaleidoscopic sign that read, "Welcome to Universal Studios, Orlando."

"All right, amigos!" announced Chris. "It looks like we're finally here."

"Show me the diamonds, show me the gold..." Sonia sang along with the stereo as she was dancing to this amazing song that only a dead – and a very dead person indeed – would not want to move to.

"Call me the answer, ohhhh yeaaah," laughed Chris as he pulled into the parking space and turned the engine off.

***

Universal Studios had totally blown our minds. The lines and the waiting time for attractions in Universal Studios had simply left all of us dumbfounded.

"Chriiiis," whined Vera, who was vigorously and aggressively waving a park brochure in front of her face. "How much longer do you think we'll have to wait? I'm about to die from this heat. It's unbearable!"

"How long do you think?" Chris raised his eyebrows in sarcastic delight and nodded towards the line.

Our faces drooped as we stared at the never-ending crowd of people determined to fly Back to The Future on board of the famous Universal attraction. It wasn't that we hadn't seen all those people before. It was just that we secretly hoped they were all – or at least half of them – going elsewhere. Perhaps this was also the line for another ride? Before that day in Universal, I honestly never even dreamed – or, rather, had a nightmare of – seeing a line that was so huge. It was akin to that life scenario that all of us face sooner or later: when you know that you are witnessing something inevitable, but still refuse to believe it, because it's too scary to be true.

"If this was in Russia," whispered Sonia, "you'd just have to lift this rope and quietly slide under it – and voilà – you're at the front of the line."

All four of us simultaneously glanced sideways at the rope, pondering this naughty yet delicious thought.

"Don't even think about it," retorted Chris. "You're not in Russia. It's not fair. Plus, the other people in line might complain and call security."

"They wouldn't do that!" chuckled Vera and immediately stopped as she caught Chris's accusatory stare.

"Okay, okay!" Diana lifted her arms in dismay, "But so you don't blame us for being tactless Russians all day long, Milo and Tom were considering that as well."

"We were not!" Tom attempted to sound convincing.

"Okay, we were," admitted Milo in this high-pitched comic tone of his, "Maybe just a little bit."

"Well, you know," I laughed, "Slovakia and Russia are closer than Slovakia and the US of A."

"And I thought English people were crazy," Chris rolled his eyes.

"No, you Brits are pretty normal," I smiled and patted Chris on the back as we fortunately moved three more inches forward in the beastly line.

"Since we're so normal –" I felt his breath on my neck. "– Do you think you'd mind sharing a hotel room with one?"

"What?" I jumped up, startled by the realization that we would have to somehow handle the sleepover situation that night. It was our first two-day trip that summer, and we had not faced this problem before.

"You know – you and me – in a hotel room, finally alone," Chris's hands were on the small of my back now, and since the line was so big and everybody was so busy making sure they didn't faint in the 110-degree heat, no one noticed his move.

I closed my eyes for a very sweet split second and thought that it actually would be quite nice. I inhaled the Floridian heat and tried to save the pleasure of his hands on my skin in my mind, so that when I was back at home and it was cold, rainy, and gloomy, and Alex was playing yet another computer game or watching yet another soccer match with his dad, I could travel back to this moment. This beautifully hot and humid weather. This fun we were having all together. And the way his touch made me feel like I was the most desired woman on the whole planet.

"You know it's not going to happen," I giggled and turned around to face him. "And look, we're almost at the end of the line. Maybe another hour and we'll be there!"

"You're getting really good at this," Chris smiled and pulled me tight, "I almost believed you."

Still trying to recover from the fact that I was so close to him I could hear his heartbeat and smell his scent (and the fact that it made me want to kiss him right there and tell him, "Yeah, sure, let's do it, the hell with it"), I caught a glimpse of Sonia crawling under the rope.

"Hmm, Chris," I cleared my throat and motioned toward Sonia with my eyes.

"Fuck," said Chris and rushed towards the girls before it was too late.

I was saved. For now.

***

You can work out quite a bit by just walking around amusement parks in America. There is so much to see and do, the whole day can go by before you know it and one minute you realize that your legs are about to fall off and the exhaustion is getting the best of you. Unless you're one of the lucky ones who operate automatic vehicles that appear to be a strange hybrid between a motorized wheelchair and a kiddy quadricycle. Okay, please, I know what you are about to say. Perhaps they can't walk. Perhaps they are disabled, overweight, or simply too elderly to handle the park on their feet. Perhaps. Like 5% of them. The rest. Hmm... Not so sure about them, but hey! I'm not here to judge, right?

The fun day in Universal was indeed flying by. It was one of those days that you want to grasp and not let go of. But the hot orange of the Florida sun started to slowly descend onto the fluffy blanket of rosy clouds and the heat began to subside. Breathing air that was at least remotely scented with coolness was a relief, and it charged us up with unexpected energy. You could almost taste the salty notes of the Atlantic breeze in the atmosphere, even though the ocean was about an hour drive away.

"So, what are we doing after we leave here? Have we decided?" I asked as I leaned against the railing.

We had been standing in line for the Mummy ride for the last forty-five minutes and my leg muscles had started to give in.

"Well, like I told you guys before, we could either go to another park tomorrow – and in that case we'd have to find a motel room here in Orlando," said Chris, "Or we could drive to Daytona Beach after we leave here and hang out on the beach tomorrow. You know – just do nothing – chill, have some frozen drinks."

"Daytona Beach!" we all screamed in unison, even Milo and Tom, because after a kick-ass day of endless Orlando entertainment and even more endless lines, nothing seems more exciting than a relaxing day of doing absolutely nothing in beach paradise.

"It's decided then!" Chris happily beamed and nodded towards the gate. "It looks like we're finally here. We made it to the Mummy!"

Feeling almost heroic after having endured so much time standing up and patiently waiting, all of us rushed toward the ride. I jumped into the first car and buckled myself up. Chris got in right next to me and gave me his typical confident and somewhat annoying grin.

"What are you smiling about?" I asked grumpily.

"Nothing," Chris shrugged and smiled even wider.

"Are you plotting against me again or something?" I furrowed my eyebrows in distrust.

"No!" exclaimed Chris in fake indignation. "Why do you always have to blame me for everything?"

"Okay, okay, I'm sorry. I didn't mean to," I apologized even though I could swear I saw him grin just as nastily one more time.

Since I could never figure out what Chris was getting up to most of the time anyway, I decided to leave him be. And this was when we felt the first bump and the car started to slowly crawl forward into the pitch-black darkness. The heart-stopping groans of the Egyptian underworld made me freeze in my seat and all of a sudden, I was afraid to move a single muscle. To my left, a decomposed skeleton with half-rotten teeth jumped out of the ancient tomb, and right in front of me, a bony face with hollow eyes and long grayish-transparent hair emerged out of nothingness and started to talk.

"Maaaaaaaaaaaaaaamaaaaaaa," I screamed and grabbed Chris's hand in desperation.

What was I thinking, sitting in the first row? I must have lost my mind! It was just the first thirty seconds of the ride and I was already almost crapping myself. It was definitely not good. I gave Chris a tentative sideways glance. Now I knew why he was grinning that way. He had probably already been on this ride and realized that I didn't know what I was getting myself into. I slid as close to him as possible and whispered, "Ok, I admit it. I'm terrified!"

"It's going to be ok, Paina. I'm here."

His lips were so close to mine, it almost made me forget that we were in the middle of the hell ride. It's amazing how miraculous horniness can be. It can give you an illusion of being safe when you are far from it, it can make you believe you are the most gorgeous woman in the world when there is lots of work that needs to be done to achieve this enviable status, and it can trigger certain courageous actions that you typically wouldn't even think of in the normal state of mind and soul. So I smiled and I kissed him. You know that you are in the serious, deep doo-doo when a French kiss turns your entire being into mush and makes you feel like a hundred daisies have just bloomed in your chest and stomach and even treacherously sprouted into the tips of your fingers. You know – even if you are trying to deny it at all costs – that there is no coming back when you are going at it in the front row of the ride and do not even care what the poor people behind you have to put up with. You know that the ever-burning eternal fire of desire is about to devour your – hold on, that was some intense fire – fire? I opened my eyes and stared at the bright-orange flames above me in shock. The ceiling *was* actually on *fire* – it was bursting with thrusting tongues of sulfurous flames and the wall in front of us was exploding with hundreds of crickety, crawling, disgusting, noisy scarabs that, unfortunately for us, looked exactly like the ones in the movie.

"Aaaaaaaahhhh!" Chris and I and the twenty others on the ride with us screamed in utter horror and dropped down in the hot fire-spitting tunnel of the underworld.

When we opened our eyes, we were already in the well-lit, familiar area where we had started our journey a few minutes before, and a crowd was staring us up and down with curiosity and ironic sneer, blissfully unaware of what was awaiting them. I followed their gazes and realized that both of my legs were rested on Chris's lap and my arms were tightly wrapped around his neck. We stared back at the people in line for a few very long moments, and then I finally took my legs off Chris's knees and blew the hair off my eyes.

"It was VERY scary," I whispered to an elderly couple at the front of the line as I got out of the car and rushed towards the exit.

***

The lambent lights of the highway were dancing in the car window as I was trying my very best not to doze off. The girls, Milo, and Tom had been snoozing contently for the last hour, and Chris was diligently driving all of us to Daytona Beach. The heart-warming notes of Jayhawks' "All the Right Reasons" was filling the car up with dreamy nostalgia. I pulled my feet up to my chest, rubbed my eyes, and rolled the window down. Sea salt in the air. The best aroma there is. The smell of the ocean.

"The ocean breeze always makes me think that we're at the tip of the continent, the edge of the Earth," I yawned and smiled at Chris. "I've always dreamt about living by the ocean."

"The ocean here is much cooler than on St. Simons," Chris smiled back, "The water is bluer and there is much more fun stuff to get up to."

"I like the ocean on St. Simons as well," I shrugged, "When you grow up inland, any beach will do."

"I guess you're right," added Chris thoughtfully.

"You are taking it for granted."

"Taking what for granted?"

"Everything," I pondered. "The ocean, warm weather, easier life."

"I guess you're right," repeated Chris and gave me a strange look. "You know you can always stay here with me," he added.

Here we go again. I sighed.

"Aha. What hotel are we going to be staying at?" I tried to avoid meeting his eyes at all costs. I was mad at him. He knew very well that I couldn't stay with him – why on Earth was he rambling on about it? Life was already complicated enough and he was making it even worse by waving the yummy bait in front of me as if I was a stupid, big-eyed mahi-mahi or something. He stared at me for a few long seconds without saying a word.

"That's what I'm trying to find. A nice, affordable hotel for us. Why don't you wake the girls up?"

Relieved by the fact that he decided not go there right at that moment, I spun around in my seat and tickled Sonia's foot.

"Wakie-wakie! Eggs and bakie," I whispered. "We're already in Daytona – get up! It's time to pick a hotel."

"Ah! What? Where? How many wine glasses do you have?" Sonia muttered and wiggled her nose, her eyes still shut tight.

I looked at Chris askew and snorted with laughter.

"I can't believe they're thinking about work after a day in Orlando," Chris chuckled back.

"If you were working triple shifts, you'd be that way as well," I grinned, "I have no clue how they're pulling it off. But let me tell you," I whispered, "Come the end of the summer, they will save much more money than I will."

"I do not doubt that at all," I could swear I heard irony in his voice.

"What do you mean by that?"

"You know what I mean! They're greedy."

"They're not greedy!" I exclaimed, "They're hard-working – and it's a totally different thing."

At that very moment, Vera stirred and opened her eyes wide.

"Are we already in Daytona?" She smiled and peered into the pitch-black darkness of the night.

"Yep. What kind of hotel are you in the mood for?" asked Chris.

"Oh, Chris," Vera stretched her back and leaned forward, her voice sounding strangely apologetic, "this is what we wanted to talk to you about... Sonia and I – can we sleep in the car?"

"What?" Chris lost control for a split second and the car swerved lightly.

"Well, you know we don't have money for hotels and such," added Vera in a whiney tone.

"What are you talking about?" Now it was my time to be surprised. "You made more than a thousand dollars after tax just last week!"

"We're saving the money to pay back our parents for the program," Sonia was suddenly awake.

"I'm doing the same thing, aren't I? I already set the money aside a long time ago, and I don't make half the money you're making!" My voice was getting louder as I was slowly but surely realizing that the girls were indeed a bit on the Scrooge side.

"We need to save the same amount for the program next year," protested Vera. "You don't have to worry about that, Elena. You're about to graduate and get married. You won't be able to come back on the J-1 visa. And us – we want to be back here next year."

From the corner of my eye I noticed Chris's face droop just a touch with the sad realization. As for me... well... Vera's words hurt me more than she'd probably intended them to. I turned around in my seat and stared at the long boring road in front of me. She was right. I wouldn't be here next year. Or the year afterwards. Or ever.

"Chris, the back of the Explorer is nice and spacious, and we brought two sleeping bags," Sonia carried on whining. "We don't want to spend the money on the hotel room."

"Sonia," Chris laughed, "the motel room would be about sixty bucks or so and we could all stay in one room. It would barely be ten bucks a person."

"We already spent an enormous amount of money on the Universal ticket," pouted Vera and crossed her arms over her chest.

"Christopher!" Milo was giggling in the back. "Just let the Russian crazies sleep in the car. Whatever! More space for us in the motel room."

"I guess you're right," Chris yawned. "I'm so tired, I don't even want to think about it. Whatever. Stay in the car. Is Diana staying with you?"

"Hell no!" Diana sat up and rubbed her eyes vigorously, "I like to work, but I'm not a half-witted tight ass."

"Shut up, Diana!" laughed Vera. "Sonia and I are going to have so much fun!"

"I don't know about you, ladies, but we are *definitely* going to have fun!" announced Chris as he pulled up in front of a beautiful tropical-themed hotel with a straw overhang above the entrance.

Through the stupid stubborn tears that I had tried to chase off for the last few minutes I stared up at the blurry edges of the hotel sign that read "Hawaiian Inn, Daytona Beach."

***

In life, we always tend to forget that the ocean is just around the corner. We drown ourselves in the drudgery of our day-to-day lives, which sometimes can be quite nice, actually, and we get so used to the scheduled existence, that the idea of doing something that is a bit out of the ordinary makes us feel lazy. I don't know whether that comes with age and the comforts that come with a better job, a better house, a better material everything, but somehow our days do not bring as much excitement and liveliness as they used to when we didn't have a better job, a better house, a better material everything. They still easily could, but we get so comfortable in our lives, we are simply too lazy to keep on exploring the different opportunities that come with the first timid rays of morning sunshine. Have you ever observed a two-year-old human being in the morning? The second they open their eyes after a good night's sleep, they are already up off the bed and ready to rock 'n' roll. They want to do different things, they want to go outside and soak in the orangeade energy of the sun, they want to live! What happens to us after that? Where does laziness come from? Where does this inner desire to explore go? Routine... the Kalashnikov that will eventually murder fun. Think about it: perhaps one day grabbing a sandwich and reading a good book by the ocean shore would be much nicer than having an expensive lunch in the company of your nice-but-not-really-giving-a-crap-about-you coworkers.

That night, I didn't need to be reminded about the ocean. Or the fun. Both of them were right there in front of me – bubbling with life and constant movement. After having checked into the hotel – which by the way was by far the best hotel I had ever stayed at – we quickly changed into our swimsuits and ran down to the swimming pool. That's what I'm talking about. Today, I would think twice if I would like to get wet and possibly chilly, and after thinking twice I'd say to myself, "Naaa, don't fancy swimming at night... A hot shower and a remote control, now that's a good idea!" But back then I didn't think so. Back then I was so excited I could swim *and* look at the ocean at the same time, I didn't even know what time of the day it was. So here we were – Chris, Milo, Tom, Diana, and I – sitting around the hot tub and getting relaxed to the point of nirvana after a hullabaloo of a day at the Universal Studios. To top things off, Chris managed to get us a few beers right before the bar closed. As you can imagine, we were in heaven.

I closed my eyes and let the salty Atlantic breeze embrace me. I was going to miss the ocean back home. I had always had a strange connection with the ocean. Even when I was a teenage girl, I could sit and stare at the sea forever. I could watch the foamy waves slowly creep up the sandy beach and roll away silently and with no resistance whatsoever. I could listen to the melodic language of the sea, and it always made me calm and accepting. And strangely enough, the sea was always different. Every day. I am yet to see the day that the ocean looks the same as it did before. Perhaps, when that day comes it will mean that I got too old and it is the time to sail off. But not yet. And hopefully not soon.

"It's weird how the ocean is so much different from the sea," I suddenly said and abruptly opened my eyes.

"Russian," giggled Milo. "Give that beer to me. It's enough for you already."

"No, I'm serious," I insisted, "It's like the sea is a child – small and naughty at times, and the ocean is like an adult – vast and calm, but when it gets angry... well, then it's no good."

"But you're missing the big point," said Chris, "They're essentially one entity. Seas and oceans – just one big body of water."

"Motherfuckers," squeaked Milo. "You're going into shit that's a bit too deep for a beer night in the hot tub, don't you think?"

"I guess we are," laughed Chris. "So, Diana, you decided not to walk it to the Cinderella Castle then?"

"Well, you didn't tell me, Christopher, that it wasn't even visible from the Universal Studios. Plus, it involved extra seventy-bucks."

"I think you just gave a definition to "another park"," smiled Tom.

I always used to forget that Tom was there. He was perpetually so quiet, it almost seemed like he was absent.

"Whatever, Tom," snapped Diana. "So, how was the check-in, Christopher?"

"It went really well, actually. As you know, I got us an ocean-view room for a very good price. The front-desk girl was very polite, and even the cop was nice."

"What cop?" asked Milo.

"There was a cop there, hanging out in the lobby. Said hello to me and everything. Asked me where in England I was from. Very cool."

"That's bizarre. I have never met a nice cop," added Tom thoughtfully.

Wow. Maybe if we kept on drinking all night long, Tom could actually tell us a bit about himself.

"Aghh... Chris, sorry, man, for interrupting, but I need to ask you a question."

We all swiftly turned around in the direction of the unfamiliar voice and saw Chris's new Hawaiian Inn buddy – the cop.

"Yes, sure, what's up?" smiled Chris.

"Do you happen to have two young foreign girls with no IDs in the trunk of your car, by any chance?"

***

"Ha ha, Chriiis, that was SO funny!" giggled Vera and extended her arm in an attempt to take a sip of my beer.

"That was NOT funny," snapped Chris and lightly pushed Vera's hand away from the beer bottle. "You nearly got me arrested for human trafficking, so – do me a favor – stay away from this god damn beer before you get thrown into jail for underage drinking, all right?"

Let me tell you, my darling reader, when Chris got serious, you knew it. There was no doubt whatsoever that his intentions were absolutely clear and there was no messing around with him. In fact, he could scare people quite a bit. He was typically so happy-go-lucky that a lot of his acquaintances were under the impression that nothing could piss him off. Well, they were wrong. Once that last straw hit Chris's back, his face changed to the point of no recognition, his eyes were drilling a hole in your skull, and you simply found yourself secretly wishing you had never been born at all. Poor Vera almost went under in that hot tub and stared at Chris with shock, confusion, and irritation.

"What on Earth has gotten into you, Chris?" she finally managed to mutter.

"I have no fucking idea what has gotten into me... I'm normally not that stupid – letting two girls sleep in my car! And where are your passports anyway?"

"At home at Island Retreat," said Sonia defiantly. "It's not a very good idea to carry such important documents around, you know?"

"Oh yeah?" Chris's eyes narrowed and the fear in Vera's and Sonia's eyes became almost palpable. "Perhaps it's not such a bad idea at all, when you're too fucking cheap and are planning to spend the night in somebody else's car! I could have lost my job, I could have gone to jail tonight and I could have ended up with a very fucking unattractive entry in my criminal record – and all that just because you were too greedy to pay ten bucks for the hotel room!"

"We're sorry, Chris," Vera was almost whispering, "we didn't think about it. In Russia it would be okay."

Different countries, different laws, different levels of obedience to those laws. That is all true. But we also sometimes tend to forget that young people simply... don't think about it. Just try to remember yourself when you were, say, eighteen. Did you remember your social security number or did you have to call your mom to ask the question that would inevitably make her silently laugh? Did you think about the consequences of your actions before you hopped in a car with the guy you met two seconds ago? Did you think that one more cocktail would not be a good idea, because you wanted to avoid an excruciating morning headache? If you did, let me assure you – you are either one of a kind, or – more likely – you are suffering from a very common type of amnesia that strikes about every lucky human being that manages to survive adolescence and marches proudly into the adulthood. Yes, we blame young people for being flighty, absent-minded, and forgetful. But stop just for one second. Stop. Remember yourself at their age. No. Honestly. Try to remember. Adult You and Young You are just one body of water, you are one entity... but something happens on our journey to the ocean. Something happens and we forget that we were a sea once – smaller, less powerful, less knowledgeable, but still somehow more confident.

Chris knew that. The moment he heard Vera apologize, the corners of his mouth drooped and his eyes became softer and warmer.

"No, I am sorry. I didn't mean to yell at you. I just got too stressed out over this situation. I probably need to go for a walk, get some fresh air."

"Okay," mumbled Sonia, her eyes lowered in shame. "We'll just go to the room. Get some sleep."

"Motherfuckas!" squeaked Milo. "What about partying on the beach? What happened to all of you?"

"Umm... let me think..." Diana mockingly placed her index finger on top of her lip. "Perhaps the party mood was spoiled a bit by a possible charge in sex trafficking? What do you think?"

"Whatever, smartass," Milo shrugged, "It's all behind us and I'm going to drink. I'll go ask the front desk girl where we could have a drink now and hang out with, you know, people who are alive."

'I'll go with you!" exclaimed Tom and caused all of us, including Milo, to jump with yet another shocking realization that Tomas was capable of speaking.

"Peace out!" Milo grinned broadly and they made their way into the lobby.

"I wish them the very best of luck with that one," smiled Chris bitterly. "Daytona Beach turned into a ghost town a long time ago. The only living people they will find here will be elderly redneck bikers who still sadly think they're king shit of turd mountain and Medicare-age transvestite prostitutes."

I glanced at his grumpy face from under my eyelashes and slowly took his hand in mine.

"I thought you wanted to go for a walk, old fart," I said gently. "Come on then!"

"Why am I an old fart?" he mumbled and cast me a suspicious glance, but still got up on his feet and followed me to the beach.

"Because you've been complaining all night long," I laughed. "Look at your face – I can already imagine you when you're seventy. You'll be horrible!"

"Well, what?" He looked at me, a flicker of his infectious smile in his gray eyes. "Daytona does really suck."

"Oh yes, it sucks," I nodded, "Look at it. Disgusting!"

He followed my gaze and then finally laughed with reluctance.

The wide open beach was a wet carpet of white sand under our feet, and the ocean was rolling infinitely with dark and playful waves. The water was almost invisible, the great unknown, but it was definitely and unavoidably there. We could taste the crystals of sea salt on our lips, we could feel the light breeze brushing coquettishly on our cheeks, and we could hear the serenade of the tide resonate somewhere deep in our rib cages. Sometimes you can't see love – perhaps, because sometimes you refuse to see it – but it doesn't make its presence less there. All your senses are involved and no matter how hard you may try to shake the feeling off, it perseveres, it survives, and, most importantly, it stubbornly stays with you forever.

"Look, a lounge chair. Let's have a seat." Chris stretched his lean body out on the chair, his head kicked back on the reclined seat, the night breeze playing with his hair.

"Wow, you are a real gentleman," I raised my eyebrows sarcastically and propped my fists against my hips.

"Easy, mama," Chris smiled. "There's plenty of space for both of us."

I stood there for a few seconds with apprehension. If I sat down in that lounge chair, with my back against his chest, his arms wrapped around my waist, and stared at the ocean in front of us, it would quite possibly be the most romantic fucking moment in my entire life. I read about it in books, I cried over the scenes like that in my favorite movies, I dreamed about it in my glittery, fluffy, pink, girly dreams. I could die for it. I could get one of my hands chopped off for it. But the guy wasn't my fiancé. A tiny little problem.

"Elena. It's just a lounge chair," Chris laughed and looked at me with those dirty, dirty eyes. *God. Or whoever is out there. Help.*

I decided that I could have a seat – after all, my legs were killing me after a long day in the park and if I sat down on the sand it would be just outright bizarre. So I laid down, my head propped against his chest, closed my eyes, and let the moon rays perform their crazy dance at the tips of my eyelashes. And we just stayed there. Lulled by the tranquil song of the rolling waves, we stayed there infinitely. The time will go by, the seconds and minutes of our lives will speed past us, people around us will change, the world that we have known will transform into something else, but we will always stay there – on that beach in Daytona, that warm and breezy night in July 2004. Because moments like that don't fade, don't disappear. They linger in our bones, they dance on the top of the pink clouds at sunset, they melt into books and movies and shape the beautiful stories of love that are passed on from generation to generation. We didn't know what the future held for us, but then again – we didn't need to know that. We had that moment and it made all our worries about the future irrelevant. Who needs the future, when you have eternity? I understood that eternal love wasn't an overly exaggerated, silly metaphor. It simply stood for something that will make the heart of a great-grandmother flutter as if she were still twenty-one. For something that will make an elderly widower taking a stroll with a cane smile boyishly. For something that will make that second when you draw your last breath joyful, meaningful, and not even a tiny little bit sad.

I looked up and he kissed me. There was a bouquet of exotic tastes in that kiss. Passion, impossibility of the future, guilt, happiness, desire, first timid seedlings of love, sadness, jealousy – all these heavy feelings covered us at once like a humongous wave that we just had to ride without any extra questions. I just rode the wave.

The surreal beauty of the moment was suddenly scratched by a strangely familiar sound that made both of us perk our ears and withdraw from each other. We looked in each other's eyes, no blinking, for a few excruciatingly long seconds.

"That sounds like... What is it?" I whispered.

"I don't know, but it sounds very familiar," Chris whispered back. "Oh shit!" he screamed as the sprinklers finally came on and sprayed us from head to toes with stinky and shockingly cold water. "Let's run!"

He took my hand in his and we ran. We ran across that wet cool sand, bathing in the salty Atlantic breeze, laughing our emotions out. Everything that we felt – all that jambalaya of confused feelings – escaped us through that silly laugh. Did it help us tackle our problems? Did it help us with Alex, Farrah, the ocean, and the border control that divided us? No. Not in the very least. But if anything – if anything – boy, we had fun!

***

I woke up to the nasty, gnawing feeling of guilt roaming through my subconscious. It was one of those mornings, when you know you did something wrong before you actually open your eyes. Now, don't pretend to be a saint, my dear reader. If you are still reading my book, I know you have been in a situation like that at least once... Right? In that particular case, I couldn't quite place why I was feeling guilty. I could sense the warmth of the sun on my eyelids, I was nicely and cozily snoozing in a very comfy bed, and I could smell the salty breeze of the Atlantic. Wait! My eyes popped open as the sudden heavy ladder of realization hit me. I looked to my right and saw Milo. I looked to my left and saw Chris. I sat up and pulled the covers all the way to my chin. I had Chris's shirt on. I winced and tried to take one of my legs over Milo to get out of the bed.

"Where do you think you're going?"

"Ay!" I yelped as I was yanked back down in bed and plunged next to Chris. "Let me out, Chris."

"It's nice to wake up next to you," he whispered in my ear and pulled me close to him. His chest burned the skin on my back, his hands were casually drawing invisible circles on my shoulder, and his lips were lightly kissing that treacherous spot under the earlobe. Girls, you know what I'm talking about.

"Well, you woke up with me and Milo," I retorted sarcastically and tried once again to wiggle out of his arms.

"Mine," I turned around to look at him and he was dead serious, "You're mine. Not Alex's, not anybody else's – mine."

I gulped for air. I was a fish thrown out on the shore of life by an unpredictable and very untimely storm.

"You sound like Gollum," I attempted a joke, but soon realized that it was to no avail. Chris was serious and intended to stay that way.

"Just stay here with me for a moment. You're so warm... It's nice just to cuddle together."

"Okay," I turned away from him with my back pressed against his chest and closed my eyes for a few seconds. It was nice to imagine that. At least for a few short moments. Waking up together to the lazy sun spots tiptoeing up the wall. Talking about a day ahead of us. Not feeling guilty about being together. Chris's embrace made me feel safe. I realized that when we were together – just cuddling like that – doing nothing wrong really –

that it was for some reason so natural, I felt safe. I realized that I didn't feel guilty. It felt good. It felt right. Now, this was scary.

"Except – it's a bit hard to cuddle with Milo in bed with us, isn't it?" I chuckled, sat up, and quickly hopped over Chris before he could get a hold of me again.

"Well, you didn't have a problem sleeping with him," laughed Chris with that annoying innate arrogance of his.

"Oh, no no no," I wagged my finger in his face, "Allow me to elaborate! We all slept in one bed together. We didn't sleep together. And that's a different thing."

"I don't know about that one, Elena," said Diana groggily as she sat up in the bed next to us and rubbed her eyes, her spiky blond hair a hot and funny mess. "Looking at you wearing a guy's shirt and jumping out of bed with two hot half-naked men in it... The only thing that comes to mind is... Well, let's put it that way – Alex probably wouldn't like it." She yawned and stared at me with the self-satisfactory grin she somehow managed to pull off a minute after waking up.

"Diana," I retorted, "you don't have a mind. So, theoretically speaking, nothing can come to it, because it doesn't exist."

"And there's no need to be so defensive!" grinned Chris.

"Listen, you people," I waved my hand angrily in the direction of the girls' bed where Vera and Sonia were still happily snoring. "When we got back in the room, you three were already sleeping. And what did it leave me with? With one bed, Chris, and Milo!"

"Russian," moaned Milo and covered his head with a pillow. "Can't you be quiet? You've been screaming for the last fifteen minutes and I'm soooo tired."

"I don't care!" I smirked. "It's time to get up, anyway."

"If you didn't want to sleep next to Chris," said Diana, her eyes glaring, "why didn't you sleep next to Milo on the edge of the bed?"

"Because Chris and Milo started whining that it was gay and they were not going to sleep next to each other," I said. "And where is Tom anyway?"

"He went to the front desk girl's house," Milo mumbled as he buried his face in the pillow.

"He did what?" all of us exclaimed in unison and stared at Milo with the expression of pure disbelief.

"You heard me. She went out with us last night and after the third Jager Bomb, she kept on saying that Euro accent was turning her on and, next thing I know, I'm there, all by myself – and Tom left with her!"

I sat down on the bedside, my arms helplessly hanging by my side. Life, and ocean, and people you meet during the journey. How unpredictable. How bitter-sweet. How bizarre.

CHAPTER SIXTEEN

Back to Earth

The other day I heard that a person that will live to be a thousand years old has already been born. Now... Stop. Ponder this thought for a second. Doesn't this scare you? I was terrified when I first heard that. Of course, we all like to philosophize about a distant theory of living forever. Being forever young. But if you were given the opportunity, would you want to? Be alive forever. Come to think of it, there is nothing too bad about it. We get to enjoy our lives for... ever. Still, something about it doesn't sound quite right. Something about it – somewhere deep in my subconscious – doesn't click. What about overpopulation? And the circle of life? And procreating and then silently slipping away? Or perhaps I am too old-fashioned? Perhaps I am getting too old and am trying desperately to hold on to that one notion that I had to learn to accept, that one day there will be no me. One day I will have to go. And now, when this could possibly change – for the better, right? – why am I holding on so strongly to that grim notion? Do I want to die?

I have always been very fond of stability and consistency. To the point of psychosis. For instance, if I did my fitness exercises one morning and liked it, I thought, "I need to be doing this every morning." Nothing bad about that. But then something happens – say, my alarm fails and I wake up too late to even brush my teeth, forget about exercising, do you think I'll happily resume my exercise routine the next day? Nope. I'll just quit it all together – to stay consistent. I am almost certain that it is a certain type of psychosis, since my logic is simply lacking logic, and yet, I still keep doing it in order to satisfy some weird, twisted part of my mind.

I believe it was the same with Alex. I wouldn't say that I had enjoyed my last two years with him. We were together, we were an item, our parents knew each other, and we already had common friends. But... when I saw him, my heart didn't start to race and my fingertips didn't get sweaty. And my brain was still functioning when he got close to me. They say that's what time does to love. It becomes such a big part of your day-to-day life, it doesn't excite you anymore. Do you believe in it? And, most importantly, do you want to believe in it?

So – back to the consistency topic. I was not intending to change my entire life simply because I got a few stray butterflies in my tummy when I woke up next to Chris. I was not going to change the life that had been going perfectly fine before I was possessed by these unnecessary emotions that surely had a very logical explanation. It was time to come back to Earth.

We actually had a lot of fun in Daytona Beach. After finally waking everybody up and making sure that Tom was safely back from his overnight adventure, we barged into an empty restaurant of the Hawaiian Inn that was already – judging by the look of pure hatred on the faces of the servers – getting ready to break down for lunch.

Chris cast a quick look at his cell phone and clicked his tongue. "Bummer, I didn't think about it. We came too late!"

"No, Christopher!" announced Diana. "It says they are open for breakfast until 11. It's only 10:57."

"Diana is right!" said Vera. "We came in just in time."

"Girls!" exclaimed Chris, a note of honest indignation in his voice. "Sometimes I can't believe you work in a restaurant!"

"What do you mean?" Sonia stared at him blankly.

I have got to say something in the girls' defense. This was the mentality we grew up with. In Russia, all business outlets tend to close a few minutes – if not more – earlier than they are supposed to. Therefore, it almost turns into a competition between a worker and a consumer – who will get who first. Ha – I got here at 4:58 and you are already locking the door! I will complain! I win! In the United States, it is considered bad taste if you choose to show up somewhere right before they close.

Now, I'm trying to be all Mrs. Let's Analyze Our Cultural Differences, but at the time, I was terrified. I was still wearing Chris's T-shirt – indigo-blue one with the turquoise logo of the Edinburgh music festival – and I had no idea why. I packed up plenty of clothes for our two-day road trip – too many, honestly – but I still chose to keep Chris's shirt on. Was this because it made me feel closer to him? Was this because I liked the look on his face when he was looking at me? Whatever the reason, it definitely was not good. Not the shirt. The concept. Of us. On the beach. As one.

"Elena!" Vera elbowed me and gave me a strange look. "Can you come back to the Earth please? For just one second? What are you going to eat?"

I looked up and saw that everybody was staring at me, including the waitress. *God, what a face.*

"Oh, I'm so sorry!" I attempted to get back to a normal polite facial expression. "I'll have two eggs over-easy please. And hash browns." I only had to hope the waitress was not going to add a sprinkling of arsenic to my breakfast. Or her spit.

As I frowned at my own thoughts, I felt Chris's hand on my knee under the table. It sent electric shivers up and down my leg and made me freeze in my seat. I couldn't do it anymore. Chris could not – under absolutely any circumstances – touch me. Anywhere. I desperately tried to chase off the memories of us in the third bedroom. But they kept persistently coming back. Dark, wet, sensual. There was no hiding from them. They were now the eternal tenants of Elena's mind. I gently pushed Chris's hand away and tried to focus exclusively on stirring the sugar in my coffee. It's a sort of yoga exercise – try to take the thoughts off your vagina to something else, like coffee.

"So, guys, what are we going to do for the rest of the day?" asked Vera.

And then, there was silence, interrupted only by an annoying cling-clang of my spoon, which was still vigorously stirring my coffee. My eyes were lowered, but I could see that Chris was staring at me with that intense look he got when he didn't get his way.

"Chris," repeated Vera. She waited this time until he finally took his eyes off my face and slowly turned to her. "Any ideas about the plans for today?"

"I had some," he said quietly, "but I don't think Elena is on the same page."

Fuck. How can he distract me from good, not-sex-obsessed thoughts and make me spiral into the wild slide-show of what I was trying not to think of by just saying something so obscure? I was pretty sure that if somebody had lit a match next to me, I would have ignited.

"Why? Elena, what do you want to do?" Diana inquired and raised her eyebrows.

"Maybe go for a walk on the beach? We could still swim in the pool, I think." I actually amazed myself that I still could think. And express my thoughts in a foreign language.

"Aaahhh, girls! This is what we are going to do!" exclaimed Sonia and pointed at the window.

"Parasailing?" Chris sounded surprised. "Are you sure you want to do that?"

"Why not? It would be so much fun!" Vera was already finishing her food in a hurry. "And memorable!"

"Yes, memorable – when you fall in and a shark will have you for lunch," laughed Chris.

"Oh, whatever, Christopher, you are such a sissy," squeaked Milo. "I'll go! Who is coming with me?"

"We are!" Vera and Sonia momentarily cleared their plates and were already disappearing through the door.

***

Back in those days, the reason I didn't go parasailing wasn't because I was scared. I wasn't really scared of anything in my early twenties. I was lazy and I wanted to lay out by the pool with a piña colada. There. Enough said.

I didn't have dark images lurking in the unknown spheres of my mind, I wasn't wondering if I had enough money (because I didn't), and I wasn't fearful of what the future day would bring me. I was ready to embrace it. That was before I realized that bad shit did happen in reality – and not just to someone, but to yourself and the people you know. It is as if, in the first part of your life, we live on the ever-so-bright-and-shiny planet called Utopia. The sun never sets there, and if it does, it is most definitely a romantic sunset designed for kissing on the beach or something along those lines, and it is protected by a highly resilient atmosphere that sends all negativity flying into outer space as if it was a teeny tiny ping pong ball. Obviously, once kicked off into the galaxy, negativity has to settle somewhere. So it goes to our alter-planet, Paranoia. It's not just negativity that travels there. We also take the mysterious inter-galactic trip. The only thing is – nobody ever warns us that the ticket was purchased and we were Paranoia-bound. One day we simply wake up in the comfort of our beds, husbands or wives, and our children, and we realize that the bloody spaceship did take us to another planet. Did it happen overnight? Did it happen during one of the drunken blur of multiple parties that had by that time all blended together? When did that happen? And how can I go back to the happy-go-lucky Utopia? If we listen to Winston Churchill, it would be foolish of us to go back to Utopia. We had grown, and the time had come to become sensible, conservative, and realistic. Time to hang on to your material possessions and your fear – in other words, get a permanent resident card on planet Paranoia, mingle with its dwellers, and throw out those strawberry-sweet distant and feather-light memories of life on Utopia out if your mind. I might be foolish, but I'm hanging on to my house at the top of the hill on Utopia. I might be one of their oldest dwellers, but who cares?

You are probably wondering why I'm rambling on again. Well, this is what this book is at times – the stream of my confused consciousness.

What I was initially planning to say was this – the trip to Daytona was like a dream come true. It was like that dream, when all your dreams come true. When all of a sudden you take off and fly up to the silky, coral clouds above your head. And when you zip through them happily, and your mind is fresh and clear, and you know that this is exactly where you want to be.

And then you drop down to earth and the pain is so excruciating and takes you by such surprise, that all you can do is, you know, just say...

"Ehhh, I believe I still have enough money saved up..." and then you scratch behind your ear and wonder... and wonder.

"You're just not thinking about it, are you?!" His voice vibrated somewhere in the back of my neck. "The reason you went to America was to save up money up for our wedding! And now you are just wasting it all, on –" He paused. "– on *Disney*," he managed to scoff in indignation, as if the word "Disney" was way below his attention.

"But –" I said, startled. And I was startled not because I didn't know what to say, but because something happened to me right there and then. Something snapped and broke. And fell, back to earth. And when it snapped, it broke free and took off again, soaring in the sky that had already turned dark, getting dangerously close to the moon, mysterious and glittery.

"Hey, are you there?" Alex asked, notes of impatience making him sound weak.

"I'm here," I said and cleared my throat. "Still here. But you know what? Diana is here – she's waiting for her turn to call. I've got to dash. I'll call you back in a few days, okay?"

"Okay, just don't blow all the money. Deal?"

"Deal."

CHAPTER SEVENTEEN

Let's Fear No More

Buddhists say that all our problems, insecurities, and fears originate from the greatest fear of all – the fear of death. I used to smirk in arrogance at this statement. I wasn't afraid of death. I was afraid of not living properly. Being afraid of death is for the weak, whiny people. But then the big change comes. You become a parent. And then you change – some of us change beyond recognition, because what we didn't realize is that one day, we will be really afraid of death. The death of our children. Even as I am typing it now, the grip of this strangling notion seems to stop my heart from beating. But after we become parents, that is what drives us – fear for our children. It can drive us one way or the other. This is when we generally break into two camps: the ones who fall into this fear and let the quick sand of horrendousness swallow them all and completely erase the people they used to be; and the ones who accept this fear, look it in the eye, and let their children become the part of this world. This world with citrus-sweet sunsets on the one hand and blood and guts, hatred and death, on the other. Yes, this world is not perfect – in fact, it's far from it, but we are here, and we have to do our absolute best to enjoy it. Writing this book helps me let my children be – it makes me remember how fearless I was, how everything I ever expected was good and there was no badness or dreadful things on my horizon.

"If I don't go let my doggies out to pee, they will do it all over my living room," yawned Chris. "You want to come with me, Elena?"

We were all hanging out in Monika's apartment, as usual, having some beers, smoking cigarettes and chit-chatting about what happened that day.

"Speaking of pissing, Christopher, did I tell you about how David pissed on our couch?" laughed Milo.

"David – your roommate David? The cook?"

"Yes! He got so wasted, he fell asleep watching telly and woke up stinking of his own piss. As is our entire apartment right now."

"No way!" Chris tilted his head back and laughed.

I wanted to kiss him.

"Yeah, I'll go with you."

"What?" Chris stopped laughing and glanced at me quizzically.

"I'll go let the dogs out with you. They need to pee."

"Yeah, I know that. I just didn't expect this answer from you."

Oh yes. I forgot to tell you a thing or two. A few days ago, under the influence of my last talk with Alex, I just decided to enjoy myself and start hanging out with whoever I felt like. It so happened that I felt like hanging out with Chris. Are you surprised?

The other night, Chris took me to Rafters – a local bar with live music. Farrah and Emma were there too, as well as lots of guys who kept on hitting on me. One of them was even trying to push Chris out of the way to talk to me, to kind of nudge him away with his elbow. Chris didn't like it a bit and even got somewhat territorial. Emma was trying to get to Chris by hitting on me and telling me that I had gorgeous eyes (strange tactic some girls use to get rid of another girl by showing an interest in her), which also didn't work. Neither on me, nor, strangely enough, on Chris.

And so here we were, delirious with booze and moonlight, in Chris's Ford Explorer parked outside my apartment. I don't really think Chris was nearly as intoxicated as I was, but he was pretending pretty well. He quickly grabbed me by the waist – in that Indiana Jones swift manner of his that made me feel all womanly, light, and super sexy – and sat me on top of him. He reached up to kiss me and my hair completely covered his face. With my back pressed against the car wheel, I was pretty much done for. "I don't think I'll get a monument to the Iron-Clad Vagina built in my honor after all," I thought, as I tried to shush my thoughts away from Chris, all of him, right there. I could sense him with every bit of my body. I reacted to him with every part of my body. One of his hands was in my hair, playing with it gently, and the other one was...

"Stop!" I said, sighing out loudly. "What are you doing?"

"I think you know what I am doing. Elena."

"Hmm," I gulped for air, stopped his hand from going any further, and looked him in the eyes. "What is it?"

"Let's go to the third bedroom. Please. It's enough – enough of these childish games. We are both grown-ups," he whispered and managed to move his hand even further. "You obviously want it as well."

"Do I?" I moved, somewhat awkwardly, and jumped up from the loud noise of the car hood that I accidentally pressed with my back.

As everything in my life, it seemed to be a sign – in this case, it was a sign that I had to stop. Plus, a nosy neighbor lady stuck her head out from her second-floor-apartment window. I laughed quietly and got back in my seat, trying to sleek my hair up a little. As I was just about to bid my good-night farewell to Chris, I saw, to my utter astonishment, that he had put the car in ignition and started driving away.

"Where are we going, Chris? I was just about to go home!"

"We are going home. Tonight, we are going to sleep together, Elena."

"You sound like a serial killer," I laughed, in spite of my semi-paralyzed state.

"Well, you know what? We went out, I wanted us to spend the night together – you want us to spend the night together – but you just wouldn't quit with that... whatever you are doing! So we are going to sleep in my place! Or you can start walking back to your place right now."

"Whatever. Psycho," I gave him a tentative glance. He was really mad. Plus, he was already half-way back at his condo, which meant that I'd have a 15-minute nighttime walk ahead of me. "Just no sex."

"No sex," He attempted a weak smile, "And you know what?"
"What?"
"When we have sex, I am going to be 100% sober. I want to remember it all, every second of it."
Now he was smiling for real. And I felt safe with him – under the sea of stars, in that velvety dark night, in the floating whirlpool of the ancient oaks above us. I felt like I could do anything, and nobody would ever know, because these protective oaks would keep my secret. But I didn't do anything that night. We just slept together. In Chris's bachelor bed, with Tex the Dalmatian happily snoring between us.

Needless to say, my darling reader, I enjoyed it immensely and – since we did nothing really (just two friends having a sleepover – it happens all the time, right?), when Chris suggested we take the doggies out the following night, I happily agreed.

So there we were, in Chris's kitchen with his yellow microwave and dancing shadows of candles on the walls. You know how sometimes you know that something that was going to happen for a long time was now ready to happen? That feeling of weird premonition? That bizarre invisible entity egging you on and whispering in your ear, "That's it... There's no going back..." At first, we both seemed to be confused that it was actually about to happen. But then, the confusion seemed to dissolve in the softly lit cream-colored room, and all we had left was the sugar-cookie sensation of anticipation in the air.

When he picked me up and sat me down on the counter, with my lower back tightly pressed to the shockingly chilly for this warm night window, he didn't seem to be confused at all. His hand traveled under my shirt and up my back, leaving me incapable of any conscious action. That tingly, wet sensation in the tips of the fingers again, one look into his eyes, one kiss – and that was it.

Oh fuck, oh fuck, oh fuck! I thought to myself as my newly bought turquoise shorts fell on the floor.

But that was enough. I didn't want to think. I was going to do it. I'd already done it a hundred times in my mind – what difference would it make? I wrapped my arms around his shoulders and kissed him back like I wanted to kiss him all summer long. Trying to share with him everything I felt – passion, confusion, happiness, pain, guilt, fear. That whole fountain of emotions that I couldn't cope with alone anymore. No more. He picked me up again, in a hurry, as if afraid I was going to change my mind, and carried me to the stairs. We stopped there again and I took his shirt off, touching his warm skin gently. My Work & Travel 2004 T-shirt fell on the steps in shame. I smiled, kissed him on the neck, jumped up, and wrapped my legs around him – and then up we went. And up, and up, and up...

***

Actually, we didn't go that far up that night. In fact, that night, nothing happened. My darling reader, I can already hear you yelling, "Whaaaat? What do you mean by 'nothing happened'?" Let me explain myself. You know how we often want something and dream about it, and imagine how it's going to be. We create that ideal plan in our minds, and God forbid the reality dares to deviate from our agenda. Did you notice that when you plan something, nothing seems to work out according to your plan? I swear, there are some sort of Olympian gods who use us for entertainment.

So, yes, back to that night. I don't know whether we got too excited, which made Chris too nervous, or whether it was the fear of making this perfect time imperfect, which in return led to it being far from perfect, or whether Zeus and Hera were indeed having their celestial fun at our expense – but nothing happened that night.

This can only happen to you, Elena. Only to you. You can't even cheat properly, I thought. I raised my hands in irritation. Strawberry splashes of the first morning sun were chasing each other on the ceiling above me, as if in mockery. "Perhaps it's a sign," I mumbled and pulled the smooth cotton bed sheet all the way to my chin.

"What sign, Elena the Paina? Are we chatting away with ourselves here?" Chris smiled as he turned towards me in bed and pecked me on the cheek.

"You know – that it didn't happen?" I blushed and looked him straight in the eyes. "Maybe it's a sign that we shouldn't be doing it."

"Bullshit!" Chris laughed and dramatically took the bed sheet off me, throwing it on the floor. "I don't believe in any crappy signs – you're mine, and that's the end of the story."

"Chris!" I squeaked. "What do you think you are doing? I'm completely naked!"

"But I saw plenty of you naked last night!"

"Yes, but it's daytime now – it's different," I muttered under my sheet, still trying to cover myself up, to no avail.

"Yeah, it's much better that way," Chris's voice got a touch hoarser as he took my hands, put them on his shoulders and then... well... you get the picture. And if you don't, it was a very nice picture indeed.

***

We were lying in bed, lulled by the calming staccato of the heavy subtropical rain. Hurricane Ivan was approaching, and we could hear the winds picking up. The outside world was about to burst in, uninvited, with all of its craziness and inevitable consequences. But so far we were there, on our safe little planet. I propped myself up on my elbow and kissed him on the mouth, taking him all in, memorizing him. I turned around and laid down on my side, with my back to him. He spooned me tight, the light whisper of his breath brushing against my neck. I closed my eyes and let the sound of the monsoon carry us away on its silver waves.

The feeling in my stomach was light and nauseating at the same time. I was floating somewhere in between the ocean and the sky. I managed to tame this enormous bird, and now I was in charge. I looked around and was immediately absorbed by the dazzling palette of neon colors around me – all colors of the rainbow and beyond, each one of them breathing with new opportunities that made my pulse beat faster and faster. And then even faster – something was about to happen. Something I was waiting for. I was enjoying every millisecond of that warm anticipation glowing inside of my chest. It was now reaching my throat. It was outgrowing me. I took a deep breath in and then it burst into an infinite number of dazzling microscopic sunflowers.

I opened my eyes and smiled at the sight of the red hair flash in front of me. I reached out for this softness and was just about to kiss him again, when –

"Elena, when did you go lesbo?"

Then I really opened my eyes, flabbergasted, and saw Vera, staring at me incredulously. I sat up and looked around. *Oh, yes. Plane. We were on the plane.*

"I thought you were Chris," I muttered under my nose, trying to chase away those hot tears that were burning in the corners of my eyes.

"Hey, Elena," Vera's voice softened. "You want to cry? Hey? Let's cry together. Come here."

And I cried there, inside that enormous steel, manmade bird, leaving wet and salty spots on Vera's bright-orange jersey. The heavy crystal rock in my throat was slowly disappearing. I don't know how much time we spent like that, but then we heard a flight attendant with the French accent say that our Air France airliner had started its descent to Moscow. I sat up and stared at the peach-colored ocean of clouds floating over the Russian capital. I saw my own eyes reflecting in the window, sitting on top of those clouds, like two sad and cold lakes. And then I saw the sun, this huge Florida orange in the sky, come up quickly over the blanket of the fluffy clouds and cast the shine and glitter on all of us. I smiled – sincerely, openly, with no fear. I was not scared anymore. But see, my darling leader, I had to go back to Russia. I had to go back home.

Epilogue

I drew a steamy heart on the foggy glass of a French door with my finger and smiled to the rain. The elements were raging in that typical August-like way that makes you feel small and powerful at the same time. Like you can't change anything, but yet you realize that you are a piece of a larger puzzle – and you fit in, you are in harmony with nature and the way of things.

I turned around just in time to duck under and avoid a Lego block flying in my direction.

"Mom!" giggles of my older son brightened the room even on this gloomy day.

"Liam Ocean," I said, trying to muster my most stern maternal look and not to laugh. (*Don't laugh, Elena, under any circumstances, just don't laugh.*) "Liam Ocean, calm down and clean up this mess. The room is a disaster."

"Who does he take after, I wonder, Elena the Paina?"

"Whatever, Chris, piss off," I laughed. "I'm trying to discipline our son here."

"Discipline? Now that's something new!" His eyes crinkled in laughter as he picked up our younger son, Max, who was diligently banging him on the head with a Buzz Lightyear gun.

I stormed off in fake indignation and snorted as Chris discreetly popped me on the bottom.

"Mommy! Are we going to the park today? You promised we'll go at 11. You said at 11!"

Oh, yes. I didn't tell you the rest of the story. In fact, I didn't tell you about a lot of things: how Chris proposed to me on a bench in Walmart with a kiddie wedding ring, how we got married under the Georgia oaks, how we were holding hands and looked at each other like we were lost and found at the same time, how I had to go back to Russia after that for a year, how we spent that year in the sky flying to see each other in different parts of the world, how I moved to America, how we had our two little boys, how every time it rains heavily here, in Georgia, I always hear their laughter woven into tropical rain drops on the window of Chris's old condo, and how I grew up – or maybe never did? How I learned that you have to get rid of fear and just dive into the unknown if that is what you want. How sometimes, just sometimes, you have to be honest with yourself and people you used to love, look them in the eyes, and tell them that the love was gone. And how you have to learn not to blame yourself for what you have done. But that is an entirely different story...

Made in the USA
San Bernardino, CA
15 April 2019